ACCESS TO WATER IN URBAN AREAS

ACCESS TO WATER IN URBAN AREAS

Indian and French Experiences

Edited by

YVES SAILLARD
GUNDAPPA SATHYANARAYANA SASTRY

Published in Association with the
French Embassy in India

MANOHAR
2012

The French version of this book was translated into English by Sheila Carrodus and Harry Forster with the collaboration of Krystyna Horko

First published 2012

ISBN 978-81-7304-978-1

Published by
Ajay Kumar Jain *for*
Manohar Publishers & Distributors
4753/23 Ansari Road, Daryaganj,
New Delhi 110 002

Printed at
Salasar Imaging Systems
Delhi 110 035

Contents

Preface

The research, 'Water Territories and Sustainable Development: Access to Water in Peri-urban Areas', that led to the publication of this book was initiated as part of the university cooperation programme ARCUS 2006-2008 – India, developed by the Rhône-Alpes Region and the Ministry of Foreign Affairs and coordinated by the University of Grenoble. Support was also received in 2006-7 and 2007-8 from the Rhône-Alpes International Mobility Scholarship Programme (MIRA, Mobilité Internationale Rhône-Alpes) for a research project entitled 'Prospective Analysis of Water Supply and Demand in Urban and Peri-urban Areas of Bengaluru and Comparative Analysis of the Situation in Mumbai and Bengaluru'.

Research undertaken by Anastasia Angueletou in the context of her doctoral thesis entitled 'Access to Water in the Peri-urban Areas of Mumbai: Water Poverty and New Urban Governance' provided an opportunity for the initial contacts with India. The study used interviews and questionnaires completed by households to examine access to water in the north, north-east and south-east peri-urban areas of Mumbai. It was funded by a scholarship from the French Ministry of Foreign Affairs, with the support of the Centre for Human Sciences (CSH) in New Delhi. The publication of the book in English was funded by the Consulate General of France in Bengaluru, India.

Under the ARCUS programme, a cooperative research project was set up between members of the Institute of International Integration and Production Economics (LEPII UMR 5252 CNRS – Université Pierre Mendès France, Grenoble) and members of the Institute for Social and Economic Change in Bengaluru. In addition to fieldwork in India and France by members of both institutes, academic exchanges were also developed as part of the programme, notably with Professor L. Venkatachalam (Madras University), who was invited to spend two months in Paris in 2007 with the support of the Maison des Sciences de l'Homme-Paris. Professor G.S. Sastry spent two months in Grenoble in November and December 2008, with the support of the Université Pierre Mendès France and the Maison des Sciences de l'Homme-Alpes.

This book was first published in French in 2010 with the title *Accès à l'eau dans les territoires urbains: expériences indiennes et françaises* by Hermès-Lavoisier, France. The translation into English has been done by Sheila Carrodus and Harry Forster, with the collaboration of Krystyna Horko. We thank them for the great care brought to this translation. As the theme of research is a topic of current significance, Professor Pierre Dumolard originally induced us with a strong motive to put the research outcome in the form of a book for its wider accessibility.

This work is dedicated to René Arrus, who was an engineer at the CNRS and expert on questions related to water. He played a vital role in setting up the research programme that led to the publication of this book. The book bears witness to our respect for the research led by René and to our affectionate memories following his untimely departure from our midst in November 2008.

EDITORS

Contributors

ANASTASIA ANGUELETOU-MARTEAU is at the Economie du Développement Durable et de l'Energie (EDDEN), Grenoble, France.

MAHFOUD BOUDIS is at the Laboratoire d'Informatique de Grenoble (LIG), Grenoble, France.

YVES SAILLARD is at the Politiques publiques, action politique, territoires (PACTE), Grenoble, France.

GUNDAPPA SATHYANARAYANA SASTRY, is at the Indian Council of Social Science Research (ICSSR), New Delhi, India.

SIVARAMAN VANATHY, is at the Madras Institute of Development Studies (MIDS), Chennai, India.

LINGAPPAM VENKATACHALAM is at the Madras Institute of Development Studies (MIDS), Chennai, India.

1

Peri-urbanization and Water Services

YVES SAILLARD AND
GUNDAPPA SATHYANARAYANA SASTRY

1.1 URBAN DEVELOPMENT AND OUT-OF-TOWN DYNAMICS

In France suburban development is associated with a preference for detached housing and the quest for better quality of life. Increasing use of motor vehicles and the difference in land prices both contribute to such behaviour. 'Urban sprawl' may be more precisely defined as 'the densification of territories at increasingly greater distances from town centres'.[1] This trend is not necessarily connected to the spread of an urban area and may occur without a rise in population, with the centre simply slipping towards the periphery. The consequences for urban development policy and access to services obviously vary a great deal. Over the last 40 years the number of urban areas in France has not significantly increased, but on the other hand, the number of urban areas ringed by peri-urban development has doubled over the same period. In the meantime the number of localities (*communes*) belonging to an urban area has increased almost fourfold, and that increase mainly concerns peri-urban localities (multiplied by a factor of seven). This peri-urban development is very different from what has occurred in Indian cities, which have tended to develop by a process of 'urban aggregation' rather than sprawl.

One feature shared by various instances of peri-urban development observed in India is that the developments have been outside conurbations, raising the question of the continuity of services and administrative management. However they seem to operate at a different scale and in a more complex way [DUP 06]. The dynamics driving peri-urban development are varied, in terms of their attraction in relation to the city and better quality urban life for middle-class people, but also through the exclusion of the inhabitants of city-centre shanty towns and the relocation of industry. These peri-urban areas may develop 'spontaneously' and unexpectedly, or on the contrary they may be planned and organized. In addition a dual movement is gradually increasing the distance between out-of-town developments and the centre, with rural areas spreading and the core-city increasing in size. A key feature of peri-urban development in India also relates to the relative importance still attached to rural life. The 2001 census revealed that less than 30 per cent of the population is urban, though this figure undoubtedly falls short of the real situation due to the classification of peri-urban inhabitants in the statistics.[2] Lastly urban populations are highly concentrated. In 2001 there were six big cities in India, each with more than 5 million inhabitants.

1.2 PERI-URBAN DEVELOPMENT IN DEVELOPING COUNTRIES AND ACCESS TO WATER

The peri-urban development process in large Indian towns leads to the formation of new transitory spaces subject to rapid change and physical, morphological, socio-economic and cultural transformation coupled with conflicting use of the land. These poorly integrated areas on the outskirts of towns lack a reliable distribution network. The water distribution system often fails to keep pace with rising population or urban growth. The type of network, the choice of technology and its capacity reflect a town's economic and social policies that vary from one territory to the other. Various social and technological changes are now calling into question the territorial distribution of networks, opening the way for a new definition of relations between public services and territory, between the extent to which demand is met and socio-economic development. The water supply in so-called 'peri-urban territories' is neither truly urban nor rural in form. On the contrary various hybrid systems of access to water have emerged, delivered by agents operating in these territories.

Water supply systems must fulfil various constraints – regarding institutional policy and organization, pricing systems and recovery of costs, infrastructure, funding and technology – in a context of rapid urbanization and constant outward expansion of city limits. The conditions for economic growth and the changes in lifestyles associated with such peri-urban development add to the complexity of the question of urban water supplies [LEE 94].

The lack of territorial identity and the necessary bodies to organize the water supply to urban and peri-urban spaces raises problems of competence. The particular feature of peri-urban areas is that they want to enjoy all the services and functions of the city without becoming an urban entity.

The widespread water shortages in the large cities of developing countries are not only due to inefficient distribution systems but they are also the result of a high rate of leakage caused by far greater problems in management, organization and social relations [LEE 94, WOR 92]. Large amounts of water are wasted because of constraints related to finance, technology and infrastructure with a bearing on water treatment and distribution. Problems in organizing and regulating the process encourage illegal access to water, which either involves unauthorized connections or diversion of water from the main network. This in turn aggravates leakage and water losses.

Considerable uncertainty, linked to unsustainable development policies, plagues the water supply in many towns. The lack of planning and management of the urban environment has depleted water reserves, permanently jeopardizing the future exploitation of resources and preventing increased supply. To meet the growing demand for water, the organizations responsible for supplying water to cities must not only exploit the existing resources to the full, but also look for alternative resources and draw water from distant sources. The necessary development work has proved costly, but it has also disturbed the water cycle and the ecosystems associated with this natural resource. Inadequate water treatment has not only led to wastage of this precious resource, but also caused serious problems for the environment and public health [HOE 01]. Furthermore the cost of water treatment has significantly increased.

All over the world the poor face serious difficulties in obtaining drinking water due to inadequate supply and problems in accessing the resource. The inefficiency of the water system supplying the poor has several major implications. The high cost of water purchases has a substantial impact on household income. Great physical effort is required to collect water, damaging the health of the poor. The resulting diseases also have economic consequences for households. Observations show that children suffer most from inadequate water supplies [UNH 03]. Various development projects worldwide have tried to cater to the basic water requirements of poor and disadvantaged people. Nevertheless, people in low-income groups carry on buying water from private vendors, paying prices between twice and 50 times more than the amount paid by high-wage earners for heavily subsidized water delivered direct to their homes [UNE 03, UNH 03]. As a result poor families spend up to a third of their income on water, whereas rich households only devote 2 per cent of income to such purchases [OKU 88]. In its overall efforts to raise living standards among the poor and enable them to meet their basic water requirements, the United Nations has set Millennium Development Goals. In particular the goal is to halve the number of people without access to safe drinking water by 2015 [UNH 03].

Efficient management of water supply and distribution in towns will require new forms of organization, technological innovation, and the transformation of infrastructures and public bodies. A change on this scale will require massive investment, quite beyond the reach of developing countries [WOR 92, HOE 01, MEI 01].

1.3 WHAT REFORMS ARE NEEDED TO ALLOW ACCESS TO SAFE DRINKING WATER IN TOWNS?

Above all access to water has a normative significance. According to the World Health Organization a person may be regarded as having access to water if he or she is served by a network or pump less than 200 m away from his/her home in an urban environment, and less than 500 m in a rural area. Over and above these global quantitative targets, it is important to look at the conditions of access to water and the many forms they take, from public distribution networks to the most informal methods. There are a great many different ways of accessing water, with specific approaches to organizing tariff systems and distributing the resource, pursuing commercial and non-commercial motives. Institutional innovation also impacts access to water. Furthermore various factors enter into assessment of the conditions of access to water: quantity, quality (of the resource itself and the regularity of access) and fairness in its distribution.

One of the main questions raised by the design of viable supply and distribution systems for shared access to drinking water in towns concerns the 'status' of the natural resource itself. There is no doubt about the scarcity of water resources. But simply because it is scarce does not make water a subject worthy of economic analysis, nor is water only an 'economic good'. Reform programmes differ primarily with regard to the economic status they attach to water.

The institutional benchmark which traditionally applies to the provision of water is defined in terms of supply, with a standard for consumption of so many litres per person per day. When water is recognized as a public good and budget constraints are increasingly tight, a series of reform scenarios present themselves quite naturally: efforts to achieve more efficient public management, decentralization of services, changes in the tariff system, various forms of private-sector intervention, and appeals for international aid. Studies of past experiments have yielded various assessment criteria.

It seems necessary to find effective policies for water tariffing in order to recover the full cost of operations and manage water resources sustainably. However, an appropriate price system should not only seek to control water consumption, but also provide incentives for conservation of the resource, which in return will increase the availability of fresh water and make it possible to cater for additional demand in the future. The water pricing policies actually deployed in various countries have difficulty in attaining this goal because of the main priorities set for economic policy and unsuitable institutional organizations [HOE 01, SAL 01, WOR 92]. The prices and tariffs fixed by these policies are supposed to cover the costs of production and distribution, but invariably they do not cover the full cost of the supply. Adjustments are consequently needed to secure the financial viability of the water sector [LEE 94, MCN 92, ROG 02, SAL 01, WHO 87, WOR 92].

The organization of water markets has been proposed as a means of efficiently managing a scarce resource. But the efficient organization of a water market requires effective enforcement of the right to water, with institutional arrangements enabling that right to be upheld. In developing countries none of these conditions are met. Setting up water markets in developing countries consequently encounters problems [SAL 01, KEM 01]. In an effort to obtain a modern, more efficient organization, several developing countries have engaged in a process of privatization. However, private-sector involvement tends to sideline social objectives expressed in terms of 'value' and to reason in terms of 'price' – an approach which particularly affects poorly paid people. The institutional model which has enjoyed the greatest success in the search for efficient management is undoubtedly the public-private partnership (PPP), which is used in several developed countries [UNE 03, OEC 03].

The overall tendency for water to acquire the status as a 'common good' is to gain more widespread recognition. The recent move towards projects making greater allowance for consumers has made development programmes more efficient and realistic. The new trend towards participation by local people is contributing to better acceptability of technical changes. This is also making it easier for governments to mobilize the resources needed to carry out such development projects. Public participation of this sort, as well as improving the effectiveness of water management, can secure the necessary control over activities concerned by the projects and reduce the costs of organization. It can also facilitate efficient upkeep of the service [DAM 01, WOR 92, LEE 94, SAL 96]. Consumer participation of this type already exists in the form of alternative water distribution systems in urban areas. Networks, neighbourhood associations and commercial systems supplying drinking water are all trying to cope with water scarcity. The main problem with alternative supply systems is, they lack effective coordination and the way they set prices, which requires careful investigation [WOR 92].

1.4 TERRITORIES AND WATER INSTITUTIONS

1.4.1 *The 'Territorialities' of Water*

Efforts to achieve consistent local management of water are often held back by social and economic processes developing at distinct scales. On the one hand, demand for water has two components: the needs of the local population and demand by production activities serving markets which are not local. On the other hand, the water supply responds to distribution constraints which require economic, technical and sanitary factors to have reached a certain level, encouraging the extension and upkeep of the networks. A single space may thus display disparities which locally favour industrial demand and business interests, or alternatively, the needs of disadvantaged inhabitants. The operation of the network consequently responds neither to the same practices nor to the same rationale, depending on the local characteristics of the space. Depending on practice and rationale, several forms of water territoriality may emerge.[3] A typical example of such a situation is the coexistence of a formal and an informal water economy in the same space, as is the case in India's megalopolises. On the one hand, there is a distribution network funded, controlled, measured and maintained by institutional players; on the other hand, a system managed directly by local people with various types of organization. Yet the two systems are interdependent: the same resource has to be shared, waste affects common areas and all the players take part in the economic and social exchanges of the space.

An understanding of the territorialities of water prompts questions about the discriminating capacity of space: how does such and such a territory connect to processes which will favour such and such a type of network and practices? The problem cannot simply be stated in terms of technology and management (harmonizing the action of the various players involved in water). It must also be stated in terms of development: how can fair access to water be achieved? We know that the informal economy gives rise to additional costs in comparison to the institutional network, despite the fact that it caters to the needs of the poorest members of the community.

The large European cities had to cope with this problem in the nineteenth century. Their counterparts in emerging countries face the same problem today, but in a more discriminating context with the unexpected potential offered by globalization.

Policies for the supply of water and local development often reach beyond a town's administrative limits. Such policies involve consideration of larger territories, for none of the problems facing today's megacities can be addressed on just one scale. But to frame regional policy it is necessary to rise above the rationale of competition between local authorities, the rivalry for power between technical advisors, between central government and local authorities, and achieve active cooperation between the formal and informal players at work in the water sector.

1.4.2 *Institutions*

One important observation that emerges from the study of the water supply in Indian towns is that the scarcity of the resource is not necessarily the main cause of failure to satisfy demand. Complex management methods, ill-adapted administrative bodies and insufficient consultation of consumers have also played a large part in this failure. The context may differ and players may pursue specific objectives, but in both Indian and French towns it is apparent that institutional factors play a decisive role. This prompts us to focus discussion on the efficiency criteria and processes of institutional innovation in relation to the contexts under study: goals related to quantity, quality and fairness to make sense when rooted in this institutional framework.

In the following section we offer a brief reminder of the overall rationale underpinning the systems deployed in water management in India and France. Each one corresponds to a different tradition of public service.

1.4.3 *Institutional Systems and Water Management Policy in India*

Since 1855 and the days of British colonial rule, the management of water resources in India has come under the larger heading of irrigation and power, as part of the Public Works Department. Following several changes in the institutional organization, under British rule but also after Independence, the Indian government established a ministry in its own right, the Ministry of Irrigation and Power, in 1952. In 1980, in view of the importance of water resources, the government set-up a separate Ministry of Irrigation. Since then the various aspects of water management have taken on decisive importance. After some changes in institutional organization, the ministry was reformed in 1985 and its name changed to Ministry of Water Resources. Since then the Ministry of Water Resources has been the sole organization in charge of planning, managing and protecting the country's water resources.

Many public service aspects of the water resources have prompted other ministries, such as the Ministry of Environment and Forests and the Ministry of Agriculture, to become involved in the management of the country's water resources, in coordination with the Ministry of Water Resources. However, in line with the rules on devolution of governance introduced by the 73rd and 74th amendments, village panchayats and urban local bodies (ULB) are responsible for the water supply and sanitation services, respectively in rural and urban areas. However, under the terms of the delegated management contract (DMC), qualified bodies may distribute water and organize sanitation services in rural and urban areas [BWS 02]. The lack of flexibility of both institutional bodies and regulations have rendered such systems ineffective. On the whole in India a specialized body set up by a government act, or by a ULB or village panchayat, manages the supply of water and sanitation services.

Water in India is treated as a common natural resource with free access for all consumers at the place where it is available. Under the constitution water resources are fully protected. Water falls within the ambit of the state, with a legislative provision in favour of central government (provision 56 of Article 246, and Article 262 on conflicts between states about rivers). Before this provision was added to the constitution there was no direct legislation to protect and manage the country's water resources. However, this concern was indirectly addressed in various laws to protect the quality of water. The first of these laws – the Shore Nuisances (Bombay and Kolaba) Act – was passed in 1853. It was followed in 1860 by the Indian Penal Code Act, which included several provisions on the protection of water quality, the River Boards Act in 1956, and the Merchant Shipping (Amendment) Act in 1970 [KUI 97]. All these regulations reflect India's concern for managing the quality of its water.

Later, with rapid growth in water pollution and associated environmental problems, the Indian government has passed several Acts designed to control environmental pollution, with a view to protecting the environment and water quality. Some of the key Acts include: the Water Pollution (Prevention and Control) Act of 1974, the Environment (Protection) Act of 1986, and the Water Cess Act of 1977, followed by the addition of a series of riders. Case law in the field of public interest and settlement in the court of disputes have significantly contributed to such policies by solving problems relating to water quality and management.

The serious problems posed by the scarcity and poor quality of water have become increasingly pressing issue with rapid population growth and industrial development. Urbanization has forced the Ministry of Water Resources to set new policy guidelines designed to manage resources more efficiently. The result is the National Water Policy, first adopted in 1987, then revised and updated in 2002. In both cases these political moves recognized that drinking water should be treated as a priority in the allocation of water resources. At the same time quality control and institutional systems were established in rural and urban areas. One interesting point is that the right to pollution-free water is now upheld as part of the fundamental right to protection of life and personal liberty, guaranteed by Article 21 of the Indian Constitution [NAT 04].

Public policies must also determine the manner in which suitable price systems for water are decided. The price must be high enough to cover operating and maintenance costs, but also the upkeep and extension of facilities. The price may be adjusted depending on the quality of the distribution service. Public policies have also encouraged the private sector to play a part in water distribution [IND 97, 02].

The institutional organization deployed in India for the supply of drinking water is, by tradition, a top-down structure, and its intention being to supply drinking water in line with a standard of so many litres per capita per day (LPCD), set by a government body. This political approach has recently shown itself to be fairly ineffective. There is now a trend towards a more bottom-up approach, with the aim of catering for the growing differentiation in water demand among the various socio-economic groups of the population. This approach encourages the population to take a larger part in the management of water and the struggle against its scarcity.

1.4.4 *Institutional and Political Arrangements for Water Management in France*

Water in France is a common heritage belonging to the nation as a whole and a resource which cannot be privately appropriated. Subject to the responsibility of the state the relevant regulations control the rights of usage. Access to water is covered by legislation which goes back to 1898 and has gradually evolved since. Initially it focused on distribution of the resource between the various forms of usage: farming, industry, and homes. Regulations concentrated mainly on setting standards for public health and water quality for use of water in industry (for production of hydroelectric power) and farming. After the Second World War there was a growing awareness that a comprehensive approach was required for the management of water resources.

The guiding principles for managing water resources were established by the Water Law of 16 December 1964. France is divided into six main river basins each supervised by an *agence de l'eau* (water agency), a public body funded by the central government and reporting to the Ministry of Ecology and Sustainable Development, and to the Ministry of Economy, Finance and Employment. The Nature Conservation Law of 1976 heralded the emergence of environmental concerns. The creation of an environment ministry brought a more quality-oriented approach to the management of water resources. A law passed in 1984 introduced the notion of aquatic environment. A subsequent law, passed in January 1992, established a framework for conservation of the aquatic environment and coordination of policies to prevent pollution. Under the provisions of this law each water agency must draw up a master plan for Water Development and Management (SDAGE). This is a planning instrument established by the relevant water commission for a fifteen-year period, setting the priorities for managing water resources. The most recent batch of SDAGE plans were completed in 1996. They are currently being updated, for completion by the end of 2009, and will cover the period from 2010 to 2015.[4] These instruments coordinate the various development schemes and must comply with European directives on water.

Water agencies receive dues paid for water usage or the resulting pollution. They allocate financial assistance to work carried out by local authorities, private companies, non-governmental organizations and farmers with the aim of making better use of water or protecting aquatic habitats. Six water agencies set-up by the French government supervise the following basins: Artois-Picardie, Rhin-Meuse, Seine-Normandie, Rhône-Méditerranée-Corse, Loire-Bretagne and Adour-Garonne.

A *comité de bassin* (basin committee) brings together local policy-makers, representatives of central government, end-users (industry and farming) and non-government organizations (consumers, fisher-men, conservationists), under the overall coordination of a *préfet de bassin* (basin prefect). The committees advise on the rate of dues levied by the relevant water agency and the programme of works decided by its board. Each committee is sub-divided to cover specific geographic sectors (nine in the case of the Rhône-Mediterranean basin) and boards to supervise local management of basins. Each basin committee has a scientific council which contributes its expertise.

Water Development and Management Schemes (SAGE) are the equivalent of SDAGEs but for a smaller area, which operate as meaningful units in terms of water resources. These instruments, which were established in 1992, set guidelines compatible with those decided for the overall SDAGE after a consultation period organized by the Local Water Commission (CLE). There are about 100 SAGE schemes in France.

European bodies play an increasingly important role in this system. A directive published in September 2000 establishes 'a framework for

Community action on water policy'. It aims to set common targets for the protection and improvement of Europe's aquatic habitats. It also fixes overall goals to be achieved by 2015. A new French law, dated 30 December 2006, is based on this framework directive and pursues the same objectives, in particular with respect to access to water and the operation of the public service for water and sanitation.

Organization of the drinking water supply is supervised by the Water Directorate at the Ministry of Ecology and Sustainable Development.[5] The central government also decides the national water policy with respect to industrial or agricultural pollution and public health. Decentralized government departments, operating at a regional or *département* level, implement the regulatory and technical aspects of such policy, under the supervision of the relevant prefect:

- *At the regional level*: Directorates tasked with monitoring the environment (DIREN), and industry, research and the environment (DRIRE);
- *At the département level*: Directorates tasked with monitoring public health and social affairs (DDASS), farming and forestry (DDAF), and public works (DDE).

All these departments are coordinated by Regional Water Technology Committees (CTRE) at the regional level and by the Interdepartmental Water Missions (MISE) at the *département* level.

However, a large part of the organization of the drinking water supply is decentralized in France. The leader of each municipal council is responsible for the distribution of drinking water, and the collection and treatment of waste water in the relevant municipality. He or she is also in charge of investment. In practice the local management of water is generally organized on an inter-municipal basis by inter-municipal syndicates or mixed syndicates representing the regional council, one or more *département* and municipalities. The local management of water resources is based on the relevant master plan (SAGE), with technical and financial assistance from the water agency and/or the various decentralized government bodies. Municipalities can also choose the form of management: direct, delegated to a municipal company, or contracted out to a private firm.

Although they are governed by the rules on delegation of pubic services, private companies play an important part in the distribution (70 per cent) and treatment (40 per cent) of water. French firms have developed their skills in water-related services, extending their reach all over the world. Veolia Environnement-Générale des Eaux and Suez now have interests in water distribution and treatment of waste water, playing a decisive role in international programmes backed by the International Monetary Fund and the World Bank.

The public service for the supply of drinking water is increasingly organized on an inter-municipal basis.[6] For various reasons, mainly related to the rationalization and streamlining of services, as well as solidarity between localities, collective management of water services increasingly plays a decisive part[7] in the form of groups of municipalities which transfer their competence to inter-municipal syndicates (urban councils, urban area or district councils) or to organizations with a separate funding system (in particular for the collection of waste water).

1.5 PLAN OF THE BOOK

The book presents the water-supply systems and corresponding experiences of four cities: Grenoble, France; and Bengaluru, Mumbai and Chennai in India. Drawing on observations relating to the various cases and the experience gained there, the book adopts a prospective stance, based on the WATER-UP method of simulation and various scenarios for future trends in the water supply to Indian megalopolises. Lastly, it outlines the challenges of public policies on water in these cities and how recent decisions have sought to resolve these issues.

Chapter 2 focuses on the city of Grenoble in France, counterbalancing the subsequent account of Indian cities. The conditions for the organization of a public water service are particularly favourable here, given the availability and quality of the natural resource, and the relatively slow demographic growth.

Chapter 3 describes the water supply for the emerging megalopolis of Bengaluru. This chapter explores every aspect of the water supply system for a large town in a developing country: the rapidly changing face of its people, and the urban and peri-urban spaces they inhabit, the risks of water shortages and the complexity of the factors involved in managing the service.

Chapter 4 focuses on the many ways of obtaining drinking water in Mumbai's peri-urban territories. Particular attention is paid to informal supply systems, the initiatives taken by consumers to find ways round the shortcomings of the public distribution network and the emergence of local water markets. This chapter highlights the diversity of the solutions which have developed.

Chapter 5 presents the lessons to be learned from the reforms introduced in Chennai, offering an appraisal guided by a neo-institutional approach. Analysis of the accumulated effects of government and market shortcomings leads to suggestions for different ways of involving stakeholders in the management of water resources, in order to move towards a more effective model of supply and distribution.

Chapter 6 is more forward-looking in its approach. Following on from the sector-oriented approach to the demand proposed by the G-EAU model, this chapter presents the WATER-UP methodology for analysing the water supply in large cities in developing countries where issues of urban and peri-urban territorialization, and the balancing of resources play a decisive role.

Chapter 7 uses the methodology presented in the previous chapter to characterize the various components of urban demand on the basis of available observations. It highlights future imbalances in access to drinking water depending on available capacity, the degree of integration of urban and peri-urban territories, and the possible changes in supply and distribution systems.

In conclusion, Chapter 8 investigates the water policies deployed in major Indian cities. The difficulties met by the public service have prompted, with inputs from international agencies, to switch-over to a more 'bottom-up' approach to water policy, focusing on demand and incentives, but also on greater private sector involvement. In particular, this chapter presents the lessons learned from experiments in public-private partnership. This appraisal raises questions about the criteria needed to define more realistic, and effective reforms.

NOTES

1. Several criteria have been successively advanced for the statistical construction of urban zoning systems in France. The rural-urban opposition regarding industrial development relates to the size of towns and/or urban areas. Industrial or urban population zones (ZPIU) refer to intermediate zones between town and country. Lastly the zoning systems in urban areas were defined precisely with the aim of apprehending the phenomenon of peri-urbanization. These systems distinguish between urban centres (with more than 5,000 jobs), urban areas (defined in terms of the continuity of their constituent localities and the proportion of jobs offered by the urban centre) and the urban periphery (localities in the urban area not part of the urban centre). All these definitions are taken from France's Office of National Statistics (Insee), http://www.insee.fr.
2. Peri-urban zones classified as 'rural' [DUP 06], p. 1.
3. By territoriality, we mean the system of relations which the individuals belonging to a group entertain with their social and spatial environment in order to satisfy their needs in an autonomous manner, inside the system.
4. GEST'EAU, 'Integrated Water Management Tools', http://www.gesteau.eaufrance.fr/.http://www.gesteau.eaufrance.fr/sdage.html .
5. http://www.eaurmc.fr/qui-sommes-nous/acteurs-eau.php
6. Ibid.
7. [MED 06].

2

The Grenoble Urban Area Water Supply System

MAHFOUD BOUDIS AND YVES SAILLARD

2.1 INTRODUCTION

This chapter aims to present the drinking water supply to the French town of Grenoble. There is no question of drawing a parallel between large cities such as Mumbai, Chennai or Bengaluru, and Grenoble, a medium-sized city by French standards, a 'small' town by Indian standards. But Grenoble enables us to describe the various levels at which a city's drinking water supply system operates, while also serving as a basis for benchmarking situations observed elsewhere.

The case of Grenoble illustrates the multi-territoriality of urban water supplies. This is due to the fact that towns are administrative entities, the place where decisions are made and public policy defined, at the crossroads of economic and social exchanges, which involve numerous spaces and form the basis of a town's development. A town's geographic space and its environment, in the broad sense, determines the availability of water. Issues related to the procurement and management of water resources, much as economic and social affairs, need to be addressed jointly with several centres of decision. Finally, the state represents the decisive public authority for the management of natural water resources.

Economic and industrial development in Grenoble has followed a pattern, with a corresponding development in the means of access to water. The changes in the way the distribution of drinking water has been managed here are an example of a series of experiments in different ways of managing a public water utility. Lastly, thanks to its exceptional geographical situation, Grenoble is determined to set high standards for the quality of its water and the quality of the public service for supply and sanitation.

2.2 THE GEOGRAPHICAL SITUATION OF GRENOBLE AND ITS DRINKING WATER SUPPLY

At the end of the nineteenth century (1885) Grenoble was connected to a supply of very high-quality water from the Drac aquifer at Rochefort, some 15 km from Grenoble. This water is naturally pure. When first commissioned, the Rochefort springs could supply 52,000 cu m of water a day to 52,000 citizens of Grenoble.[1]

The industrial and urban development of Grenoble during the twentieth century brought changes to the original system, with extensive work on the catchment and mains network between 1963 and 1971. Thanks to the quality of the facilities and the characteristics of the Rochefort source and other sites,[2] Grenoble may be cited as an example for the analysis of urban water supplies.

The exceptional quality of Grenoble's water is largely due to the position of the Drac aquifer, which means it is naturally filtered. The aquifer is fed by the Drac river basin which extends over 3,000 sq km.

The Rochefort catchment consists of five wells (three radial wells and two seepage wells) which draw water from a depth of 30 cu m. The facility has two reservoirs: the Rochefort reservoir (at 252 m above sea level), with a capacity of 3,500 cu m, sufficient to feed the pumps at the lifting station. The Bresson reservoir (elevation 372 m), with a capacity of 40,000 cu m, stores approximately one day's consumption. The two reservoirs are high enough for the water to be distributed by natural gravitation; furthermore the end users are located at a relatively low altitude, ranging from 214 to 272 m. The automated machinery at the Rochefort site can process up to 137,000 cu m a day. It is estimated to have the potential to cater to the needs of half a million people.

The quality of the water from the Drac aquifer is equivalent to that of mineral water, due to the fact that it is filtered by alluvial deposits. A certificate of public utility (DUP) was issued on 9 October 2007, defining a protective perimeter, encompassing an area of 2,300 ha, to protect the natural quality of the water. The 500-ha fully protected area (marked in red in Figure 2.1) is owned by Grenoble City Council.

The water supply to the Grenoble urban area is comparable, in chemical terms, to bottled mineral water commonly consumed in France. Water quality is checked regularly by the Regional Water Laboratory, certified by the Ministry of Health. The largely favourable conditions prevailing over the catchment area are summarized in Table 2.1.

The aquifers are refilled by the mountain and glacier environment. The average annual rainfall over the last 30 years has been 929.8 mm

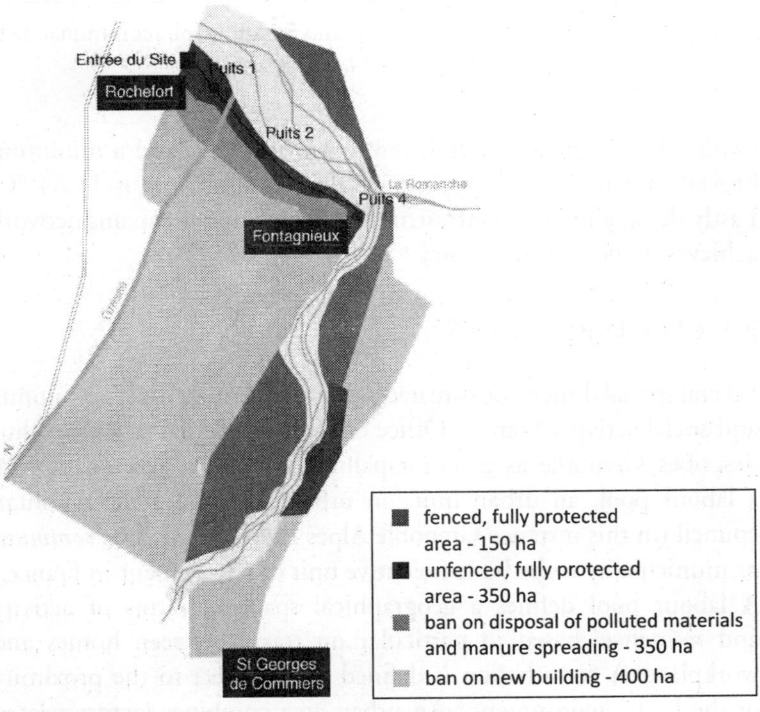

Source: Régie des Eaux de Grenoble, 2006 annual report.

FIGURE 2.1: THE ROCHEFORT SITE AND ITS PROTECTIVE PERIMETERS

TABLE 2.1: THE MAIN PARAMETERS FOR GAUGING WATER QUALITY IN THE GRENOBLE URBAN AREA

Bacteria	G and AG: Very good quality water, in compliance with quality standards without additional disinfectants
Nitrates	Quality standard: 50 mg/l Average content observed: 4.2 mg (G), 3.1 mg (AG)
Pesticides	Quality standard: 0.1 µg/l Maximum content: Below detection threshold
Hardness	No quality standard Average content: 20.9° (G), 19° (AG) – average mineral content
Fluorine	Quality standard: 1.5 mg/l Observed content: 0.08 mg/l (G) – low fluorine content
Other parameters	All the results for other parameters comply with quality standards (undesirable, toxic substances, etc.) (G)

Source: Régie des Eaux de Grenoble (G) and Syndicat Intercommunal de la Région Grenobloise (AG).

(with a maximum value of 1,288.6 mm in 1977, and a minimum of 480 mm in 1989). The average daily temperature is 11.64 °C. Lastly the quality of the infrastructure is such that the mains network achieves 93 per cent efficiency.[4]

2.3 CITY TERRITORIES

Several spatial dimensions are necessary to describe a town's economic and social activity. France's Office of National Statistics (Insee) thus describes Grenoble as a municipality (but also a 'town-canton'[5]), a labour pool, an urban unit, an urban area and a metropolitan council (in this instance Grenoble Alpes Métropole[6]). The *commune* or municipality is the basic executive unit of government in France.[7] A labour pool defines a geographical space in terms of activity and residence, based in particular on travel between homes and workplace. A conurbation is defined with respect to the proximity of the built environment.[8] An urban area combines factors related to the continuity of the built environment and of employment, also encompassing the concept of an urban centre and the neighbouring localities connected to it.[9] Finally, a *communauté d'agglomération*, or metropolitan council, is an administrative body (not a statistical construct), much as a municipality, canton or region. This body is an *établissement public de coopération intercommunale* (EPCI), or public establishment for intermunicipal cooperation, brought about by voluntary regrouping of municipalities to carry out joint projects. This type of organization, made possible by a recent law (on consolidating and simplifying intermunicipal cooperation, dated 12 July 1999) reflects the need to pool resources for the running of services and amenities. Municipalities and cantons, established in 1789, are part of the basic administrative organization of the French state.

These spaces describe dimensions of the city, all of which are meaningful for the supply and management of a natural resource: administrative districts for decisions on supply, distribution and equipment; statistical groupings for the assessment of demand and the development of networks. Table 2.2 presents Grenoble's various urban territories with their population and size.

The population of the Grenoble conurbation registered its highest growth between 1954 and 1975 (with 3.6 per cent average annual growth), a period which saw a boom in the electrical and mechanical engineering industry, the development of integrated circuit manufacturing and the setting up of a laboratory belonging to France's Atomic Energy Commission (CEA) in 1962. After 1975

TABLE 2.2: GRENOBLE TERRITORIES, 2006 DATA

Territory	Population	Area (sq km)	Density (pop. per sq km)
Municipality	156,107	18.1	8,610.4
Conurbation	396,657	307.1	1,291.5
Urban unit	427,659	324.8	1,316.8
Urban area	531,440	1,567.9	338.9
Labour pool	584,395	3,322.5	175.9

Source: Insee, Statistiques locales.

average annual demographic growth fell to 0.2 per cent,[10] and the conurbation only saw relatively slow, moderate changes, suggesting that demand for water was relatively stable. Despite its high-tech image Grenoble depends primarily on the service sector (accounting for 77 per cent of all jobs), in which health care (including the university teaching hospital), local government (prefecture, Isère Departmental Council, City Council) and state education are the main employers.

The conurbation is a highly urbanized territory, with an average density of nearly 1,300 people per sq km. The Grenoble conurbation is not subject to demographic pressure but it is undergoing significant internal changes, between generations and between the localities that make up its territory.

The peri-urban development of Grenoble followed a pattern that is fairly common for large and medium-sized towns, with a negative migration balance in the centre of the conurbation[11] and a positive balance in the outskirts.[12] The demographic trends of the city are also characterized by net negative flows[13] towards France's major centres of business and employment. The executives and intermediate professions trained by Grenoble's large higher education facilities often find work elsewhere. The negative migration flows are also due to people moving to the nearby Mediterranean coast when they retire. On the other hand, Grenoble is extremely attractive for students, with about 50,000 students either at university or in one of the graduate engineering or business schools. Grenoble consequently enjoys the image of a 'youthful' city, with roughly one-fifth of its population aged 20 to 29 years.

The disparities in the lifestyle, standard of living and housing observed across the conurbation are due in part to the presence of two clearly differentiated sub-groups: senior managers and members of the professions with relatively high incomes, and students often with part-time jobs. Collective housing accounts for about three-quarters of first homes, on average. However, there are significant disparities between the centre and some localities in its immediate vicinity, and peripheral localities where detached housing is predominant.

2.4 ORGANIZATION OF THE PUBLIC WATER SERVICE IN GRENOBLE

In the middle of the 1980s significant changes were made to the way the drinking water supply in Grenoble was organized. It had traditionally operated as a municipal public service, but switched to a system of water distribution and sanitation delegated to the private sector. Initially the poor efficiency of this organization and the crisis it brought about led to renegotiation of the contract between the municipality and the private companies tasked with managing the water supply. The contract was subsequently terminated and management by a municipal company was restored. The effectiveness of the waste-water processing plant was called into question. Tighter public supervision was enforced and disposal operations, organized at a regional level, were separated from waste-water processing and transferred back to municipal management. This series of *in vivo* experiments makes Grenoble something of an exemplary case for illustrating a discussion on governance of a public service and more specifically the organization of public-private partnerships for the procurement and distribution of drinking water.

The organization of the public water service fits into the larger framework of national bodies (see following section). It draws a distinction between the water procurement and distribution services, which are organized at a municipal level, and the sanitation service which is organized at an intermunicipal level. This complex organization is both a justification for greater consumer consultation and an illustration of the 'multi-territoriality' of water.

2.4.1 *The Bodies of National Organization*

On account of its geographical situation in relation to various river basins, the management of Grenoble's natural water resources is primarily dependent on the Rhône-Mediterranean and Corsica Water Agency (EauRMC), which by law is a public, state-sponsored body reporting to the Ministry of Ecology and Sustainable Development, and to the Ministry of Economy, Finance and Employment. The mission of this agency is to 'initiate rational use of water resources in its catchment basin, combat their pollution and protect aquatic habitats'.[14] It provides municipalities with financial assistance to build the necessary structures to protect resources and subsidizes work on drinking water supply networks in rural localities. EauRMC focuses on three main issues:[15] combating (domestic, industrial and agricultural) pollution, preserving and managing water resources, and outreach operations in the service of education and public awareness.

The Rhône-Mediterranean and Corsica basins[16] cover 130,000 sq km, accounting for roughly a quarter of mainland France. The two basins' water resources represent 44 per cent of all run-off, carried by 6,500 streams exceeding 2 km in length and lakes such as Geneva, Annecy and Le Bourget, more than 70,000 sq km of wetlands, and 15.5 billion cu m accumulated in glaciers. The two basins serve nearly 14 million people. The average density of this geographical space is about 100 inhabitants/sq km, but with very large disparities, ranging from conurbations to very sparsely populated mountain areas. This part of France accounts for half the country's tourist activity. Grenoble is one of the industrial centres in an area where significant numbers of people are still engaged in arable farming and stock raising.

The Drac-Romanche Water Management and Development Scheme (Sage)[17] sets water resource guidelines to be followed by public bodies, local and national government. The plan for the Drac and Romanche rivers covers more than 2,500 sq km and concerns 119 localities. It was framed between December 2002 and March 2007[18] and is the result of work by the local water committee, which brings together everyone with a stake in water: policy makers, consumers, public bodies and technical partners.

In each French department the Directorate of Public Health and Social Affairs (DDASS) monitors water quality and checks compliance with legal requirements set by decree no. 89-3 of 3 January 1989, on water for human consumption. Samples are taken regularly and analysed by a regional water analysis laboratory certified by the Ministry of Health.

Regarding the organization at the municipal level, Grenoble's water and sanitation services were operated by a municipal company until 1989. They were privatized in 1990, then reorganized as a *société d'économie mixte*, a form of quasi-public company, in 1997. Three years later the water service returned to public management. The Régie des Eaux de Grenoble (REG), a municipal company invested with 'moral' legal personality and financial independence, was set up. Its statutes are those of an *établissement public industriel et commercial*, a publicly owned industrial and trading company. The Metropolitan Council is now responsible for sanitation. The public water service for Grenoble is consequently based on two organizations with different perimeters and management methods:

- Water procurement and distribution for the city of Grenoble (and two neighbouring localities of Sassenage and La Tronche);
- Sanitation for the whole of the area governed by the metropolitan council.

2.4.2 *Drinking Water Procurement and Distribution*

The procurement and distribution of drinking water in the Grenoble urban area are organized in accordance with a spatial division, between the core city and surrounding localities, but with considerable interconnection of services.

The city of Grenoble[19] owns the pumping station for drawing water from the Drac aquifer, as well as 500 ha of protected land around the Rochefort catchment. The city also manages water consumption by municipal buildings and all consumption for public usage (fire hydrants, fountains, water outlets for street cleaning, etc.).

A *régie*, or municipal company, is responsible for operating the drinking water procurement and distribution service. The work of Régie des Eaux de Grenoble (REG) concerns the following fields:[20]

- Water protection, catchment, production and conveyance;
- Allocation and effective use of the drinking water resource;
- Water distribution and quality assurance;
- Management of consumer connections and relations.

REG[21] is governed by a board with 12 members, including eight city councillors, one of whom is elected to chair the board. The four remaining members of the board are selected for their technical input. The board sets the main policy guidelines for the company and supervises its activity. A manager-coordinator put forward by the leader of the City Council is appointed by the City Council following due debate to take charge of the everyday running of the company.

REG employs about 85 permanent staff, including 16 municipal employees seconded by the City Council. REG has implemented quality processes enabling it to obtain ISO 9001 certification for the quality of its services, the water it supplies and its consumer service.

At the end of 2007 REG had 51,130 consumer connections on its books. It was operating a 240-km network of water mains, with 13,100 branch connections. It distributed 11.9 million cu m of water in 1997 (source: Régie des Eaux de Grenoble).

Consumption by the various categories of subscribers is detailed in Table 2.3.

Other municipalities in the conurbation have delegated the procurement and/or distribution of drinking water to the Syndicat Intercommunal des Eaux de la Région Grenobloise (SIERG).[22] This intermunicipal agency, or EPCI (see section 2.3), is governed by the Code Général des Collectivités Territoriales, a set of regulations for local authorities. SIERG is empowered 'to carry out work on

Table 2.3: Breakdown of Water Consumption Between the Various REG Subscribers

Category of consumer*	Volume of water consumed (2006), cu m
Residential	3,459,563
Large consumers	5,770,274
Outside sales	1,630,681
Municipal usage	1,290,086
TOTAL	12,150,604

Note: * Residential refers to households; Large consumers comprises blocks of flats (mainly social housing), administrative bodies, commerce and industry; Outside sales covers sales to other localities; and Municipal usage refers to council consumption (parks and gardens, fire hydrants, etc.).

Source: Régie des Eaux de Grenoble, 2006 Annual Report [REG 06]

behalf of member municipalities in its field of competency, which covers the production, transport and storage of drinking water but excludes distribution which remains within the remit of member municipalities'.[23]

SIERG serves 32 localities, with 2,00,000 consumers. It was set up after the Second World War, in 1947, at the instigation of seven municipalities (including Grenoble). The increasing number of localities concerned and the economic development of the urban area prompted SIERG to extend the scope of the water resources under its management, adding the lower reaches of the Romanche river (1948-58), then the Pré-Grivel catchment, Plaine de Jouchy (starting in 1965), the Oz-en-Oisans catchment (in 1975) and the Olle aquifer, which came to serve as the emergency groundwater supply for SIERG.

SIERG applies the overall guidelines on security of supply and water quality at an inter-municipal level. SIERG is supervised by a board comprising representatives of the 32 municipalities concerned (two delegates for each municipality). For the committee to be able to deliberate and take valid decisions, a quorum is required, consisting of a majority of committee members. Exactly the same method, proportionate to the amount of water consumed by each locality, is used to calculate how much each municipality contributes to the SIERG budget. SIERG operates as an instrument of intermunicipal solidarity. It pays for the expenditure required for its operations but also invests in maintaining and extending its network and purchasing new land, exercising a pre-emption right to protect the immediate environment of the catchment.

SIERG organized the distribution of 18 million cu m of water in 2006, with a network comprising 67 reservoirs and 110 km of mains. Each locality has an average reserve equivalent to two days' consumption.

Five interconnection networks link the REG and SIERG networks enabling them to solve any temporary problems for the water supply in the Grenoble urban area. Backup connections also link the network to its highland counterpart, the Syndicat Intercommunal des Eaux de Casserousse (SIEC). For example, over a three-month period in 2003, REG supplied 8,00,000 cu m of water to assist neighbouring localities: Echirolles, Saint Martin d'Hères, Eybens, Fontaine, Seyssinet-Pariset, Saint-Martin le Vinoux and Gières.

2.4.3 *Treatment of Waste Water*

The treatment of waste water is organized at an inter-municipal level, serving the city of Grenoble and surrounding localities.

The *communauté d'agglomération*, or metropolitan council (known as Grenoble Alpes Métropole, or Metro) is responsible for sanitation.[24] Since 1 January 2005 the metropolitan council has represented 26 localities in the Grenoble urban area. It is responsible for the entire public sanitation service: collecting, transporting and processing waste water. This includes investing in, maintaining and operating drains and three sewage stations. The council is also responsible for rainwater drainage (except for flooding).

The various municipalities delegate their powers to the metropolitan council for the organization of the public sanitation service. This arrangement does not only concern municipalities represented in the council, but also 28 localities outside the urban area which are connected to one of the three sewage stations operated by the council.

The metropolitan council enjoys full ownership of certain facilities[25] and operates others transferred to it by the municipalities. The facilities wholly owned by the council comprise a (40 km) network of inter-municipal drains, 39 pumping stations and two sewage stations (Le Fontanil, dates from 1977 and has a capacity equivalent to 35,000 people; Aquapole was commissioned in 1989 and has a capacity equivalent to 5,00,000 people). The facilities transferred by municipalities include drains (1,700 sq km[26]) and about 100 subsidiary structures.

The inter-municipal public sanitation service is operated by a financially independent municipal company, with the metropolitan council retaining its moral personality. The council on the advise of its board is empowered to take decisions on pricing policy, budgeting, tendering and other agreements.

The public sanitation service is operated as a municipal company,

Régie d'Assainissement (RdA), under direct council control except for a few services which are covered by an agreement delegating the public service to an outside operator, under the supervision and technical control of the RdA. Operation of the two sewage stations (Le Fontanil and Aquapole) and the inter-municipal main sewers is delegated to Société Dauphinoise d'Assainissement (SDA). The Gières municipality has delegated its sanitation and rainwater drainage services to SEM des Eaux de la Région Grenobloise et d'Assainissement du Drac Inférieur (SERGADI), a quasi-public company.

The sanitation company is responsible for various tasks. It carries out work for the upkeep and maintenance of waste water collection and pumping structures. Two-thirds of its interventions concern blockages on the network, the rest focusing mainly on various forms of pollution or damage (2007 sanitation annual report). Sanitation services also include large-scale upkeep and replacement work, and operations to extend or build new sanitation facilities all over the area for which the metropolitan council is responsible. A specific (electro-mechanical) department monitors and operates round the clock 100 pumping and injection stations which are an integral part of the sanitation system. RdA is also responsible for inlets to the sanitation networks.

The sewage stations are operated by an outside contractor. Treatment of the waste water removes pollutants before releasing it into the natural environment. For example, the Aquapole sewage station reported 72.7 per cent efficiency for 2007, between the raw waste water entering the plant and the water released into the Isère River.

Figure 2.2 below presents, in simplified form, the multi-territoriality of water in the Grenoble area in terms of methods of procurement and management.

2.4.4 *Coordinating the Various Players and Consumer Representatives*

Given the large number of players involved in the public water service, organizations are needed to coordinate operations and monitor consumer satisfaction.

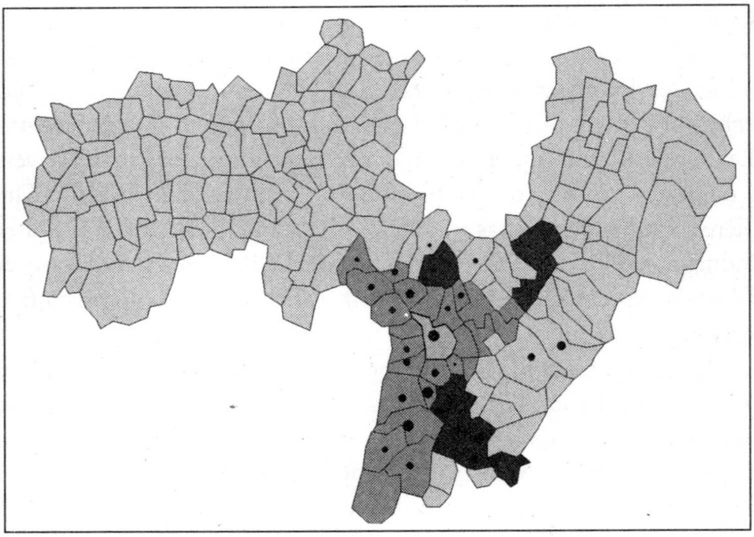

City of Grenoble
Localities in the Grenoble Urban Region (RUG) covered by the relevant master plan, except for localities in the Beaurepaire area.
Metro localities represented on the Grenoble Metropolitan Council.
Non-metro localities served by SIERG.
Well for metro localities (size of circle proportionate to amount drawn in 2006)

Sources: The outline maps used here were produced by BD Carto © IGN; for the perimeter of the Grenoble Urban Region, http://www.aurg.org/, on 23/10/2009; for details of metropolitan council localities, www.lametro.fr, on 23/10/2009; and localities served by SIERG, www.sierg.org, on 23/10/2009. The locations and volume of water procurement are based on data for 2006 from EauRMC, www.eaurmc.fr.

FIGURE 2.2A: MULTI-TERRITORIAL WATER NETWORK: GRENOBLE URBAN AREA AND NEIGHBOURING LOCALITIES

In 1996 the Grenoble Water and Sanitation Users Committee (CUEAG) was set up. It advises the City Council on the operations of the public water service. In 2002 an agreement was signed between the committee and the municipal water company, REG.[27] Under its terms the committee is required to meet every two months, holding a joint meeting with REG twice a year. It advises on decisions on

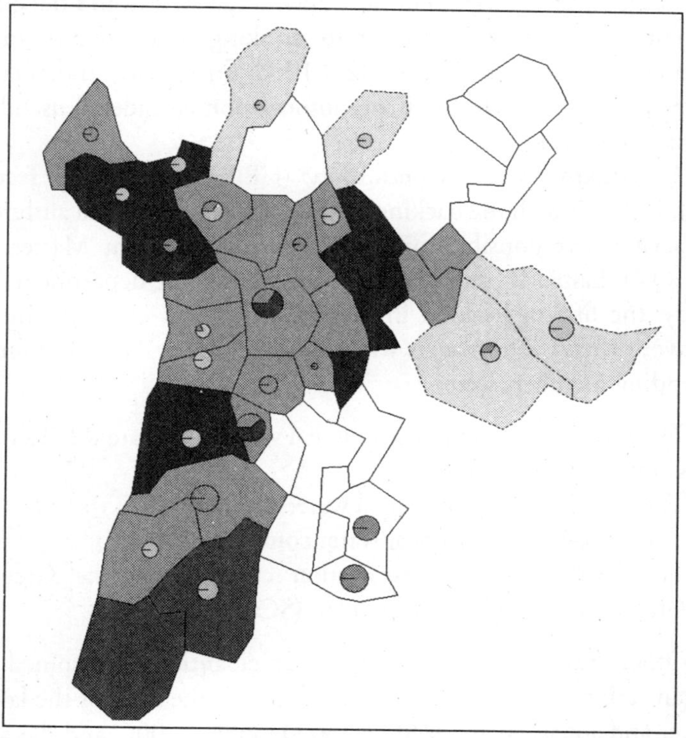

- Metro localities where public water supply is operated by an outside contractor.
- Metro localities where public water supply is operated by a metropolitan-owned municipal company.
- Metro localities where public water supply is operated by a municipal-owned municipal company.
- Localities outside the metropolitan urban area with wells supplying metro localities.
- Localities outside the metropolitan urban area with a water supply operated by SIERG.

- Water from underground aquifer
- Water from underground springs
- Surface river water

Sources: BDcarto@IGN for outline map; EauRMC, REG, Metro and SIERG for data.

FIGURE 2.2B: MULTI-TERRITORIAL WATER NETWORK: TYPE OF OPERATIONS IN 2006 investment, the operation of the public water service and the quality of consumer care with respect to drinking water distribution. It also reviews the draft REG budget. REG, for its part, undertakes to provide the committee with any information considered useful and to assist its work.

A Drinking Water Community (CEP)[28] was set up recently (4 July 2007) with the backing of the *syndicat mixte* (local authorities association) responsible for the Urban Development Master Plan (SCOT), EauRMC and the Prefecture of the Isère department. This body, the first of its kind in France, serves as a coordinating link between the various players with a stake in water. The community's founding members were:

- The Grenoble-area inter-municipal water syndicate (SIERG);
- Grenoble City Council;
- The Grenoble-city municipal water company (REG);
- The Drac-Romanche local water commission (CLE);
- The local authorities association coordinating the Grenoble Urban Development Master Plan (SCOT).

Other water associations and municipalities have joined this organization since its inception. In line with the aims of the law on water and aquatic habitats, dated 30 December 2006, and the ninth EauRMC programme, CRP seeks to consolidate the public water service and increase its efficiency by developing closer ties between territories and supporting local authorities.

The work of CEP is managing drinking water in 243 localities and 22 organizations in the Isère department. The work is mainly related to various forms of action in the public interest, the safety of networks, protection of resources and the price of water. CEP seeks to obtain concerted control of water prices and quality. In all, its work concerns 6,86,000 people in the Grenoble urban area (residents and visitors). The community is coordinated by the SCOT organization, funded by its members and EauRMC. Its prime objective is to make public action more effective and to build closer links between territories.

In addition, other organizations play an important part in consolidating and assessing the public water service. The Fédération

Nationale des Collectivités Concédantes et Régies (National Federation of Contracting Authorities and Municipal Companies [FNCCR] acts as a forum for local authorities organizing public services, in particular water supply (but also energy and environmental services). This non-profit organization, set up in 1934, supports local councillors in their work organizing local public services operated under various forms. It encourages municipalities to pool their services better to control the technical complexity of the task and the management of public services. Both REG and RdA belong to FNCCR.

FNCCR represents the interests of local authorities in their dealings with national and European authorities, and with contracting companies. It also operates as a centre for training and sharing of experience gained by local authorities. It devotes much of its energy to designing and disseminating benchmarks for the performance of water and sanitation services with the support of local authorities and the Ministry of Ecology and Sustainable Development (water directorate).[29]

2.5 THE COST OF THE PUBLIC WATER SERVICE IN THE GRENOBLE AREA

As we have seen in the previous section the public water service is split between two separate departments: procurement and distribution on the one hand, sanitation and waste water treatment on the other. The amount charged to consumers covers the complete service. We shall now look at how the overall price is calculated, focusing mainly on the city of Grenoble, without detailing the pricing methods of other localities in the urban area.

The price of water, corresponding to the 'consumption' item in the REG budget, is re-calculated every year[30] on the basis of the estimated inflation in the water sector, based in turn on increases in specific prices (mains, drains, connections, supplies and pipes; the overall public works index for all categories of work; and conventional underground works) and on weighting coefficients derived from the REG cost structure.[31] Forecasts are also made for the level of investments and their funding, payroll trends, and the sliding scale of charges for large consumers. A distinction is drawn between fixed items (connection and meter hire) and variable items appearing in water bills which are directly related to consumption.

One way of presenting the water price structure is to look at the breakdown between the main players in the public water service, as shown in Table 2.4. With this approach, the price structure of Grenoble water for 2009 is as given in Table 2.4 (based on annual invoiced consumption of 120 cu m for a four-person household).

These data mean that the total price of water for residential use, including distribution, sanitation and taxes was set at €2.41 per cu m in 2009.

The price of water differs depending on whether it is for residential use (calculated as shown in Table 2.4) or destined for large consumers. This impacts on both the fixed part of the price and the variable part linked to consumption. Table 2.5 shows these differences for REG's share of the water price (procurement and distribution).

TABLE 2.4: PRICE STRUCTURE OF GRENOBLE WATER IN 2009, ACCORDING TO PUBLIC WATER SERVICE PLAYERS

Beneficiary	Amount in €	%
REG		
Consumer connection	16.90	
Hire and upkeep of meter	7.38	
Consumption	88.80	
Total	113.08	39.1
Water agency		
Standard charge	7.26	
Anti-pollution measures	22.80	
Modernization of network	15.60	
Total	45.66	15.8
SDA (standard charge)	36.396	12.6
Metro (standard charge)	79.008	27.3
VAT	15.07	5.2
TOTAL per 120 cu m	289.214	100.0

Source: Régie des Eaux de Grenoble, http://www.reg-grenoble.fr/Default.aspx?tabid=90 (accessed in August 2009).

TABLE 2.5: DIFFERENCES IN WATER TARIFFS APPLIED BY REG BETWEEN RESIDENTIAL USERS AND LARGE CONSUMERS

Tariffs from 1/01/2006 to 31/12/2006		
Basic price before tax (VAT at 5.5%)		Amount in €
Tariff for residential use		
Fixed part per half-year		7.51
Price of water per cu m		0.6381
Tariff for large consumers		
Fixed part per quarter-year		
Consumption < 6,000 cu m a year		3.77
Consumption > 6,000 cu m a year		15.05
Price of water per cu m		
0 to 24,000 cu m a month		0.6381
24,001 to 36,000 cu m a month		0.5775
Over 36,000 cu m a month		0.5220
Meter hire		€/half-year
	∅ 10, 12, 15 mm	3.18
	...	
	∅ 250 mm	281.57
	Swan neck	3.18

Source: 2006 Annual Report, Régie des Eaux de Grenoble, p. 55 [REG 06].

The structure of water prices can be presented in such a way as to highlight the various functions of a water management system (distribution, drainage and sanitation) and the various types of cost (Figure 2.4).

As we can see the overall price of water covers three main functions: procurement and distribution of water (41 per cent), drainage and treatment of waste water (41 per cent), and taxes and other duty (18 per cent).

A distinction is made in the share of the price allocated to procurement and distribution between fixed and variable costs. Fixed costs (connection, hire and upkeep of meters) are calculated over six-month periods. Variable costs are mainly made up of the net price fixed by REG, but also of the standard charge paid to EauRMC. The cost of waste water drainage and treatment is split between two items: a standard charge paid to SDA, which operates the Aquapole sewage station; and the standard charge paid to the Metro inter-municipal

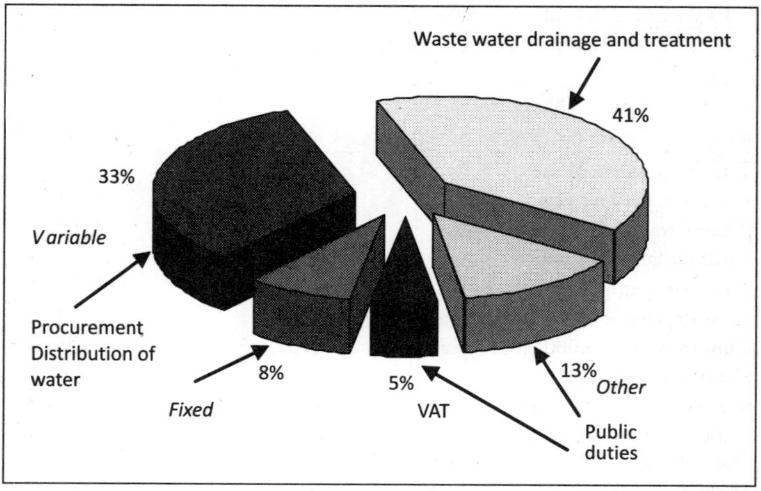

Source: Régie des Eaux de Grenoble, http://www.reg-grenoble.fr/Default.aspx?tabid=90 (consulted in August 2009), on the basis of water price as invoiced.

FIGURE 2.4: PRICE STRUCTURE OF GRENOBLE WATER BY FUNCTION AND TYPE OF COST

organization. Public duties concern the standard charge levied by EauRMC which helps local authorities to combat pollution (Other), and VAT, at a rate of 5 per cent, which is due on each item of pre-tax cost.

The changes in the pricing of Grenoble water reflect a close link between the price of water and the way the public water service is organized [LOB 06]. Grenoble has experimented with a series of management systems: loosely controlled private management (up to 1995), then renegotiation of the contracts and partly private management (up to 2000), finally restoring the system hinging on a *régie*, or municipal company. The variations in the price per cubic metre clearly reflect these changes. The return to public management has brought down the costs of procuring and distributing water to the city of Grenoble (see Figure 2.5).

The price of water in Grenoble can be compared with the prices in other localities around the city and with other French towns.

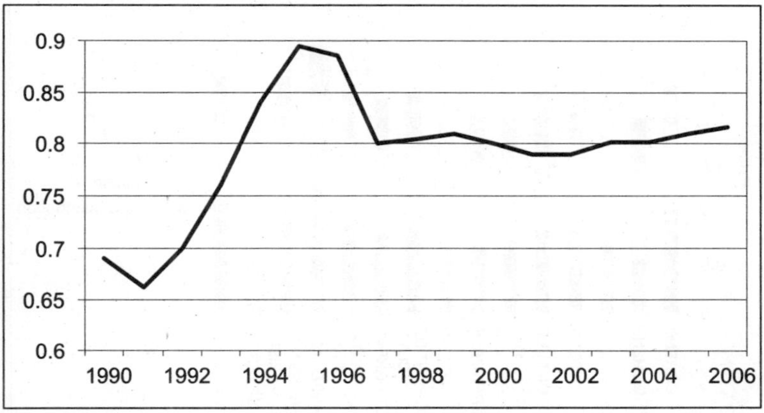

Source: Régie des Eaux de Grenoble, 2006 Annual Report, p. 4 [REG 06].
Note: The INSEE consumer price inflation index for all households has been deducted from the price of water (spring water distribution function).

FIGURE 2.5: VARIATION IN THE PRICE, BEFORE TAX, PER CUBIC METRE OF WATER, IN INFLATION-ADJUSTED EUROS (BASE 2006)

The EauRMC agency carries out regular surveys of water prices in the various localities within its remit.[32] Much as for the data from REG (preceding charts), the data obtained from these surveys is based on the supply in each surveyed locality of a standard volume of 120 cu m consumed in the course of the year. The chart in Figure 2.6 uses data from the survey for 15 (out of 26) localities in the Grenoble urban area, for which data was collated. The price of water in Grenoble is lower than the prices charged in the various localities in the urban area, though in 2005 there were no major variations. For the whole of the urban area, the price of water varies between €2 and 3 per cu m.

The same EauRMC survey shows that average residential water consumption does not vary a great deal, ranging from 45 to 75 cu m per person per year (in 2005) on average, as shown in Figure 2.7. The pricing system does not seem to establish a link between the level of consumption and the price charged.

The price of water in Grenoble is generally considered to be one of the lowest for a large town in France. According to FNCCR[33] and

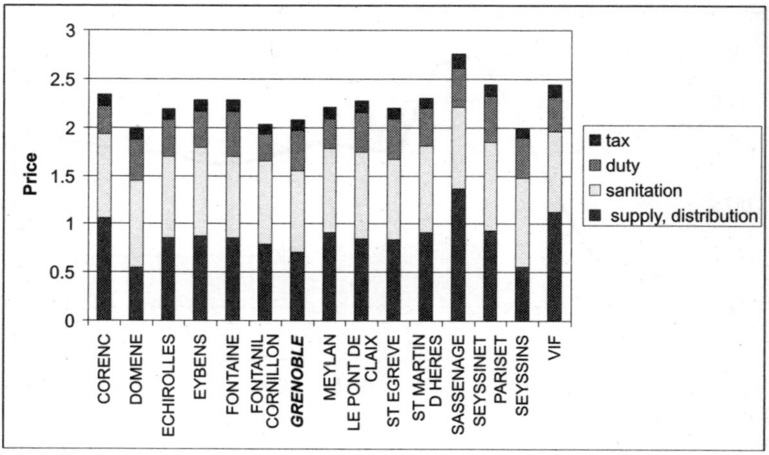

Source: l'Agence de l'eau du Bassin Rhône-Méditerranée-Corse

FIGURE 2.6. THE PRICE OF WATER IN CERTAIN LOCALITIES OF THE GRENOBLE URBAN AREA

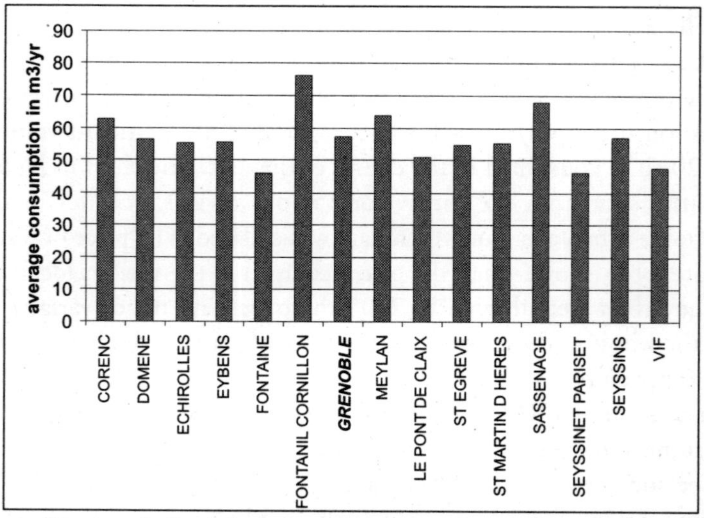

Source: l'Agence de l'eau du Bassin Rhône-Méditerranée-Corse

FIGURE 2.7. AVERAGE CONSUMPTION IN cu m FOR VARIOUS LOCALITIES IN THE GRENOBLE URBAN AREA

Nantes Métropole, quoted in an REG document, Grenoble is one of the French towns where the price of water is lowest,[34] as shown in Figure 2.8.

2.6 GRENOBLE: A BENCHMARK FOR ACCESS TO DRINKING WATER?

The geographical situation and tradition of public service in the water supply make Grenoble something of a benchmark for the organization of water supply. The city enjoys the availability of plentiful, good-quality water resources. There is no interruption in distribution. There is little pressure from population growth. Urban development is not upsetting the balance between the city and the peri-urban environment. Grenoble is thus able to distribute water of excellent quality, with one of the lowest prices among large French towns.

The long-term sustainability of this form of urban procurement does, however, raise three types of issue: the renewal of infrastructure, the consistency of public policies and the anticipation of climate change.

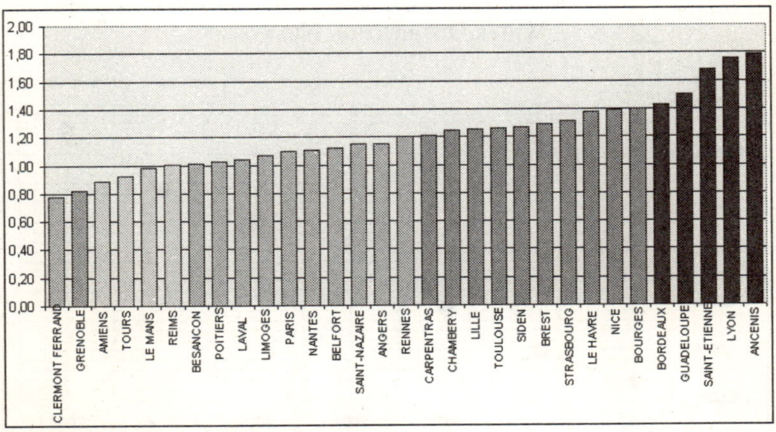

Source: FNCCR and Nantes Métropole.

FIGURE 2.8: AVERAGE PRICE PER cu m IN 2006 FOR LOCALITIES WITH MORE THAN 1,00,000 INHABITANTS (AVERAGE PRICE BEFORE TAX PER cu m FOR THE WATER PART OF A 120 cu m INVOICE, NOT INCLUDING FIXED CHARGES; NOT INCLUDING SANITATION, TAXES AND STANDARD LEVIES)

When Grenoble's water distribution network was first built its capacity exceeded the demands of the 1960s population. With changes in the network it is now necessary to replace certain facilities and extend the network to keep up with the spread of the urban area.

According to the 2006 and 2007 annual reports published by REG the water distribution network was in the following state in 2006 (Figure 2.9a), despite efforts to replace the mains (Figure 2.9b).

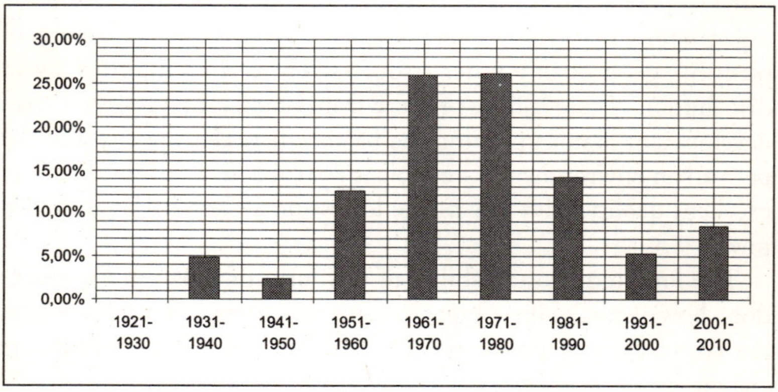

FIGURE 2.9A: RELATIVE AGE OF THE GRENOBLE WATER DISTRIBUTION NETWORK

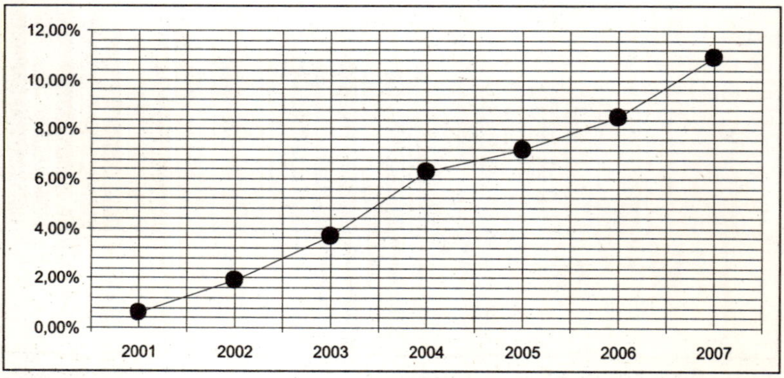

Source: Régie des Eaux de Grenoble, 2006 and 2007 Annual Reports, [REG 06], [REG 07].

FIGURE 2.9B: PROPORTION OF GRENOBLE MAINS LESS THAN 10 YEARS OLD

In some localities the relative age of facilities is already causing problems of leakage, due to holes in water mains,[35] and the rate of the network's replacement will have to be speeded up over the next 20 years. Renewal work will also be required to comply with European standards on the use of lead pipes.[36] Modernizing old water mains could have a significant impact on prices.

Although the major part of Grenoble's water distribution network, is in public ownership, may yield to free-market pressures in line with changes in the political colour of the city council, as has occurred in the past. However, the current trend is towards greater inter-municipal coordination, with consumers playing a larger part in water governance. The main issue is to achieve a more consistent whole, adjusting the existing price system to reflect efforts to control demand. Residential consumption stands at about 200 litres a day (daily average per subscriber, excluding wholesale and large consumers)[37] and REG wants to convince users to consume less. Reducing the level of consumption would enable REG to commit itself to supplying water to other localities in the urban area with additional connections to the distribution network.

The current system for managing water for the Grenoble urban area is complex, involving a large number of different players, with various bodies tasked with their coordination. This begs the question of whether it might be preferable to shift towards a more integrated management system encompassing the whole urban area. This would mean extending REG's remit to all the water resources of the urban area, harmonizing water prices, and integrating procurement, distribution and sanitation services. It is also at the urban-area level that the priority given to various forms of water usage can be effectively defined, in particular the top priority given to drinking water.[38]

Although the supply of drinking water is not thought to be a problem in France, the prospect of climate change could have a negative impact. In recent years Electricité De France (EDF), which uses the water of the Drac, has received various requests to release water to top up the aquifer.[39] A growing number of crossover connections are being fitted between the various networks serving the Grenoble urban area to guarantee the standard of water distribution in the urban area. A borehole 200 m in depth was drilled in 2009 to determine the limits of the aquifer.[40] A project is under study to stockpile bottled water in preparation for natural or technological hazards.[41] Furthermore restrictions on water usage have become a regular fixture in France: in September 2009 more than half of French departments had taken measures to restrict the use of water for at least one river basin.[42] According to the same source, at the same time of the year in 2003, under drought conditions, three-quarters of all departments were affected by similar measures.

NOTES

1. Histoire de l'eau de Grenoble, Régie des Eaux de Grenoble website, http://www.reg-grenoble.fr, accessed on 30 October 2009.
2. Exploitation of other sites in the Drac-Romanche River basin.
3. This description of the equipment at the Rochefort site is taken from the Régie des Eaux de Grenoble website, Le site exceptionnel de Rochefort, http://www.reg-grenoble.fr, accessed on 30 October 2009.
4. In 2006, primary efficiency (supply) was rated at 93.30 per cent and technical efficiency (distribution) at 81.23 per cent. The water agency considers that in an urban environment, a yield of between 70 and 80 per cent is acceptable. Régie des Eaux de Grenoble, 2006 annual report, pp. 89-90.
5. According to the definitions set by Insee, a town-canton is a group of complete localities, whereas a canton (the term is used in France for a constituency in elections for the *conseil général* [departmental council]) may bring together fractions of localities. In urban areas a town-canton consists of the core town. So in the present case the town-canton of Grenoble corresponds to the locality of Grenoble.
6. As explained under the Statistiques locales heading, on the Insee website, http://www.insee.fr/fr/, accessed on 30 October 2009.
7. It is, according to Insee, the smallest administrative sub-division in France and also the oldest, having replaced the towns and parishes of the Middle Ages. The *commune* came into existence in 1789, gaining a degree of political autonomy thanks to the law of 5 April 1884, which defined its rights and obligations. See http://www.insee.fr/fr/methodes/default.asp?page=definitions/commune.htm, accessed on 30 October 2009.
8. This process takes as its starting point the 'urban units', according to the Insee definition, which may be found at: http://www.insee.fr/fr/methodes/default.asp?page=definitions/unite-urbaine.htm, accessed on 30 October 2009. These units consist of one or more localities with continuous built-up urban fabric (without a break of more than 200 m between two structures) and are home

to at least 2,000 people. A locality belongs to an urban unit if more than half of its population lives inside the built-up area. A multi-locality urban area refers to an urban unit comprising several localities.

9. More exactly, an urban area brings together an urban centre, an urban unit offering at least 5,000 jobs and 'without any enclaves and all in one piece', and rural localities or urban units other than the urban centre, 'of which at least 40% of the resident population with a job works in the urban centre or one of the localities attracted by it'.
10. The statistical data quoted in this section and all the data presenting the Grenoble urban area were collated by Insee Rhône-Alpes [INS 05].
11. The 'centre' is defined by Insee as a circle with a radius of 8 km around Grenoble.
12. The peri-urban zone of the conurbation is defined as a circle with a radius of between 8 and 30 km around Grenoble.
13. [INS 05].
14. http://www.eaurmc.fr
15. http://www.eaurmc.fr/qui-sommes-nous/mission1.php
16. http://www.eaurmc.fr/agence-bassin-rmc/bassin.php
17. http://www.drac-romanche.com
18. The Sage is an integrated instrument for water management based on the EU Water Framework Directive, passed by the European Parliament in 2000, and transformed into French law in 2004. The Directive aims to achieve a good state of water resources by 2015, http://www.water.europa.eu/
19. http://www.grenoble.fr/jsp/site/Portal.jsp?page_id=546, accessed on 30 October 2009.
20. http://www.reg-grenoble.fr/Default.aspx?tabid=46, accessed on 30 October 2009.
21. http://www.reg-grenoble.fr/Default.aspx?tabid=131, accessed on 30 October 2009.
22. http://www.sierg.org.
23. The new statutes of SIERG, 30 November 2005: http://www.sierg.org/60-les-statuts-du-sierg.htm
24. We have used the description of this department as presented by Grenoble-Alpes-Métropole [GAM 07].
25. Ibid., pp. 4-5.
26. More exactly: waste water network 669 km, rainwater network 678 km, all-in-one networks 368 km, making 1,715 km in all; source: SIE 07.
27. Agreement between Régie des Eaux de Grenoble and the Grenoble Water and Sanitation Users Committee, 17 September 2002.
28. http://www.region-grenoble.org/index.php/fr/communaute_de_l_eau_potable
29. http://www.servicedeau.com
30. Extract from the record of decisions of the Board of Régie des Eaux de Grenoble, 14 November 2007, p. 57 [REG 07].

31. The forecasts serve to update the tariff system for various REG services over the coming year; source as above, p. 61.
32. The 2004-5 survey investigated 1,556 localities (20 per cent of the localities in the basin). The survey included all localities with more than 10,000 inhabitants and achieved a response rate of nearly 90 per cent. The sample concerns a population of 1,03,47,000, or 74 per cent of the total population of the river basins [AGE 06].
33. Fédération Nationale des Collectivités Concédantes et Régies.
34. The data from this comparison of French towns cannot necessarily be compared with data on the Grenoble conurbation: the date is not the same (2006 in the present case, 2004-5 for the previous survey) and here the price of water is given before tax and only covers distribution and supply services.
35. Grenoble City Council has installed equipment to locate and detect leakage by acoustic correlation [REG 07], pp. 82-6.
36. In the EU Drinking Water Directive, revised in 1998, the standard for the lead content of drinking water was cut from 50 µg/l to 10 µg/l.
37. Source: Régie des Eaux de Grenoble, 2006 annual report [REG 06].
38. Priority set by the Sage.
39. Under an agreement between EDF and Grenoble City Council Régie des Eaux de Grenoble is entitled to draw off water from the Drac river. Similarly if the aquifer drops to a certain level EDF releases water from its upstream reservoirs. In 2007 a steady volume of water was released, at 1.5 cu m per second, without interruption from 6 June to 9 July. When the level of the aquifer drops below a certain level EDF is under an obligation to release additional water to recharge the aquifer. This trend, already observed over the four previous years, was even more significant in 2007, Régie des Eaux de Grenoble, 2007 annual report, pp. 28-9 [REG 07].
40. Borehole initiated by Régie des Eaux de Grenoble (tender issued in 2008).
41. A study of options for building up a strategic reserve was carried out to secure the drinking water supply to the city of Grenoble. Packaging of an emergency water reserve in large bottles, with several storage depots in Grenoble, is among the options adopted by Régie des Eaux de Grenoble, 2006 annual report, pp. 86-7 [REG 06].
42. Source: Eau France web site, Bulletin de situation hydrologique, September 2009, p. 12 (www.eaufrance.fr/docs/bsh/2009/09/bsh_2009-09.pdf).

3

Supplying Water to an Emerging Megalopolis
The Case of Bengaluru

GUNDAPPA SATHYANARAYANA SASTRY

3.1 INTRODUCTION

The scarcity of water in the world is less a matter of quantitative limits than poor management of resources [SAL 04]. While this problem exists in many countries, irrespective of their levels of development, it is more acute in developing countries and especially in urban areas because of increased demand, poor availability and constraints on infrastructure and institutions. The present study highlights such problems in Bengaluru's water supply system along with the associated environmental issues, and outlines measures that would improve the efficiency of the current system. The study recalls the history of Bengaluru's water supply system and the sources of the water. It identifies the characteristics of water demand, supply and quality, and describes how the distribution system functions and production and delivery costs are established. Here an attempt is also made to describe the water supply situation in the peri-urban area of the city.

Bengaluru is the capital of Karnataka state and a prominent metropolis of India. In recent decades, the city has experienced rapid economic growth based on the concentration of industrial and service activities that have made the city the IT and technology capital of India. This rapid transformation has had a major impact on lifestyle and urban growth. The population of Bengaluru rose by 38.6 per cent between 1991 and 2001 to reach the 6 million mark in 2001. At present the population is closer to 7.5 million. The city's activities are mainly focused on industrial production. While Bengaluru is highly specialized in the development and export of software-related products, it also carries out traditional industrial activities. A major share of employment is concentrated in production (45.8 per cent), while trade and services account for an equal share (27.1 per cent each).

Bengaluru's technological specialization has attracted highly qualified professionals and workers from throughout India as well as from abroad. The rapid immigration process triggered by the city's development has increased the demand for services and, more importantly for quality services. The rapidly growing migrant population has been posing serious infrastructure problems to the city in general and the peri-urban zones in particular. This economic and demographic growth has led to the emergence of 'Greater Bengaluru' with an area of 741 sq km. This consists of seven City Municipal Councils (CMC), one Town Municipal Council (TMC), and approximately 110 villages situated adjoining the city boundary [Figure 3.1; SAS 07a]. The expansion of the city limits has posed serious limitations on the service provision of the existing infrastructure and services, and hence, led to numerous malfunctions. The water supply is one of the services impaired by the city's intense and rapid transformation.

3.2 BENGALURU'S DEVELOPMENT AND WATER REQUIREMENTS

Bengaluru is situated at an altitude of approximately 940 m above sea level, in an area that is structurally short of water. There are no perennial surface water resources around Bengaluru that could provide the city with a continuous and sufficient supply of water, with the exception of Arkavathi River, a tributary of the Cauvery which is one of the main rivers in southern India. In 1896, the Hesaraghatta Lake Reservoir was built at a distance of 18 km to the north of the city to provide Bengaluru with potable water. This had a potential of 22.5 million litres of water per day (mld). In 1933, with demand

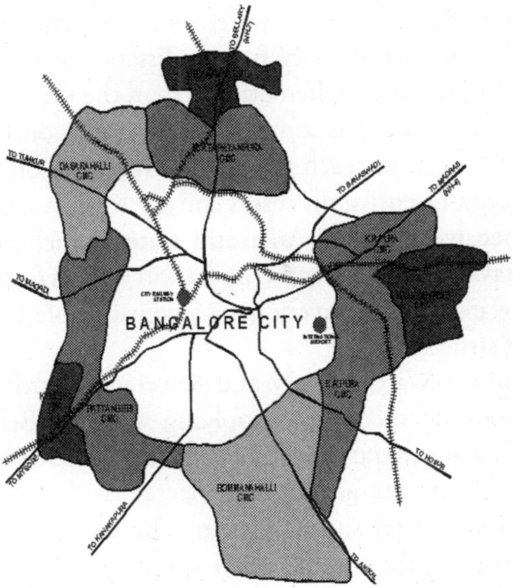

Source: City of Bengaluru.

FIGURE 3.1: MAP OF BENGALURU

already growing, a second reservoir was built at Thippagondanahalli which is about 28 km to the north-west of the city. This reservoir has contributed an additional potential of 143 mld. Both these reservoirs obtain water from the Arkavathi River.

After the implementation of these initial measures to supply water to Bengaluru, the city launched its growth dynamics based on rapid industrialization, encouraged by the Government of India and the Karnataka state. In terms of future potential water source, until mid-1960s, the Cauvery River was considered to be the stable and lasting source of water for dealing with the growing urban population of Bengaluru and the consequent rise in water demand. Indeed, the river Cauvery has been contributing to the city's water demand ever since its inception. However, water from the Cauvery has to be shared among several south Indian states. The Karnataka government, with the authorization of the Indian government, has reserved 19 tmc[1] of water for the city of Bengaluru to enable the city to meet its growing demand for drinking water [AUS 01a]. The first stage for harnessing the Cauvery water for Bengaluru began in 1974. It delivered 135 mld to the city from a distance of 98 km. Because Bengaluru is located at a higher altitude than the Cauvery River, the water after its treatment has to be pumped continuously against the head reach of 500 m to reach the city for distribution, which is an extremely energy-intensive process. Cauvery River water is therefore far more expensive than the Arkavathi water, which is distributed by natural gravity. Obviously, the operation and maintenance costs for drawing water from Cauvery have a considerable impact on the water pricing structure.

The Bengaluru Water Supply and Sewerage Board (BWSSB) is the official body charged with supplying water to Bengaluru and disposal of sewage generated in the city. The Board was established in 1964 by a Karnataka government decree, with a set of specific objectives towards water supply system. The first and the foremost objective is to organize potable water supply and ensure necessary measures towards disposal of sewage generated in the existing urban zones or those being built in the Bengaluru metropolitan area. The BWSSB needs to supply water for domestic use on a priority basis in metropolitan Bengaluru. The Board prepares and implements plans for the city's domestic water supply and sewage disposal in line with the required standards It sets the water tariff and bills on a 'no loss, no profit' basis. The BWSSB is an autonomous organization advised by a 10-member consultative committee formed by the Karnataka government [BWS 02]. Although autonomous, the BWSSB has to obtain Karnataka government's approval for fixation and revision of water tariffs, and execution of all major water development projects.

Bengaluru's economic development based on information technologies and related services have acted as a magnet and the city has grown considerably. The increased demand for water since 1974 has led to a periodic augmentation of Cauvery River water through several programmes (I to IV stages, see Table 3.1). In 2007, the BWSSB supplied 957.9 mld of water from the combined Cauvery and Arkavathi sources to satisfy the city demand [BWS 07]. In addition, water was delivered from 6,248 bore wells maintained by the BWSSB, which are vital for serving the city areas that do not have access to the network. The water from these wells represents only a small fraction of the total groundwater extraction in the city by the BWSSB in particular and the Karnataka state in general. Other potential water sources identified and may be mobilized by the city authorities according to the future needs include groundwater (between 130 and 260 mld), rainwater harvesting (between 20-50 mld) and the use of treated waste water (from 170 to 220 mld). These resources are only considered 'water potentials' (Table 3.1)

TABLE 3.1: BENGALURU WATER RESOURCES IN 2007

Source	Year of installation	Distance from Bengaluru (in km)	Other potential resources (in mld**) around 2025	Water delivered (in mld**) in 2007
Arkavathi River	1896	18	22.5	0.0
Hesaraghatta Reservoir	1933	28	143.0	83.2
RG Halli Reservoir				
Arkavathi River	–	–	165.5	83.2
Cauvery River				
Stage I	1974	98	135.0	145.5
Stage II	1982	98	135.0	146.5
Stage III	1993	98	270.0	324.1
Stage IV				
Phase I	2004	98	270.0	249.2
Phase II	2012	98	515.0	–
Phase III	(underway) 2025		*686.0	–
Cauvery River		98	2,011.0	874.7
Other potential sources				–
Groundwater			130-260	–
Rainwater			20-50	–
Waste water treatment			170-220	
Total other sources (taking the maximum limits)			320-530	–
Total water resources			2,706.5	957.9

Notes: * Subject to the Cauvery Water Dispute Tribunal (CWDT) decision
** mld: million litres per day

Source: AUSAID, 2001; BWSSB Annual Performance Reports, 1997, 1998, 2001, 2006-7.

and do not appear in the quantities of 'water delivered'. Among the potential sources, both ground water and treated wastewater will play significant role in fulfilling future needs, provided they are protected with adequate regulations.

At present (stage I to Phase 1 of Stage IV of the Cauvery River Project), the various potential water resources available for Bengaluru stand between 1,295.5 and 1,505.5 mld, depending on whether we use the lower or upper limits of each of the 'other potential resources'. By 2025 (including Phase III of Stage IV of the Cauvery River Project), the total potential water resources could reach between 2,496.5 and 2,706.5 mld, again depending on whether we use the lower or upper limits of the other potential resources. However, part of this potential supply is subject to discretion by the CWDT. If the city does not obtain this additional 686 mld from the river, the potential water resources would be reduced by approximately one quarter by 2025.

By 2025, on the basis of per capita consumption norm of 150 lpcd, by integrated management of all the available potential water resources, Bengaluru city can support 16.64-18.04 million population if the Cauvery Water Dispute Tribunal accords permission for 686 mld of water, and on the other hand, 12.07-13.47 million if the Cauvery Water Dispute Tribunal negates the permission. Hence, under the said assumptions, the available potential water resource has prescribed the population size limits for the city by 2025. Therefore, it is high time that the policy makers and administrators in charge of long-term growth and development perspective of the city of Bengaluru have to make a special note while promoting the future growth, expansion and development of the city.

3.3 THE STATE OF WATER SUPPLY AND DEMAND

Demand estimates are carried out on the basis of a per capita consumption of 150 litres per capita per day, which is the standard used for metropolitan cities by the Central Public Health and Environmental Engineering Organization (CPHEEO). In 2007 the city's water requirement calculated according to the said benchmark and demographic growth estimates, was 1,072.5 mld,[2] whereas only 957.9 mld was actually delivered. By this estimate, therefore, the population's requirements were not being met.

Despite the planned increase in water resources with successive Cauvery projects and the greater exploitation of the Arkavathi River, the city still suffers from water shortage. The prime reason is obviously rapid development and demographic growth. Between 1971 and 1981, the population of Bengaluru rose by nearly 76.8 per cent, making it Asia's fastest growing city. The gap between demand and potential supply – not to mention real supply – continued until 2001. This gap reached an alarming level around 1991, and imposed an immediate increase in the city's water supply capacity. The water drawn from the Cauvery River in the period 1991-2001 reduced this gap considerably. However, on the basis of the future consumption patterns of the various socio-economic groups of the urban population, and likely conservation measures to be adopted by the consumers using new technologies, it seems that water demand may increase moderately in the future.

Another very strong factor for water shortage is the gap between the water delivered and the inhabitants' real water consumption, which reveals the amount of unaccounted-for water (UFW). In Bengaluru, the percentage of UFW is high. In 1996 it was estimated at 29.35 per cent but between 1996 and 2007 it rose sharply to reach 42.54 per cent. As a result the supply system in 2007 was in a more critical situation (Figure 3.2). The most worrying aspect of this situation is that although water from the Cauvery is very expensive, an estimated 44 per cent of the total river water intake is lost [AUS 02a]. Therefore, as per the water intake for distribution, although 129 lpcd[3] of water was delivered in 2007 (estimated from the total amount of water extracted divided by the total number of inhabitants), which is already below the standard of 150 lpcd), actual consumption after loss would only be 73 lpcd (Figure 3.2). While mobilization of potential resources with huge investment has increased per capita daily consumption and brought it closer to accepted standards, the actual per capita consumption level has fallen mechanically as a result of uncontrolled water loss (Figure 3.2).

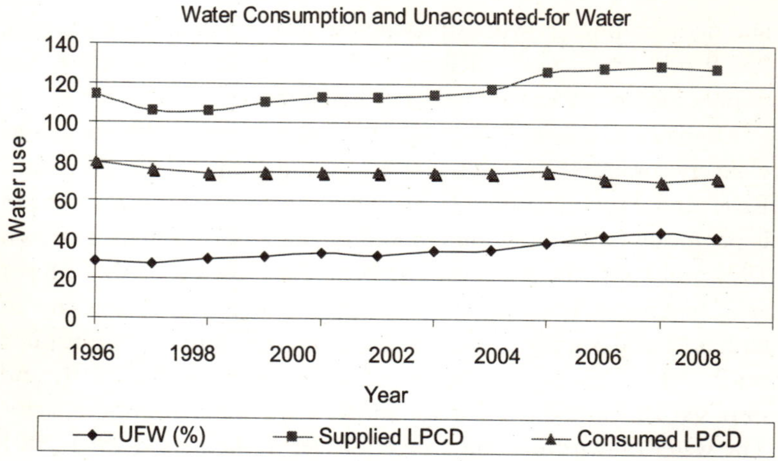

FIGURE 3.2: UNACCOUNTED-FOR WATER CONSUMPTION

It is estimated that an increase in existing supply capacity by 1 million litres would add only 50 per cent to the capacity on account of prevailing UFW situation [SAS 07b]. It is therefore clear that constant increase in water resources potential without proper control over the magnitude of unaccounted for water, is not a viable solution for long-term management of urban water supply for Bengaluru. Appropriate strategies need to be implemented to improve the efficiency of the existing system, and in this regard the first and the foremost executive policy decision required is to bring down water losses to a minimum.

The issues of per capita water consumption and water loss also hold true for other major Indian cities. With the exception of Chennai (76), the quantity of water distributed in lpcd are satisfactory in Mumbai (208), Kolkata (228), Delhi (258) and Hyderabad (242), without taking into account water losses. According to estimates (which, however, date back to some ten years), losses in each of these cities are considerable: Mumbai (18 per cent), Chennai (20 per cent), Kolkata (50 per cent), Delhi (26 per cent) [RUE 01], and Hyderabad (51 per cent) [SAL 97]. Water losses are also a problem in numerous other Asian cities, with estimates in the region of 55-65 per cent for

Manila and 50 per cent for Jakarta. The loss rate has been estimated at 50 per cent for Mexico City [LEE 94].

Large quantity of water loss in the city water system is the result of poor infrastructure and organizational problems in the urban water management bodies. While experience shows that water loss can never be eliminated completely, the acceptable level is generally considered to be 15 per cent [AUS 02a]. For a given standard per capita consumption, greater water loss would mechanically impose additional quantity of water, which implies larger amount of water to be treated, stored and distributed. To accommodate additional volume of water, the network needs to be expanded and, so does the infrastructure required for distribution. To satisfy these needs new equipment and more expensive operating and maintenance systems are necessary. When demand is not met, consumers have to seek alternative supply sources to fill the gap between supply and real consumption, which has major financial implications for households. These costs are in addition to the high prices set by the water utility authorities to finance the investment required for increasing their network capacity.

The shortage of water, created artificially by poor management and inadequate infrastructure by the BWSSB has resolved in a most irrational measure to provide water intermittently to consumers. This decision has been the most difficult solution to get accepted by the consumers. This in turn has led the population to develop alternative strategies to acquire water according to their socio-economic background.

Accordingly, households with intermediary or high income have turned to private sources to satisfy their water requirements. Depending on the opportunities available to them, they either dig wells on their land or in commercial or industrial locations. This strategy has been developed with no regulatory framework to govern the criteria for digging bore wells such as the permissible distance between wells, the quantity of water to be extracted, the depth of the well or the sustainability of the number of wells relative to the groundwater availability and its renewal, etc. The number of privately managed wells in the city is estimated to be around 1,00,000 and it will continue to rise at the rate of 1,000 new wells every year. In addition to these 'private' wells, there are 6,248 wells spread across the city and are maintained by the BWSSB to make up for shortfalls in inaccessible areas of the city. This rampant situation has obviously affected the city's ground water table which is dropping fast. Poor households and the most destitute segment of the population, on the other hand, are obliged to resort to independent water vendors to satisfy their needs.

It is important to note that there existed a legislation: The Karnataka Groundwater (Regulation for Protection of Sources of Drinking Water) Act, 1999 introduced as per the instructions from the Government of India and came into effect on 27 October 2003. The rapid depletion of the precious water resource as a result of uncontrolled exploitation for domestic, industrial and commercial purposes has, however, triggered for more comprehensive legislation to regulate the groundwater exploitation activities. Thus, in 2007 the Karnataka Groundwater (Regulation and Control Development and Management) Bill was placed on the Karnataka state government's agenda. Later, in continuation of this legal spirit, the Karnataka Groundwater (Regulation and Control Development and Management) Act, 2011 came into existence on 7 April 2011.

3.4 THE CONDITIONS FOR ACCESSING DRINKING WATER

The Board supplies water to the entire metropolitan Bengaluru, which covers an area of 595 sq km. For operational reasons, the BWSSB has divided the metropolitan area into five divisions: central, east, west, north and south. The Board's principal function is to supply water to households from the city's available 40,99,959 connections which includes domestic and non-domestic categories. Some serve households directly, while others, including public fountains, serve them indirectly. Approximately 95 per cent of the total connections have been dedicated to domestic use with a meagre share of 5 per cent to non-domestic purposes. The Board also supplies water to industries, defence and railways as bulk supply. In the process of inefficient institutional activities, the Board also served 22,894 unauthorized connections which were legalized between 2005 and 2006 [BWS 06].

3.4.1 *Water Usage*

The break-up of water consumption by type of usage shows that the highest proportion (35.59 per cent) of usage is by households followed by public fountains (15.70 per cent), the remaining usage being insignificant (Table 3.2). In our observation period (1996-2007), the domestic share of consumption remained high and even rose slightly, whereas non-domestic and industrial consumption tend to fall slightly. These inverse evolutions reveal BWSSB's deliberate policy to favour domestic consumption. To pursue this objective, the Board discouraged non-domestic consumers from using its water through appropriate economic instrument by setting very high tariff for non-domestic use. Despite reduction in non-domestic consumption, the share of domestic consumption practically remained constant between 1996 and 2007, with a slight increase in 2007. The share of public fountains in total water consumption fell sharply in the same period, even though low-income households and slum dwellers depend on them for their water requirements [AUS

TABLE 3.2 BREAKDOWN OF WATER CONSUMPTION PER TYPE OF USAGE (%)

Year	Domestic	Public Fountains	Non-domestic	Industry	Other Types of Usage	Total Water Consumption	Water Loss
1996	34.49	26.62	4.37	2.49	2.67	70.64	29.36
1998	33.78	26.20	4.16	2.01	3.18	69.32	30.68
2000	34.47	23.29	3.81	1.79	2.97	66.73	33.27
2002	35.67	21.11	2.94	1.64	3.54	64.92	35.08
2004	34.20	17.89	2.91	1.68	4.08	60.76	39.24
2007	35.59	15.70	0.87	1.29	4.01	57.46	42.54

Source: BWSSB Annual Performance Reports 1995-6 to 2005-7.

02b]. Taken together, these two developments are disturbing both BWSSB and consumers. The share of domestic consumption did not rise significantly because the share of water loss also increased. The reason for reduction in the share of fountain water in total consumption is that measures were taken to encourage low-income households and slum dwellers to connect to the distribution network through individual connections to improve their water access. This interpretation has confirmed on account of significant increase in the share of the two lowest consumption blocks (0-25,000 litres and 25,000-50,000 litres) among the major water consumption blocks between 1991 and 2007. However, this drop in consumption may also be due to the fact that many public fountains are no longer operational. Furthermore, the growing demand from the railway and defence sectors has led to a regular increase in demand from 'Other' categories. As indicated, the share of water loss has been increasing at an alarming rate at the cost of huge project cost and consumer welfare.

3.4.2 *Different Ways to Access Drinking Water*

Domestic consumption, which is the largest consumption segment in the city, varies considerably by divisions defined by the BWSSB. The share of domestic consumption is highest in the south division, followed by the west. Conversely, the central division has the lowest domestic consumption (see Table 3.3). The south division is composed of well-known residential areas such as Chamarajpet, Basavanagudi, Jayanagar, Banashankari, Hanumantanagar as well as new extensions like J.P. Nagar and Koramangala, with very high housing density. Residential density is also very high in the west division with residential areas such as Vijayanagara, Rajajinagar, Nandini Layout, Kethamaranahalli, West of Chard Road, Magadi Road and Mysore Road. Consumption in the central division is mainly non-domestic, with a heavy concentration of large commercial activities, such as those to be found in the Shivajinagar district, Commercial Street, Brigade Road and M.G. Road. The preponderance of industry in the east division explains the high level of industrial water usage there

(Table 3.3). Thus, the differences in water consumption pattern among divisions are mainly associated with the land use pattern prevailing in those divisions, but they contradict BWSSB's main objective which is to focus on the domestic sector.

Globalization and international competition have significant impact on the industrial sector of Bengaluru. As a result, several large, medium and small industrial establishments and in particular sector-specific units under electrical (including the public sector units such as New Government Electric Factory [NGEF], Mysore Lamps, and Kirloskar Electrical) and textile (Binny Mills, Raja Mills) along with the well-known public-sector companies like Hindustan Machine Tools (HMT) to mention some prominent ones, have closed down their operations in the city. As a result, industrial districts are gradually being transformed into residential areas, with a tendency to transfer water consumption to domestic usage, thereby returning to BWSSB's original policy of dedication of its service to the domestic sector. However, special treatment is reserved for commercial activities whose presence is strongly correlated with the residential areas and housing density. Another strategy followed by the BWSSB for balancing water distribution with priority for domestic service is differential pricing mechanism. Non-domestic water is more expensive than domestic; the strategy that ensures the Board's financial viability to a some extent. Therefore, BWSSB

TABLE 3.3: BREAKDOWN OF BENGALURU'S WATER CONSUMPTION BY DIVISION AND TYPE OF CONSUMPTION (2007)

Divisions	Domestic use	Non-domestic use	Public fountains	Industry	Other
Central	8.00	19.36	8.28	0.29	18.94
East	17.10	24.06	17.80	75.00	43.97
West	27.41	18.06	19.00	2.95	0.83
South	32.32	31.86	36.31	6.97	0.52
North	15.17	6.66	18.61	14.79	35.74

Source: BWSSB, Handbook of Statistics, 2003-4, 2004-5, 2005-6, 2006-7.

needs to follow a consistent and balanced policy that serves domestic users for their household needs and activities, as well as the other consumers.

The Board is focusing on water supply to households (domestic sector and public fountains) in which 95 per cent of its connections, taking up 51.3 per cent of the city's water. However, there are major differences in the quantity consumed and the number of connections according to the consumption blocks. In 1991 as in 2007, the majority of connections (respectively 69.7 and 64.5 per cent of total connections) went to the lowest consumption block (from 0 to 25,000 litres). The two lowest ones alone represented more than 90 per cent of total domestic connections (Table 3.4). This situation has considerable implications both on the quantity of water consumed and on the possibility of recovering the distribution and equipment costs. In the period 1991-2007, the 25,000-50,000 litre block rose fastest and became the primary one, followed by the block just above it (50,000-75,000 litres). However, the highest con-

TABLE 3.4: DISTRIBUTION AND EVOLUTION OF CONNECTIONS AND DOMESTIC CONSUMPTION BY CONSUMPTION BLOCK, 1991 AND 2007 (IN PERCENTAGES)

Consumption block (in litres per year)	Number of connections			Consumption (in million litres)		
	1991	2007	• (%)	1991	2007	• (%)
0-25,000	1,55,986 (69.7)	3,22,473 (64.5)	106.73	41,963 (36.7)	1,22,030 (34.9)	190.80
25,000-50,000	51,697 (23.1)	1,42,988 (28.6)	176.56	40,705 (35.6)	1,53,150 (43.8)	276.24
50,000-75,000	11,861 (5.3)	28,498 (5.7)	140.27	16,808 (14.7)	50,700 (14.5)	201.64
75,000-1,00,000	3,133 (1.4)	4,500 (0.9)	43.63	6,517 (5.7)	11,889 (3.4)	82.43
More than 1,00,000	1,119 (0.5)	1,500 (to 0.3)	34.05	8,346 (7.3)	11,889 (3.4)	42.45
Total	2,23,797 (100.0)	4,99,959 (100.0)	123.40	1,14,341 (100.0)	3,49,658 (100.0)	205.80

Source: BWSSB Handbook of Statistics, 1991-2, 1992-3; 2003-4, 2004-5, 2005-6, 2006-7.

sumption block (more than 75,000 litres) fell in relative terms. The continued increase in the medium consumption blocks may be the result of a deliberate policy to discourage the use of public fountains, as well as the relative increase in the number of households in these segments.

The first two blocks clearly dominate (Table 3.4), since they represent more than 73 per cent of the total water consumption. The 50,000-75,000 litre block is also significant (14 per cent of total consumption). In line with connections, consumption in the 25,000-50,000 litre block rose sharply between 1991 and 2007. The high density of connections and, to a lesser extent, the amount of consumption in the first two blocks, indicates that most of the BWSSB's supply is to low-consumption users and low- or very low-income households. In relative terms, consumption in the high water consumption blocks declined. This trend appears to be due to the consumers in the high consumption segment resorting to the private sector for their water requirements, for simple reasons of quality, reliability and accessibility of their water resources. These consumers belong to relatively high-income social categories and may prefer to use private water resources. Private water vendors make considerable profits by supplying to this demand by charging exorbitant prices. The BWSSB has a high proportion of low and very low-income consumers and a falling share of relatively high-income consumers, and therefore facing stupendous task in matching fair water allocation with financial viability. In this very tricky situation, the main question is, how should the distribution system be organized and pricing system be developed? The Board is obliged to balance its finances when supply is concerned, though it is mainly serving the lowest consumption segments. It is supposed to be guided by principles of equity and financial viability but fails to recover costs or satisfy consumers' basic water requirements.

3.5 THE QUALITY OF ACCESS TO DRINKING WATER

The BWSSB supplies consumers with water throughout its distribution area on alternate days. The usual method in the city is to provide water for three days a week for a limited number of hours in a day. The east division is the most favoured with a minimum three-day distribution period. Interestingly, nearly 27 per cent of households in this division receive water everyday and many households have water for four or five days in a week. The east division is the centre of Bengaluru's high-tech industry and therefore equipped with modern water distribution and storage infrastructure, thus making water access far easier. The central and south divisions have more restricted access although the south also benefits in part from the presence of high-tech companies. The west and north divisions are the most disadvantaged. The main reason for distribution restrictions in the north division is that it is served by the TG Halli and Hesaraghatta reservoirs, which have a very limited capacity, although Cauvery River water has gradually been added to improve supplies. Some 16 per cent of households across the city have daily water access, but the variations between divisions are considerable, ranging from 11 per cent in the north to 27 per cent in the east (Table 3.5). Although daily access to clean water is not guaranteed by the BWSSB, some households, depending on their water-friendly locations do actually benefit from this location pattern.

Water is usually available for two to four hours per day on all distribution days, and in areas with location advantage for four to six hours. Distribution times vary according to the dry or rainy season. There are disparities in hours between divisions, but these are less marked than the number of distribution days. For instance, the west division appears to be relatively 'privileged', with a fairly high

TABLE 3.5: DISTRIBUTION OF HOUSEHOLDS BY NUMBER OF DAYS PER WEEK THEY ACCESS DRINKING WATER (%)

No. of days per week	East division	West division	North division	South division	Central division	Total
2 days	1	2	1	2	4	2
3 days	33	66	83	49	59	57
4 days	24	17	5	29	19	20
5 days	12	1	–	2	3	4
Everyday	27	13	11	17	14	16

Source: AUSAID, 2002c.

proportion of households having access to water for more than six hours per day. However, this includes different types of access, such as public fountains. The criteria for easy access to drinking water are not taken into account. Access to water from public fountains is not always suitable and conceals considerable variations between social groups. Problems occur more frequently in the central division where most households have access to water for a maximum of six hours (Table 3.6.) Another problem related to the limited number of hours, especially in the case of water from a public fountain, is the waiting time involved with the risk that households may not obtain sufficient water for their needs. Such constraints would further encourage people to resort to private vendors or illegal means for obtaining the required water. This is clearly one of the reasons for the large number of unauthorized connections in the city recorded by the BWSSB.

In most divisions, drinking water is made available in the very early hours of the morning and very late at night (Table 3.7) and these hours add to the physical and mental stress of households, with loss of sleep and the associated problems due to waiting time involved. These constraints occur throughout the city, and seem to be worse in the central division, leading to water hoarding and wastage. One solution might be to vary the water distribution hours during different periods of the day according to the division, rather

TABLE 3.6: PERCENTAGE DISTRIBUTION OF HOUSEHOLDS BY NUMBER OF HOURS OF WATER DISTRIBUTION AND BY SEASON IN 2001

No. of distribution hours	Dry season by division					Rainy season by division					Total	
	E	W	N	S	C	E	W	N	S	C	Dry	Rainy
2-4	33	24	31	30	41	24	21	21	26	26	31	27
4-6	24	21	23	28	41	26	17	20	22	25	24	22
6-8	12	15	11	12	6	19	15	17	17	9	11	16
8-10	4	10	4	5	6	6	14	8	5	7	6	9
>10	7	12	10	9	5	11	19	16	12	6	9	13
Average	5	6	5	6	5	6	7	7	6	5	4	7

Note: E: East; W: West; N: North; S: South; C: Central.
Source: [AUS 02c].

TABLE 3.7: BREAKDOWN OF HOUSEHOLDS BY WATER DISTRIBUTION PERIOD (%)

Different times in the day	East division	West division	North division	South division	Central division	Total
Early in the morning	31	22	23	26	36	27
Morning	25	18	14	24	26	21
Noon	9	14	8	14	6	11
Evening	5	13	10	7	6	9
Early night	11	15	23	14	9	14
Late night	16	18	23	14	16	17

Source: [AUS 02c].

than having set hours. Furthermore, cultural practices and work rhythms are not easily adapted to the arbitrary limitations of the water distribution hours. In a context of distribution constraints, a method based on two time periods, one early in the morning and one late at night, with limited distribution hours, would be preferable and could encourage households to save water.

In the absence of a guaranteed access to drinking water, slum-dwellers and low-income households depend on a plethora of alternative supply methods such as private connections, buying water from vendors and using public fountains. Mostly this is for domestic use, which represents the majority of consumption in all divisions. The most used public water supplies are the standpipes provided by the BWSSB. However, this method of sharing water only functions during restricted periods and can only supply a limited quantity that may be insufficient to cover all the requirements of households. Large number of people use the standpipes, the average being 223 per standpipe, ranging from 163 in the east division to 314 in the south (Table 3.8). Consequently households in the poorest social categories are obliged to buy water or resort to illegal means to cover their needs, such as diverting public or private resources. With the increasing standpipes-dependent population due to combined effects such as growing number of households with limited hours of water access, greater demographic concentration, and a larger proportion

TABLE 3.8: BREAKDOWN OF PUBLIC FOUNTAINS BY CATEGORY AND BWSSB DIVISION

Categories	Central division	East division	North division	West division	South division	City
Standpipes	1,801	3,904	2,213	4,338	2,926	15,182
Hand pumps	314	607	657	1,168	606	3,352
Water pumped from wells	15	23	32	20	6	96
Total operational public fountains	2,130	4,534	2,902	5,526	3,538	18,630
Total non-operational public fountains	320	1,957	394	1,225	808	4,704
Average no. of inhabitants reliant on public fountains	218	163	235	212	314	223
Per capita consumption	114	117	104	73	109	100

Source: Data gathered from AUSAID, 2002b Public Fountain Study and the BWSSB Handbook of Statistical Tables 1997-8 and 1998-9.

of public fountains being out of order, we can only expect the unauthorized connections to increase.

3.6 THE QUALITY OF DRINKING WATER IN BENGALURU

The function of the BWSSB is to distribute quality water, according to national criteria, to all its consumers. Quality control is carried out at two levels. First, raw water treatment is monitored continuously and, second, analyses are carried out at regular intervals on random samples from the distribution system (Table 3.9).

Quality control is carried out by frequent sampling and testing for biological characteristics and residual chlorine. Results of these tests over several years show that water quality is ensured. Only a small proportion of the total samples analysed do not meet the criteria. The results were relatively poor in 2002-3 and in 2003-4.

TABLE 3.9: WATER QUALITY PARAMETERS CONTROLLED BY THE BWSSB IN BENGALURU

Parameters	Units	Desired values
1. Appearance		Clear
2. Colour	–	Colourless
3. Odour	–	Odourless
4. Turbidity	–	10 Maximum
5. pH		7.0–8.50
6. Alkalinity mg/l	mg/l	Limits not set
7. Acidity		Limits not set
8. Suspended matter mg/l	mg/l	500 Maximum
9. Electrical conductivity	Microgrammes/cm	Limits not set
10. Total hardness	mg/l	300 Maximum
11. Chloride	mg/l	Limits not set
12. Calcium	mg/l	75 Maximum
13. Magnesium	mg/l	30 Maximum
14. Iron	mg/l	0.3 mg/1
15. Phosphates	mg/l	Should be none
16. Albuminuria ammonia		Limits not set
17. Ammonium	mg/l	Should be none
18. Nitrates	mg/l	20
19. Nitrite	mg/l	Should be none
20. 27 degrees C – in 4 hours Oxygen chloride		Limits not set
21. Chloride	mg/l	250 Maximum
22. Residual chlorine	mg/l	Limits not set
23. Agar-agar in 24 hours 48 hours	mg/l	10
24. Lactose ferments Most probable number/ 100 ml		Should be none

Source: BWSSB, 2009.

Between 2005 and 2006, the proportion of samples with biological characteristics that failed to comply with standards fell sharply. However, the proportion of samples indicating levels of excessive residual chlorine rose (Table 3.10). Any failure to comply with the

TABLE 3.10: RESULTS OF WATER QUALITY TESTS ON THE DISTRIBUTION NETWORK

Year	No. of tests	% of tests below par	No. of tests	% of tests failing to comply with quality standards
	Biological characteristics		Residual chlorine in suspension	
2002-3	16,087	4.0	1,633	10.1
2003-4	18,207	4.0	2,007	11.0
2005-6	19,523	2.0	2,971	15.2

Source: BWSSB, Annual Performance Reports: 2002-3, 2003-4 & 2005-6.

regulatory water quality standards is immediately dealt with by the BWSSB by taking efforts to improve the quality in the divisions where this had occurred.

3.7 WATER ACCESS IN THE PERI-URBAN TERRITORIES

The water supply system in Bengaluru city proper is fairly well-organized while peripheral areas lack in several aspects. The spatial spread of the benefits of urbanization in developing countries is a subject of considerable debate. We believe that these effects are very limited in the case of Bengaluru with respect to water supply to the adjacent peri-urban territories. There are eight Urban Local Bodies (ULB) of equal size in Bengaluru's peri-urban area. Each ULB has its own urban management system according to the Indian Constitution. It manages its own services and utilities, including water, and develops its own urban infrastructure. The main source of water for all the peri-urban ULBs is the groundwater and it is managed under specific water programmes. The water extracted from wells, water towers, water tanks are distributed through limited water networks for domestic and non-domestic consumption. The quality of the water from these ground-water installations is assumed to be of potable quality. However, it cannot be guaranteed since there are no treatment facilities provided to the ULBs' water supply system.

The various ULBs have relatively similar supply and demand characteristics (Table 3.11). The limitations of their supply have

TABLE 3.11: WATER SUPPLY AND DEMAND IN BENGALURU'S PERI-URBAN ULB

ULB	Population in 2001	Water demand in mld	Current supply in mld	Per capita supply in lpcd	Distri-bution hours	No. of distribution days
Bommanahalli	201,220	27	8	40	2-3	Alternate days
Byatarayanapura	180,931	28	8	44	2	Alternate days
Dasarahalli	263,636	58	27	102	3-4	Daily
Kengeri	42,386	4	3	71	2	3 days/week
Krishnarajapura	187,453	25	5	27	3-4	Alternate days
Mahadevapura	135,597	18	7	52	45 minutes – 1 hr	2-4 days/ week
Rajarajeshwari-nagar	95,769	14	7	67	2	Daily
Yelahanka	93,263	14	3	32	2	Alternate days

Source: Consulting Services for Improved Quality of Urban Water Supply Services: Water Demand Assessment for Eight ULBs around Bengaluru, Operation Research Group, 2004.

obliged both domestic and non-domestic consumers to depend on other resources, the most obvious being to purchase water from the private market. On average, consumers spend Rs.248[4] per month in addition to what they pay for ULB water. The ULB rate covers production costs, distribution and water supply system maintenance. ULBs charge a flat rate of Rs.45 for domestic connections and Rs.90 for non-domestic per month. From the institutional side, the annual expenditure on maintenance and repairs varies for ULBs and it ranges from Rs.4.2 million in Krishnarajapura to Rs.27 million in Byatrayanapura. Unlike in the case of city water supply, it is very difficult to comment on the cost recovery for the water supply system by the ULBs in the peri-urban region.

3.8 THE COST OF SUPPLYING WATER TO BENGALURU

Although water is a freely available natural resource, its treatment and delivery entail specific costs [UNE 03]. During 2006-7 the total production and distribution cost for 3,49,658 million litres of drinking water supplied to Bengaluru was Rs.7,101.42 million. This may be broken down into Rs 2,008.24 million for equipment (28.28 per cent) and Rs 5,093.19 million for operating costs (71.72 per cent). Between 1997 and 2007, the total production and distribution costs increased by 478.57 per cent to satisfy the growing water demand of Bengaluru consumers. The equipment and operating costs rose by 376.77 per cent (34.28 per cent per year) and 531.76 per cent (48.34 per cent per year) respectively over the same period. The higher rise in operating costs was mainly due to the increase in maintenance costs as a result of ageing equipments, energy use as well as the cost of personnel.

Significant rise in operating costs is largely due to repairs, maintenance, administrative and energy costs whose unit costs are subject to considerable annual variations. In particular, the interest charges on loans towards projects and related investments and the expenditure on energy required for pumping the water greatly contributed to the increase in expenditure. During 1997-2007, energy expenditure rose by 164 per cent, and similarly all the other three components have also experienced price hike. At the beginning of the period operating costs tracked the evolution of total costs. But, later it had slowed down in line with the more gradual rise in equipment costs before rising sharply again at the end of the period (Figure 3.3). At the beginning of the period the water came from the Hesaraghatta and Thipagondanahalli reservoirs (with a capacity of 165 mld) and both the sources were close to the city thus, requiring no major investment. Operating costs therefore pursued their 'normal' trend. The sharp increase in total production costs was principally due to heavy interest rate charges for loans raised to increase water supply capacity (Figure 3.3). Equipment costs also rose significantly between 1997 and 2007. Total investment for Stages I and II of the Cauvery River Project was Rs.1.15 billion, whereas the cost of Stage

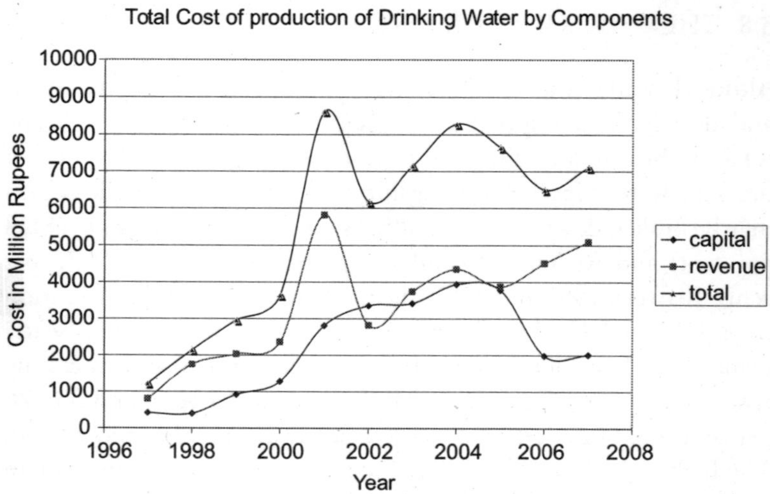

Source: BWSSB, Annual Reports 1996-2008.

FIGURE 3.3: COST OF BENGALURU'S DRINKING WATER BETWEEN 1992 AND 2008

III is estimated to be Rs.2.40 billion. Further, according to BWSSB sources, the total cost of phases I and II of Stage IV alone is estimated to be Rs.34.72 billion [BWS 01, p.13].

Investment costs rose sharply with the development of the Cauvery Project to satisfy growing water demand, and were almost on par with operating costs. If investments are required to develop alternative resources in the future, the same cost phenomenon may occur in the future as well. If we look at the current trend in project costing, any future project for increasing available resources is bound to be very expensive. In the context of the existing cost recovery policy, the future higher investment costs may not be borne equally by the entire population, as it will make water more expensive which would contradict the BWSSB's social equity objectives.

All these problems are mainly attributed to ever increasing population of Bengaluru for its obvious attractive situation and opportunities created by the policy makers. Therefore, it is a development issue of top priority that the Government of Karnataka need to analyse and understand the emerging complex issues of ever-growing Bengaluru and evolve a comprehensive policy such that Bengaluru's growth is diverted to the next order centres thereby achieving two prime objectives: (a) promoting Bengaluru to be an ecologically progressive centre by containing all the characteristics of a balanced urban ecosystem, and (b) promoting balanced regional development there by diffusing the benefits of urbanization to a larger region.

On the basis of the total amount of water produced (3,49,658 million litres) and the total expenditure required for its production and distribution (Rs.7,101.43 million in 2007), the unit production cost of water per kilolitre in Bengaluru is Rs.20.31. This corresponds to the cost incurred (drawing water from the source, treatment and distribution) per kilolitre of water to deliver water to the consumers through their network connections. The unit production cost, which stood at Rs.6.10 in 1997, more than trebled between 1997 and 2007, with annual growth of 21.18 per cent (cost 1 in Figure 3.4). This cost was arrived at on the basis of the total amount of treated water delivered to the distribution network without adjustments for water losses and this is extremely high. For comparative purposes, the cost is Rs.2.17 in Mumbai and Rs.5.73 in Chennai [CHA 03]. Over the same period, the consumer price index for the urban population rose from 361 points to 596,[5] representing an average annual increase of 5.1 per cent.

We need to estimate two more production costs by including total as well as minimum shares of unaccounted-for water in deriving the unit production costs. In 2007, the BWSSB lost 1,48,759 million litres (42.54 per cent) of treated water as unaccounted-for water. These losses rose phenomenally between 1997 and 2007, and should be included in the cost calculations to reflect the real cost. Accordingly, the unit production and distribution cost of drinking water in the city after correction for unaccounted-for water was therefore Rs.35.35 in 2007. In 1997 this cost was Rs.8.46. The price has therefore more than quadrupled, resulting in a far higher figure than the increase in uncorrected production costs ('cost 2' in Figure 3.4). The production cost of water by excluding the magnitude of unaccounted for water which is higher by Rs.15.04 per kilolitre than normal production cost in 2007 is a considerable burden on BWSSB, in addition to imposing water restrictions on consumers. Between 1997 and 2007, the gap between the corrected and uncorrected cost of water losses rose from Rs.2.36 to 15.04, with an obvious impact on the price structure. If the BWSSB had taken appropriate measures to reduce water losses to the acceptable levels of 15 per cent, the cost of the kilolitre would have reduced to Rs.27.24 (cost 3, Figure 3.4). The per kilolitre charge would thus reduce by Rs.8.11, which would result in significant savings on all water expenditure. On account of a gradual increase in the quantum of water distributed to the consumers, all the three costs have risen, whether water losses were taken into account or not. The growing share of unaccounted-for water could contribute to groundwater renewal and strengthen its base [AUS 02a], however, this may not lead to real compensation for the water losses. Furthermore, production costs per kilolitre vary according to the source of the supply and the stages of the Cauvery Project [THI 03].

Operating cost trends may be analysed more precisely on the basis of the changes in their cost components, which are the true reflections of water management methods. The main components are the administrative costs, repairs and maintenance, energy and interest on loans, and the biggest of these are the administrative

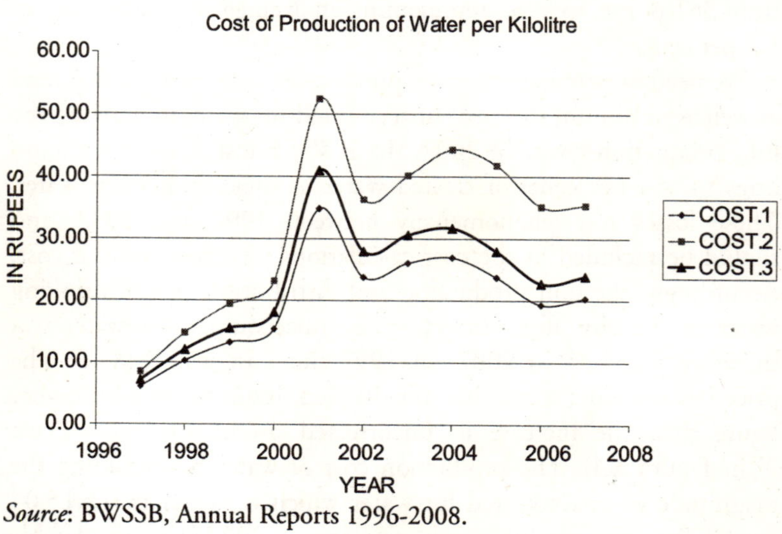

Source: BWSSB, Annual Reports 1996-2008.

FIGURE. 3.4: WATER PRODUCTION COSTS PER KILOLITRE

and energy costs. Water from the Cauvery has to be pumped over a distance of nearly 100 km to an elevation of approximately 500 m, which entails high energy costs.[6] The share of energy-related costs has fallen since 1997, but this type of cost is unpredictable with no clear trend and varies with consumption and frequent energy price reviews. The trend may further increase in the future with the greater use of Cauvery water on completion of Stages III and IV. This is the most worrying aspect for the resource and the environment. With the prevailing water distribution system, the increase in consumption would mean an automatic increase in even unaccounted-for water, which in turn would contribute to rise in the total energy consumption.

In the absence of any financial resources of its own and with the expected higher intake of Cauvery water, the BWSSB is obliged to borrow a great deal of money to finance its investments. In 2001 the Board's interest charges were high but fell sharply over the following years, only to reach a new peak in 2006 (Figure 3.5). This explains the rise in the unit production cost and the overall water production cost. This rise may continue with the final stages of the Cauvery Project, unless sufficient provisions are made for additional infrastructure. The cost of borrowing may be reduced with improved cost recovery, which is generally required for efficient water management and better financial viability. Bengaluru consumers have already indicated that they are ready to pay more for a better water supply, and this may contribute to a gradual recovery of costs which in turn, reduce borrowing and hence, the magnitude of interest. The share of payroll costs, which fluctuated at first and then rose after 2002, justified the cautious measures taken by the BWSSB to make this expenditure more manageable (progressive staff cuts). New water management technologies were recently introduced, such as the deployment of a Geographic Information System (GIS), and launched training programmes, notably to develop managerial skills for promoting more efficient use of resources. Maintenance and repairs represent the smallest share of the total operational and maintenance costs. However, one of the main reasons for the increase in unaccounted-for water is the poor quality of the distribution network. Since the BWSSB intends to replace the old network, network maintenance has not been a priority in the maintenance and repair costs, with the exception of the peak observed in 2006 and 2007. The 'Other' costs mainly relate to depreciation and vary considerably (Figure 3.5).

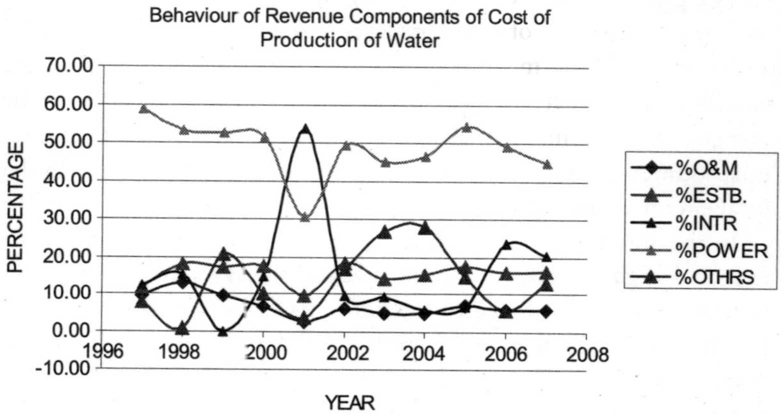

Source: BWSSB, Annual Reports 1996-2008.

FIGURE 3.5: REVENUE COMPONENTS IN THE COST OF WATER PRODUCTION IN BENGALURU

3.9 WATER PRICING AND COST RECOVERY

The priority objective for any water supply body must be to ensure its financial stability and viability. This objective can be achieved if the managing body follows a generally accepted policy of recovering its production and distribution costs. This implies an efficient pricing policy of the organization in charge of the water system and most importantly its implementation with rigour. The most delicate issue here, and one that is most debated in urban water supply organization is the pricing method. The price has several factors in countless components. Pricing must cover a variety of costs including production, maintenance, management, depreciation, interest charges on loans, and provisions for repayment of loans and more significantly environment and resource costs. Tariffs must also be such that water is accessible to all socio-economic segments of the population, so that the vital needs of all individuals are satisfied and at the same time the most precious resource is efficiently used and conserved.

If we consider public fountain water as being used for the domestic sector in Bengaluru, 51.29 per cent of the total water supplied is used for domestic purposes. This estimate includes unaccounted-for water (42.54 per cent). The production cost for a kilolitre of water is Rs.20.31 (including water losses) and the cost per kilolitre of water consumed is Rs.35.35 (excluding water losses). At present the BWSSB uses a block pricing structure whereby the largest water consumers subsidize the small ones. In practice this means users in the first consumption block obtain a 50 per cent price subsidy on domestic water consumption, whereas those in the second one have a 30 per cent subsidy. Starting with the third-block, consumers are paying the real cost of production. In this system, loss of income from the first two consumption blocks is offset by the consumers in the higher consumption blocks [AUS 01b]. The most recent tariffs announced in January 2005 follow the same principle. According to this, consumers pay between Rs.6 and 36 per kilolitre of water for their domestic consumption, depending on their consumption block. Non-domestic consumers pay between Rs.36-60 per kilolitre, while industry pays a set price of Rs.60 per kilolitre of water consumed.

Thus, the price paid by non-domestic users is six times the price paid by domestic users in the first consumption block. Industry pays ten times more. If we compare this price range with the production costs, approximately 70 per cent of water consumption – which basically consists of the first two blocks – is subsidized, whereas the 'normal' production cost is Rs.20.31, and the rates applied to users in the two lowest consumption blocks are respectively Rs.6 and 9. This minimum tariff appears affordable, at least for households with low income, and this is the only accessibility criterion for low income households, that fulfills Bengaluru's water pricing policy [RAG 02]. If we look at the minimum rate for the second consumption block, the BWSSB loses approximately Rs.11.31 per kilolitre. Furthermore, the average overall cost recovery rate is Rs.13.93, which is far from the production cost of Rs.20.31. This rate is even worse if we include unaccounted-for water (Rs.35.35) (see Figure 3.6). When the biggest consumers account for a small proportion of consumption, it is difficult to offset subsidies with the high consumption blocks. The BWSSB has to bear lasting losses with this pricing method and to avoid a major financial crisis, it will have to review its pricing and cost recovery policy – unless the Karnataka government continues to subsidize the Board. Water is clearly undervalued in Bengaluru.[7]

The BWSSB frequently revised the water tariffs in order to maintain its financial viability and did so in 1991, 1996, 2000, 2002, and recently in 2005. A comparison of the pricing structures prevailing in the various periods clearly shows that 1996 was a turning point in the awareness that water is a precious resource, an economic asset and a unique environmental resource that needs to be preserved. During the period 1991-6 there was a hike in the minimum rate, and the cost of water rose significantly for all consumption blocks, and especially the second and fifth. By comparison, the 1996-2000 price rise was insignificant, and in 2000-2 there was another tariff increase. In particular, over the period of ten years from 1991 to 2002 the water tariff rose in all consumption categories and the

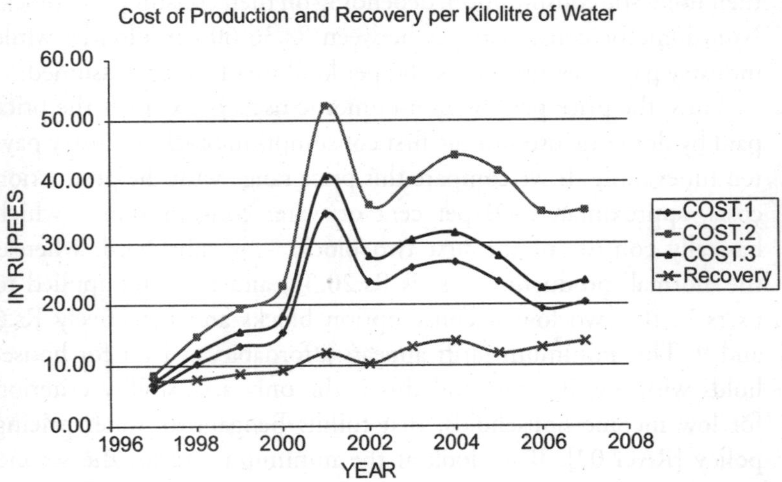

Source: BWSSB, Annual Reports 1996-2008.

FIGURE 3.6: PRODUCTION AND RECOVERY COSTS PER KILOLITRE OF WATER

lowest consumption blocks were especially affected, followed by the second and the third blocks (Table 3.12). Even in the 2005 tariff hike, the 'medium-low' category was the worst affected consumption block. It is clear from the pricing policy being followed by the BWSSB that the least water-consumption blocks are the ones which are constantly subject to price rise. These are the consumers who are the most vulnerable and they are very badly in need of government support for satisfying their water requirements. This is precisely the reference made by the MDGs in achieving the water accessibility target. Although the users in these segments are supposed to benefit from the government's principle of consumer solidarity, successive price rises have totally nullified this advantage. Experience shows that this section of the population spends a relatively high amount of their income and energy in obtaining water.

In the non-domestic usage, we see the emergence of the same process that exacerbates the vulnerability of the lowest categories of users (Table 3.13). However, unlike in the case of domestic use, the lowest non-domestic users do not benefit from the block pricing distribution. Users in the lowest non-domestic consumption blocks are the most badly hit by frequent price hikes. However, since their consumption is oriented to commercial activities, with well-known business tactics or strategies, they cleverly pass on their water price shocks to customers and nullify the impact.

The BWSSB's pricing and cost recovery policy is supposed to enable it to cover production, operating and maintenance costs. Coverage of operating costs improved at the end of the 1990s before falling again and then improved once again between 2003 and 2007. This was because the Board took several simple measures, including facilitating payment by various means such as bank transfers, 24/7 counters, kiosks, etc. However, till the presence of unaccounted-for water and therefore unbilled water is included, any evaluation method of BWSSB's financial situation, the problem of cost recovery remains. During the reference period 1997-2007, the average recovery rate for the total water production costs stood at 62 per cent. As with the recovery of operating costs, this improved at the beginning of the period but only reached 34.59 per cent in 2000-1. It then rose to 68.61 per cent in 2006-7. The financial

TABLE 3.12: DOMESTIC WATER PRICES FOR BENGALURU IN 1991, 1996, 2000, 2002 AND 2005

Consumption block (in litres)	1991 (in Rs.)	1996 (in Rs.)	2000 (in Rs.)	2002 (in Rs.)	2005 (in Rs.)	% change			
						1991-6	1996-2000	1991-2002	1991-2005
Minimum	12.50	60	65	100	48	380	8.33	700.00	397.04
0-8,000					6				
8,001-25,000					9				
0-15,000				5.00	–	–	–	–	
0-25,000	0.50	2.40	3.50	6.50	–	380	45.83	1,200.00	
25,000-50,000	1.20	5.00	7.00	10.00	15	317	40	733.33	1,150
50,000- 75,000	3.00	15.00	19.00	25.00	30	400	27	733.33	900
75,000-100,000	4.50	20.00	26.00	30.00	36	344	30	566.67	700
100,000-200,000	6.00	25.00	33.00	–	36	317	32	450.00	500
More than 200,000	6.00	25.00				317	–	–	

Source: BWSSB, Annual Reports: 1991, 1996, 2000 and 2005.

TABLE 3.13: PRICING FOR NON-DOMESTIC WATER USE IN BENGALURU 1991, 1996, 2000, 2002 AND 2005

Consumption block (in litres)	1991 (Rs.)	1996 (Rs.)	2000 (Rs.)	2002 (Rs.)	2005 (Rs.)	1991-6 %	1996-2000 %	1991-2005 %
Minimum	60.00	250.00	275.00	330.00	–	317	10	–
0-10,000	6.00	25.00	33.00	33.00	36.00	317	32	500.00
10,000-20,000	6.00	30.00	39.00	39.00	39.00	400	30	550.00
20,000-40,000	9.50	35.00	44.00	44.00	44.00	268	26	363.16
40,000-60,000	12.00	40.00	51.00	51.00	51.00	233	27	325.00
60,000-100,000	12.00	45.00	57.00	57.00	57.00	275	27	375.00
100,000-200,000	12.75		60.00	60.00	60.00	233	380	370.59
More than 200,000	15.00	50.00					20	–
Industry	15.00	50.00	60.00	60.00	60.00	233	20	–

Source: BWSSB, Annual reports: 1991, 1996, 2000, 2002 and 2005.

viability of any urban water sector is based on the assumption that operating costs relating to maintenance and repairs are covered. Fortunately, the BWSSB does succeed in this by covering 90 per cent of its operating costs. However it still only covers 62 per cent of the total cost. This poor performance shows that the pricing policy used will not allow the Board to recover its real costs. The main problem is therefore to determine how it would be possible to finance the cost cf on-going projects as well as increasing cost of future projects. The urban water supply system in Bengaluru, as elsewhere in the world, does not succeed in being self-financed.

The cost recovery problem may even deteriorate further with the considerable investment expected for the Cauvery River projects. The BWSSB has been legally charged with the responsibility of satisfying the drinking water requirements of the citizens of Bengaluru. It must therefore take difficult decisions and explore the various possibilities that would enable it to finance its costs from its own resources, without longing for outside assistance. One way forward was examined by testing consumer willingness to pay for the development of projects to improve access to drinking water. A recent study on the willingness to pay towards improved water supply by Bengaluru consumers shows that households in all segments (including slum-dwellers and all income categories) would be ready to pay more towards improved water supply. This financial option is worth examining in detail. The various other possibilities open for cost recovery are: (a) to integrate the cost of investment into monthly water consumption and include it in the pricing; (b) to issue bonds with attractive interest rates to encourage the general public to finance investment; (c) to tax water at country or state level in order to finance the necessary investment in the urban water supply system. While the first two options could be managed by the state through appropriate legislation, the third option requires far more complex legal arrangements.

3.10 ARE ALTERNATIVE POLICIES POSSIBLE FOR BENGALURU?

Bengaluru's population is growing faster and its territories have expanded in consequence. Being located in a region with limited natural-resource endowment, the city's water supply raises serious issues. The inefficiency of the existing system, which results in only 57 per cent of treated quality water being accounted for, exacerbates the situation. At the same time, the BWSSB has regularly increased the levels of potential water resources without taking any real measures to contain loss levels, at the risk of allowing it to lose part of these additional resources.

An appropriate policy to deal with these issues is a priority. A comprehensive policy on Bengaluru's development needs to be evolved such that it contains Bengaluru's growth, and thereby makes it possible to achieve threefold objectives: (a) controlled growth and expansion of Bengaluru, (b) efficient infrastructure and service provision to the Bengaluru metropolitan area, and (c) promotion of balanced regional development by diverting Bengaluru's growth to its neighbouring growth centres.

According to the various drinking water access scenarios, Bengaluru does not meet any of the UN Habitat[8] and UNESCO accessibility criteria in terms of (a) security, (b) sufficiency, (c) regularity, (d) ease of access, and (e) availability at a reasonable price [UNH 03], [UNE 03]. The reasons for this are that while the quality of water seems to be acceptable, the gap between supply and real consumption is too large. Distribution is assured intermittently and consumer studies show that the distribution system is not consistent with public policy objectives. The availability of water seems better managed for low income group of households as more than 70 per cent of the total water delivered to the city is consumed by the least two consumption blocks, the most vulnerable population. However, due to restricted supply, increasing share of unaccounted for water and limited infrastructure, the most vulnerable population is obliged to resort to illegal tapping to obtain water, which contributes to further increase in the share of unaccounted-for water. Finally our analysis on water tariff structure and change reveals that consumers in the low consumption segments are the most affected group. Thus access to water, according to UN Habitat and UNESCO standards, is not implemented in a suitable way by Bengaluru's existing water supply system.

The current cost recovery policy of the BWSSB is inefficient in a context of major and expensive investment programmes, both current and future. The present pricing method is neither effective nor equitable. Instead a renewed pricing base would avoid frequent price reviews.

The current institutional approach should be altered to allow consumers to take part at all levels of water management. Such a system would ensure proper monitoring of resources, infrastructure and promote in arriving at a well accepted water tariff structure. In addition, people participation in the urban water supply system would control the system's administrative costs.

Integrated water management is necessary to mobilize all the available water resources (surface water, groundwater, rainwater and wastewater treatment). Only this kind of change in the water supply organization could satisfy the growing demand being experienced in the metropolitan Bengaluru area over time.

NOTES

1. thousand million cubic feet (tmc) = 28,317 m cu m.
2. In the hypothesis of approximately 7 million inhabitants.
3. Lpcd = litre per capita and per day.
4. At 24 January 2009 one Indian rupee (INR) was worth €0.015.
5. Source: www.labourbureau.nic.in
6. It has been estimated that between 2 and 3 per cent of the world's energy consumption is used to pump and treat water for urban residents and industry. In developing countries, energy costs devoted to delivering water represent up to 50 per cent of municipal budgets. It is the second largest item of expenditure after payroll costs for these countries. [USA 02].
7. In comparison, cost recovery is Rs.3.13 in Mumbai and Rs.10.74 in Chennai [CHA 03].
8. United Nations Habitat and Settlement Programme.

4

Diversification of Access to Water in Mumbai's Peri-urban Territories

ANASTASIA ANGUELETOU-MARTEAU

Mumbai[1] and its peri-urban territories make up India's largest metropolis, with a current population of nearly 19 million people. The changes in the Mumbai metropolitan area are emblematic of the rapid spread of India's megalopolises.

The changes underway in Mumbai's peri-urban territories display both the 'degenerated peripheralization' described by Kundu et al.,[2] and the peri-urban development leading to segmentation defined by Dupont.[3] The city is mainly sprawling horizontally, populating peripheral zones and rapidly absorbing rural or peri-urban localities into the urban fabric, rather than increasing the density of urban centres. The advantage of this process is that it reduces congestion at the core of major cities but on the downside it tends to produce increasingly vast metropolitan areas.

The small and medium-sized towns of Mumbai's peri-urban territories will play a decisive part in the region's development. The economic and political reforms, which started in the 1980s and gathered momentum in the 1990s, have given the towns responsibility over urban infrastructure, but without allocating them sufficient funds to achieve their goals. With the growing urbanization of these territories and the municipalities' inability to provide a satisfactory water supply, there has been growing supply-side diversification in these territories. A whole range of organizations have emerged as a possible source of supply, some drawing on the mains network, others on surface or underground sources, associated with arrangements for which a charge is made (in a market served by small operators) or not (customary access).

We shall start by presenting the territories around Mumbai, their scope and complexity. We shall then characterize the overall situation as regards the water supply in the Mumbai megalopolis. We shall then analyse, drawing on a specific survey, how various forms of water supply can develop to cope with the shortcomings of the public network in the peri-urban towns of Vasai-Virar.

4.1 THE PERI-URBAN TERRITORIES OF MUMBAI

The city of Mumbai and its peri-urban territories form the Mumbai Metropolitan Region (MMR), extending over 4,355 sq km and bringing together four municipal corporations[4] (Mumbai, Thane, Kalyan, Navi Mumbai), 19 municipal councils, 7 gram panchayats and 995 villages. The administrative limits of the metropolitan region cover the Mumbai district[5] and part of the Thane and Raigar districts, as may be seen in Figure 4.1.

The perimeter of the MMR has been changing for 40 years, integrating Mumbai's growing sphere of influence.

Up to 1968 a large share of urbanization in the region was contained within Mumbai's city limits. In the 1970s the idea was to promote balanced, planned regional development throughout the territory, in order to prevent the formation of large cities and counter a massive, uncontrollable trend towards rural migration [MIL 01]. Multi-nodal development of the metropolitan region was to be encouraged with the start of a series of self-sufficient towns that could accommodate the overspill of population and industry. In keeping with this rationale the Government of Maharashtra (GoM) decided to build a new town (Navi Mumbai) on the other side of Thane creek to relieve congestion in the megalopolis.

Mumbai's peri-urban territories have not all developed at the same rate, nor have they all undergone the same process of urbanization. Three factors have been decisive in the choice of development strategy: the initial degree of development of the relevant zone, property values and the system of ownership, and the type of urban development

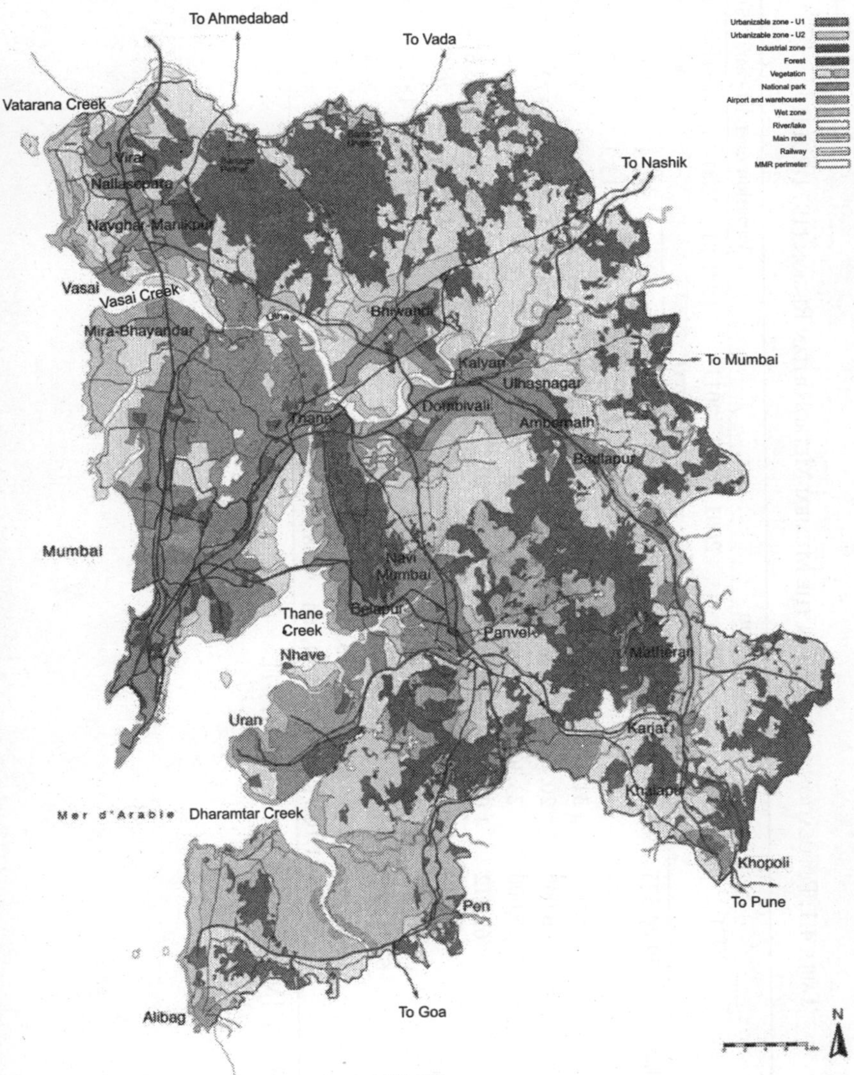

Source: [BMR 95], map produced by the author.

FIGURE 4.1: THE MUMBAI METROPOLITAN REGION (MMR)

TABLE 4.1: POPULATION VARIATIONS IN THE MUMBAI METROPOLITAN REGION (1971-2011)

Towns	Population					Variation over 10 years (%)			
	1971	1981	1991	2001	2011 (prev)	1971-81	1981-91	1991-2001	2001-11 (prev)
Greater Mumbai	59,70,575	82,43,405	9,925,891	11,914,98	12,931,000	38.1	20.4	20.0	8.5
Vasai	30,594	34,940	39,781	49,346	65,000	14.2	13.9	24.0	31.7
Navghar-Manikpur	9,000	31,494	59,324	1,16,723	1,85,000	249.9	88.4	96.8	58.5
Nallasopara	6,000	20,724	67,732	1,84,538	3,15,000	245.4	226.8	172.5	70.7
Virar	15,000	23,303	57,600	118,945	2,95,000	55.4	147.2	106.5	148.0
Panvel	69,112	1,01,623	1,58,362	172,349	1,99,625	47	55.8	8.8	15.8
Kalyan	2,46,038	440,310	8,20,584	1,400,348	17,66,503	79.0	86.4	70.7	26.1
New Mumbai	46,200	97,018	3,18,199	9,15,513	15,40,995	110	228.0	187.7	68.3
Urban MMR	67,11,247	98,37,116	1,33,78,249	1,78,45,935		46.6	36.0	33.4	
Rural MMR	10,80,341	12,54,676	11,56,115	10,47,124		16.1	-7.9	-9.4	
MMR	77,91,588	1,10,91,792	1,45,34,364	1,88,93,059		42.4	31.0	30.0	

Source: [BMR 95], [MMR 03], [COI 91], [COI 01].

sought. Various more or less centralized or devolutionary policies were deployed [ANG 08].

Population growth in the MMR followed its spatial expansion towards the north, east and southeast. It reached out along transport routes, particularly railway lines, initially (in the 1970s) towards Mira-Bhayander and Vasai-Virar, but also towards Thane and Kalyan, then subsequently (since 1983) towards Vashi, New Mumbai and Panvel. The urbanization process alleviated congestion[6] in the city centre but gave rise to an increasingly vast metropolitan area.

The Vasai-Virar region[7] which we shall look at in greater detail is one of the peri-urban territories to the northeast of Mumbai. It extends over 380 sq km and comprises four towns (Vasai, Navghar-Manikpur, Nallasopara, Virar), each of which has a municipal council, 47 villages, 2 industrial estates, farm land, forest and salt marshes. The region's economic and urban development started in the 1970s. Application of the Urban Land Ceiling and Regulation Act[8] and the extension of the rail network encouraged development and rapid urbanization. The steep demographic growth of Vasai-Virar sprang from on a sustained birth rate and the influx of two groups of population: people moving out of Mumbai towards the city's perimeter, and others from the hinterland drawing closer to the outskirts of Mumbai in the hope of finding work.

One powerful trend observed throughout the Mumbai metropolitan area is the fragmentation of these territories. This urban fragmentation combines various components, some spatial (physical disconnection and discontinuity in the morphology of buildings and infrastructure), others social (residential segregation, bunker mentality of specific communities) or economic (dispersed forms of employment), but above all political, with growing dispersal and profusion of players involved in urban management and regulation [JAG 01]. Although territorial fragmentation is not a formal process, it implies sub-integration of towns and neighbourhoods through the MMR.

Property speculation in the city of Mumbai is forcing people to settle increasingly far from the centre. The motives behind the choice of site are linked to a trade-off between the price of land, the cost of transport and services, and the quality of the environment or even security, which varies between neighbourhoods [DUP 07]. The richest households carefully choose their homes, while dumping the poorest families in places where they do not want to be. This process is gradually changing the city's social geography and structure [VER 06], resulting in renewed segregation between a prosperous population and low-income groups in poorly equipped peripheral zones. In keeping with the key trends emerging in the peri-urban territories of Mumbai, the towns of Navi Mumbai, Kalyan, Thane and Vashi attract upper and middle-class people, whereas the Vasai-Virar area attracts the middle classes and the poor.

The other characteristic of the region is its anarchic urban development. Without a zoning plan approved by the municipal councils, and strict regulations on housing, but above all given the difficulty of enforcing planning regulations, irregular forms of housing construction have developed in the area under study. This involves urbanization that disregards regulations, sometimes without a building permit, or without any official property title to the land it occupies, and sometimes both. The development of informal housing concerns both very poor people settling in slums and building their own homes, and prosperous families moving into luxury housing in residential neighbourhoods with no building permit. We consider that the form of urbanization observed in small and medium-sized India towns, with its fragmentation between 'physical' (alternating built and empty plots) and 'statutory' housing (alternating formal and informal housing) prevents the installation of an efficient water network covering the whole territory and encourages the development of other sources of supply.

Mumbai's satellite towns should have formed separate economic centres, complementing the development of the metropolis. But today we see them as dormitory towns. The study by the Mumbai Metropolitan Regional Development Authority (MMRDA) [MMR 05] shows that half the inhabitants of the city's peri-urban territories travel into Mumbai every day to work. The peripheral towns have not managed to create enough jobs to restrict the constant ebb and flow of commuters.

4.2 ACCESS TO WATER IN THE MUMBAI METROPOLITAN AREA

The fragmentation of the built environment in India's towns affects the quantity and quality of the water supply. Two trends are apparent in these territories: (i) fragmentation of service to the extent of complete breakdown; (ii) differentiation of service as a function of the specific characteristics of localized demand. In fact the service is selectively restricted to scattered urban housing units. There is considerable diversity in infrastructure and quality of service between towns and within individual towns. This diversity concerns access to water but also other urban services (electricity, sanitation, transport, etc.).

In the short term the public services alone cannot meet the demands of a growing urban population. The organizations operating the water supply should adopt much more pragmatic, less conventional methods for supplying urban households. Given the disparity of demand in peri-urban territories it seems advisable to diversify the forms of supply. This diversified offering may be provided by a single public utility, by a range of independent (private-sector) suppliers in competition in the territory, or by direct access to private and public resources. But to diversify the service to this extent involves setting up different technical solutions which in turn impact on the quantity and quality of service.

4.2.1 *Overall Organization of Water Procurement*

Each state in India has its own agencies and departments[9] for policy-making in this field. The government agencies concerned by the development and procurement of water in the MMR are the Maharashtra Jeevan Pratikaran, the Maharashtra Industrial Development Corporation, the Municipal Corporation of Greater Mumbai and the Groundwater Survey and Development Authority. All these agencies are committed to developing resources in order to meet their own needs, but without any coordination with the others.

Following the adoption in 1992 of the 74th Amendment to the

Constitution, responsibility for the urban water supply and sanitation was delegated to local government. In a small number of towns the municipal council is responsible for the whole supply cycle, operating along similar lines to France's *régies* (municipal companies). Only the town of Panvel (south-east corner of the MMR) has adopted this solution. Other towns often work with public or semi-public agencies, and private bodies at various levels of the urban water supply cycle.

In 2005 the GoM established the Maharashtra Water Resources Regulatory Authority, an independent agency set up to facilitate and guarantee the management, allocation and fair, sustainable use of water. The creation of a regulatory authority is a major step forward in terms of the institutional organization of the water sector in India.

4.2.2 *Imbalance in Supply and Demand at Issue*

The MMR draws most of its water supply from two river basins (Vaitarna and Ulhas), mainly in the form of surface water. One estimate of the potential water resources available to the MMR for domestic and industrial use amounts to 10,333 MLD, with a further 2,740 MLD which could be used in the Damanganga basin (shared between the states of Maharashtra and Gujarat).

Despite these resources being available, major infrastructure works is needed to enable them to be actually used. One of the recurrent problems is the delay in launching such work. In 1979 the Maharashtra Water Supply and Sewerage Project I (MWSSP-I) was launched to supply the towns round the perimeter of Mumbai, where the first wave of urbanization had occurred (Thane, Bhiwandi, Kalyan, Dombivali, Ulhasnagar and Mira-Bhayandar). The project was finally approved in 1992. Framed in 1989, the next phase (MWSSP-II) was designed to supply the area in and around Vasai-Virar, Thane, Bhiwandi, Mira-Bhayandar, Kalyan, Navi Mumbai and Uran [GOM 03]. This phase was launched nine years behind schedule. Due to these massive delays the projects were under-specified and do not correspond to population growth in the towns and growing demand for water.

Table 4.2 shows the disparity between supply and demand for water in 1991, covering the whole Mumbai metropolitan area. Additional resources will have to be found in the years to come. The water balance presented for 2001 may look reassuring, but it conceals some significant errors. For example, the water supply to the Vasai-Virar area was supposed to improve with completion of the Surya project. But the data for 2001 provided by the MMRDA does not reflect the real situation in the field. The supply is over-estimated and by 2008 the Surya project was only partly operational. In practice the Vasai-Virar area is subject to serious shortages.

Domestic demand alone in the MMR is forecast to rise from 3,453 mld in 1991 to 6,415 mld in 2011. To obtain these estimates, we used the standards of the Central Public Health and Environmental Engineering Organization, increased to allow for leakage from the mains estimated as 25 per cent up to 2001 and 20 per cent up to 2011. The annual growth in demand is estimated as 2.28 per cent. Although the rate of population growth is supposed to drop after 2011, it is estimated that demand for water will continue to rise at the same rate. This assumption is mainly justified by rising living

TABLE 4.2: TRENDS FOR WATER SUPPLY AND DEMAND IN THE MMR

Towns	Estimate of domestic and industrial demand (mld)								
	1991			2001			2011		
	Demand	Supply	Deficit/ Surplus	Demand	Supply	Deficit/ Surplus	Demand	Supply	Deficit/ Surplus
Mumbai	3,026	2,502	-524	3,848	3,810	-38	4,471	4,412	-59
Vasai and Navghar-Manukpur	21	3	-18	33	33	0	48	45	-3
Nallasopara	17	6	-11	53	53	0	106	98	-8
Virar	13	1	-12	37	37	0	66	66	0
MMR	4,457	3,804	-653	6,354	6,283	-72	7,961	7,855	-107

Source: [MUM 03]
mld: million litres per day.

standards and increased water availability. On the basis of these assumptions, demand for water in the MMR will reach 9,972 mld in 2021 and 12,493 mld in 2031. The estimates consequently conclude that the potential resources should be sufficient to satisfy demand in the MMR up to that time. However, allowance should be made for the possibility of major local disparities between supply and demand at certain times. Shortages may occur in some areas if work is not carried out in time.

In the next section we shall focus on the problems for water supply in peripheral areas and how the development of other forms of supply, in addition to the network, respond to rising demand for water.

4.3 ACCESS TO WATER IN TOWNS IN THE VASAI-VIRAR AREA

We carried out a field study of six towns in the peri-urban territories of Mumbai, to gain a better understanding of access to water in India's small and medium-sized towns. The aim of the survey was to investigate the relation between changes in public water services and urbanized space, and to understand the forms of water supply chosen by households depending on the various available sources and their degree of satisfaction. We drew up a questionnaire and polled 601 households. We also held semi-directive interviews with (public and private) players involved in supplying water and planning territorial development, as well as policy makers and members of civil society.

In 1986 the four municipalities in the Vasai-Virar region launched new water infrastructure projects (Pelhar and Usgaon). Another project, the Surya water supply scheme, is currently underway. The first phase of the project, which was started in 1996, was expected to supply the four towns with some 100 mld by 2006. The supply quotas for each town were expected to more than triple, compared with the level in 2005. In the spring of 2005 the towns (except Vasai) started to draw on the Surya scheme, to the detriment of other sources, which are now supplying surrounding villages but maintaining the same level of service. But in practice the Surya supply has so far remained very limited.

4.3.1 *Quality of Service*

The water supply to the towns covered by our survey does not really take an urban or rural form. The baseline remains a mains water supply serving each household, but due to the lack of financial resources and political determination, and the delay in planning, the towns do not have a reliable water supply. A large part of the network is secondary. It is consequently difficult to adapt it to the growth or densification of certain central neighbourhoods, or to its extension into recently urbanized districts. Furthermore the network is often old and badly maintained with very high losses.[10] In answer to our questions the municipalities estimated losses at 5 per cent, but in practice wastage probably ranges from 25 to 50 per cent. The rate of urban development far exceeds the ability of the competent authorities to deliver a service to new customers, or even maintain the same level of service to existing customers.

Extension of the network initially follows the development of new regularized districts,[11] subsequently serving illegal settlements. Several studies have shown that the informal nature of land ownership is an obstacle to access public services. Our study revealed a different picture. All four municipalities are prepared to supply households in illegally developed neighbourhoods, providing they pay local property taxes.

The region enjoys a high level of coverage but this does not mean the service is adequate. Connection to the water main is no guarantee of good-quality or dependable service.

The service is intermittent, available once a day or once every two days, above all in summer, and only lasts a few hours. All households, rich and poor, are affected by the irregular supply. It makes no difference whether they are in regularized or 'marginal' areas. Contrary to what the municipalities claim with their data, the Indian standard[12] of 70 lpcd for small towns without a sanitation system is not met.

Water distribution is uneven between households, depending on the type of dwelling and connection (group or individual connection, stand-pipe) and its size (1/2 inch,[13] 3/4 inch). The supply is organized on the basis of a zoning system. As a fixed amount of

TABLE 4.3: SOURCES OF SUPPLY TO THE VASAI-VIRAR REGION

Towns	Allocations		Municipal supply				Supply as observed	
	Present	Future (Surya)	Network coverage	Quantity (lpcd)	Frequency	Times	Quantity (lpcd)	Time (min)
Vasai	2 mld: Usgaon 2 mld	10 mld	40%	100	Daily	Once daily, 7:00 to 8:30	51.4	78.3
Navghar-Manikpur	7.5 mld: Usgaon 3.5 mld, Pelhar 4 mld	25 mld since 05/05 10.5 mld*	95%	62	Daily, alternate days in summer	Once daily about 1hr 15	51.1	62.8
Nallasopara	7 mld: Usgaon 4 mld, Pelhar 3 mld	35 mld since 02/05 8 mld*	83%	40	Daily, alternate days in summer	Once daily < 1 hour	41.7	71
Virar	12 mld: Usgaon 10 mld, various underground sources 2 mld	30 mld since 02/05 4 mld	approx. 100%	84	Daily, alternate days in summer	Once daily about 1hr 30 to 2hr	51.3	67.6 (alternate days)

Notes: (*) Towns no longer draw water from the previous sources.
mld: million litres per day
lpcd: litres per capita per day

Source: Calculations by author, data provided by the four municipalities.

water is distributed to the town, some neighbourhoods receive more water over a longer time than specified in their daily quota, others less. The quality of the water itself is mediocre. The water is treated, but the intermittent service, cracks in the mains and leakage, and low pressure on the mains supply all contribute to reduce the quality perceived by the end user. This type of problem is directly related to poor management by the water department. It is badly organized and fails to keep to the agreed time slots for supplying water to each part of the town, resulting in an irregular service.

The municipalities have a clientelist-type of policy, which means that certain favoured residential sectors are better supplied than other parts of town. The quality of the network and its lasting existence depend on investments in infrastructure, preventive maintenance and upkeep.

4.3.2 *Cost of Access to the Network*

Over and above the right of access to the network, access is often conditional on connection costs and the pricing system. Connection charges depend on the size of the connection, the existence of a meter, or not, the category of consumer (household, business, etc.), the position of the dwelling (town centre or outskirts), etc. [ADB 08]. Our study reveals two decisive new factors affecting connection charges: the type of dwelling (house, block of flats, temporary structure); and building materials (*pucca*,[14] *semi-pucca*[15] or *katcha*[16] dwellings).

A study by the Asian Development Bank of 20 Indian cities [ADB 07] reveals considerable variation in connection expenses in different towns, with an average cost of Rs.1,584. The Bank considers Rs.2,500 an appropriate amount, but the municipalities covered by our study charge more.

Excessively high connection costs may exclude low-income households and encourage illegal connections. In contrast, low connection costs make it easier for a large number of households to connect, but deprive municipalities of the funds they need to extend the network.

Network accessibility also depends on the pricing structure. Indian towns use several methods for calculating prices. The majority of the municipalities under study apply a monthly flat rate, a price that may integrate several variables: the size of the dwelling, the number of occupants, etc. Our study shows that the price is determined according to the type of dwelling (house, block of flats, temporary structure), the building materials and the size of the pipe. The advantage of the flat rate system is that it is simple, but it makes it difficult to monitor consumption. Moreover households are required to pay a monthly charge regardless of the actual availability of the resource and any interruptions in service. Several studies show that metered connections can be a solution which reduces wastage while permitting payment for the service rendered. The fitting of meters in the four towns was a precondition for obtaining funding for the Surya scheme. The local authorities nevertheless disregarded their commitment and are still reluctant to charge the proper price for water. The trend in these peri-urban territories is towards an end to free water, the local authorities having committed themselves to remove stand-pipes and make widespread use of private connections, even in slums.

The aim of the pricing system should be to enable the service to produce sufficient financial resources to cover its operating costs. But recovering costs is a major problem in several Indian cities which has delayed improvements to services. In the MMR, only the water department of Mumbai itself operates with a budget surplus. Everywhere else the sector is largely subsidized.

4.3.3 *Development of Small Private Suppliers*

Several studies,[17] carried out from the 1990s onwards, revealed the existence in many parts of the world of a very wide variety of small private operators supplying water. Despite the plentiful literature, little work[18] has been done on private operators and use of free supplies in Indian towns. Their presence is nevertheless indisputable, though certainly underestimated by local authorities.

There is no standard definition to describe and classify such activities and the corresponding small private suppliers, who complement the official operators (municipalities or private organizations operating under contract). The local authorities do not officially recognize the water suppliers, which operate independently, with no legal connection to either the local authorities or the larger operators. We have treated any source of supply outside the municipal network as a supplementary source, including customary access to wells, public and private boreholes, lakes and rainwater.

For a long time it was assumed that these operators, often dismissed as informal, paid no attention to prevailing regulations. In fact it is unusual to find wholly informal activities – in the sense that they completely ignore the regulations. For that matter, entirely formal activities – in the sense that they comply with all the regulations in force – are also extremely unusual. In practice any organization may have, to a varying extent, on a permanent or temporary basis, all or part of its activities outside the framework of the legal, fiscal or statistic control of the state [MIR 80], because its activities fulfil some but not all regulatory requirements. One way of gauging the degree of formality or informality is business status (operating as a registered company, belonging to a trade association, sub-contracting for a local authority, etc.). Another approach is to focus on the conditions under which work is done (having a permit to draw water from underground springs, paying business and land taxes, and transport dues).

Studies show that small private suppliers offer a solution to a large share of the urban population of developing countries. They also show that the role of independent operators may be regarded as competing or cooperating with that of the competent authority. In a large number of studies these operators supply the poor population of the urban periphery, but other studies show that they are active wherever there is a shortage of water, regardless of the legal status of housing or the standard of living of households.

4.3.4 *Complementary Forms of Supply in the Vasai-Virar Area*

In the Vasai-Virar area we identified several forms of complementary supply which fill the gaps left by the municipal service. On the one hand there is a (marginal) local practice of gifts of water between neighbours, access to communal sources (lakes and rivers), public water outlets (wells and bore-holes), and recovery of rainwater. On the other hand, there are various forms of paid supply governed by market forces. For several years now private markets for ground or municipal water have been developing. There are also markets for the transfer of water from farming to towns. Water markets and customary access have developed due to urbanization, the region's rapid growth and the incompetence of the municipalities.

The main characteristic of developing countries, and more specifically the area under study, is the frequent coexistence of several types of supply, regarded as formal or informal, operating in parallel and serving various market segments inside the same town or neighbourhood. Table 4.4 details the various types of alternative supply, which supplement the municipal network in the Vasai-Virar area.

Home water-producers are households who draw and consume water from a well or bore-hole they own. Although they are not actually breaking a law, we consider this form of supply to be informal

TABLE 4.4: ALTERNATIVE WATER SUPPLY ARRANGEMENTS IN THE VASAI-VIRAR AREA

<table>
<tr><th rowspan="2">Arrange-ments</th><th colspan="7">Activities</th></tr>
<tr><th>Catchment</th><th>Pumped</th><th>Transport</th><th>Treat-ment</th><th>Storage</th><th>Distri-bution</th><th>Operation & upkeep</th></tr>
<tr><td>1</td><td colspan="3">Tanker-truck</td><td colspan="2">n/a*</td><td colspan="2">Tanker-truck</td></tr>
<tr><td>2</td><td>Groundwater reseller</td><td colspan="2">Tanker-truck</td><td colspan="2">n/a</td><td colspan="2">Tanker-truck</td></tr>
<tr><td>3</td><td colspan="2">Groundwater reseller</td><td colspan="2">n/a</td><td colspan="3">Groundwater reseller</td></tr>
<tr><td>4</td><td>Groundwater reseller</td><td colspan="4">n/a</td><td colspan="2">Groundwater reseller</td></tr>
<tr><td>5</td><td>Municipal government</td><td>n/a</td><td colspan="3">Municipal government</td><td colspan="2">Reseller connected to municipal network</td></tr>
<tr><td>6</td><td>Free sources</td><td colspan="5">n/a</td><td>Municipal government (sometimes)</td></tr>
</table>

Note: n/a: not applicable

Source: Compiled by author.

because no systematic inspection[19] is carried out of the quality and permanence of the resource. Supplies of this sort are found in all four towns. Having met their own needs, the owners of an underground source sometimes sell water to neighbouring households.

Such sales only account for a marginal share of total consumption in the area, particularly since the 2000s, thanks to the extension of the municipal network. Sales of home-produced water are most common in the poorest districts (Nallasopara), where families can neither afford to connect to the mains supply nor invest in an underground water supply.

The resellers of municipal water consist of households living in detached houses with access to water mains, who sell water to neighbouring families. Resellers of this sort are mainly located in Nallasopara and the eastern part of Navghar-Manikpur. Once they have filled their storage reservoir from the mains supply, such resellers let neighbours draw mains water from a tap outside their house. The administration tends to turn a blind eye to such practices, despite their complete illegality, because they suit consumers who benefit from a water supply close to home, as well as the resellers themselves, who make a profit, and even the municipalities.

The first firms operating tanker-trucks appeared in the mid-1980s. By 2005, 320 tankers operated by 80 companies were supplying the towns of Nallasopara and Navghar-Manikpur. These are small concerns (one to three vehicles), not registered companies, but organized in two trade federations. Each federation organizes the tanker water supply within the perimeter of a town, negotiating and setting prices, protecting the business of individual concerns, limiting the arrival of new contractors and sharing out the consumer base. The market is well organized and tightly controlled. Tanker-truck firms must register with the Road Traffic Officer and pay road tax. The local authorities are aware of the existence of these firms but do nothing to limit their activities.

By free-access sources we refer to public sources. Everyone may access public wells and boreholes, lakes, ponds and rivers. We should add another seasonal source of supply, rainwater. Although the World Health Organization defines it [WHO 00] as 'sustainable access to safe drinking water', we have treated it as an informal source because there is no control over the quality of the resource, nor yet its availability during the monsoon.

4.3.5 *The Outlets for Small Private Operators*

It is very difficult to assess the size of the market outlets for private operators supplying water. One criterion is the number of households involved in at least one market or free-access source. To give some indication of the situation, of the 541 households surveyed in the four towns, 43.1 per cent depended for their supply exclusively on the municipal network. The others combined two (31.8 per cent) or three (4.4 per cent) sources of supply. A second criterion could be the quantity of water sold on a daily basis, but there are no records containing such data for the towns under study, so we have had to make estimates. In 2005 the amount of groundwater sold per day by tankers ranged from 30 mld (Maharashtra Jeevan Pratikaran data[20]) to 80 mld (City and Industrial Development Corporation data[21]), or 96 mld according to our calculations. The volume of revenue could be a third possible criterion for assessing the size of the market, but data is scarce and its reliability is open to dispute. When surveyed both the tanker firms and the resellers, they were very reluctant to reveal such information.

The complementary forms of supply are not uniform, but specific to a town or certain neighbourhoods, sometimes even limited to certain times of the year. The small private operators identified in our survey do not cover the whole area under study, and the services they offer vary a great deal in terms of water quantity, quality and price.

The presence of complementary sources depends on resource availability, accessibility, physical character (natural or artificial) and period. The supply depends on the amount of rainfall, the rate of groundwater recharge, availability and cost of energy. Furthermore supply capacity depends on where demand is located, the type of housing and what households can afford.

There are consequently considerable disparities between town centres and outlying neighbourhoods, depending on resource availability and demand. For example, in the town of Vasai, more than half the population draws water from wells and private

TABLE 4.5: CHARACTERISTICS OF PRIVATE WATER OPERATORS IN THE VASAI-VIRAR AREA

Characteristics of service	Characteristics of private operators in the Vasai-Virar area				
	Tanker-trucks	Consumer-resellers	Private wells and bore-holes	Resellers with an underground source	Free sources
Towns served	Nallasopara, Navghar-Manikpur, Virar	Nallasopara, Navghar-Manikpur, Virar	Nallasopara, Navghar-Manikpur, Vasai, Virar	Nallasopara	Nallasopara, Navghar-Manikpur, Virar
Relation to resource	Independent (private property)	Dependent (public property)	Independent (private property)	Independent (private property)	Independent (public property)
Technology in use	Mobile distributor	Fixed source	Fixed source	Fixed source	Fixed source
Source of supply	Underground sources, quarries, lakes, dams	Municipal network	Underground sources (well or bore-hole)	Underground sources (well or bore-hole)	Underground sources (well or bore-hole), lakes, rainwater
Service technology	Home delivery	Collected from reseller/Supply by flexible pipes at home	Own use	Collected from reseller	Collected from source, Use near source
Uses	All uses, except drinking water	Drinking water and cooking (primarily)	All uses	All uses	Washing clothes and dishes, toilets, bodily hygiene (primarily)
Water quality	Poor	Good	Good, depends on season	Good, depends on season	Depends on season
Times	All day	Same time as municipal supply	No set time, when the electric pump is working	All day, when the electric pump is working	All day

(Contd.)

TABLE 4.5 *(contd.)*

Characteristics of service	Characteristics of private operators in the Vasai-Virar area				
	Tanker-trucks	Consumer-resellers	Private wells and bore-holes	Resellers with an underground source	Free sources
Treatment	By end user	By end user	By end user	By end user	By end user
Reason for supply	To remedy network shortcomings	To remedy lack of network	Availability of source	To remedy lack of network	To remedy network shortcomings
Payment	Monthly	Monthly	n/a	Monthly	n/a
Investments	Purchase of vehicle Rs.25,000 (second-hand)	Cost of mains connection. Varies with town	Construction costs depending on depth. Rs.16,000 to 20,000 to drill 30 to 35 metres	Construction costs depending on depth. Rs.16,000 to 20,000 to drill 30 to 35 metres	0
Operating expenses	Rs.17,000 a year for road tax and wages	Monthly bill	No electrical expenses (if electrical pump), cleaning of well Rs.320 a year	No electrical expenses (if electrical pump), cleaning of well Rs.320 a year	0
Average price per litre (Rs/l)	0.2189	0.106	0.0182	0.0739	0

Note: n/a: not applicable
Source: Compiled by author.

boreholes. The town's underground sources are relatively shallow but supply plenty of good-quality water all year round, unlike the western part of the region where several wells and boreholes dry up at the beginning of the summer.

The various complementary forms of supply adjust to the demand. They proliferate in informal neighbourhoods (slums and luxury blocks of flats) not covered by the public service, but also in areas where the service cannot cope with high demand. The service provided by small private operators thus contributes to the spread of urban services into new residential districts and slums which the mains supply has not yet reached.

The different forms of supply cater for specific demands in terms of quantity, quality, price and time of delivery. They can adapt to local conditions, both physical (steeply sloping or flood-prone areas) and climatic (drought, flooding), and to exceptional circumstances (celebrations, weddings and such). But they also increase the fragmentation of the town in terms of public services [BAR 08] by supplying a fragmented product on a small scale [HUG 80].

Water quality depends on the source of supply (private or public; surface or underground). Households often complain about the poor quality of water, particularly in summer and during the monsoon, and about its brackish flavour. Tanker firms pay little attention to the quality of the water they supply, often falling back on the argument that they are providing an essential service, the only solution for local people.

In the Vasai-Virar area the municipality is the main official supplier (operating the mains network). Small private operators invest in various niche markets, forming sub-oligopolies at specific locations, each one setting its own prices [LOV 93]. The small firms focus on small market segments in terms of product and customer base. This is not a highly competitive market organization and there are only a limited number of operators, so the business is profitable. Neither the local authorities nor other independent operators constitute a threat to these sub-oligopolies.

Under no pressure from rival firms, the small private operators make no attempt to improve their efficiency. Indeed there is a certain understanding between each category of small private operator with regard to tariffs. In principle this situation is bad for consumers, due to the lack of competition.

Access to these niche markets is restricted, with barriers raised by the informal operators to control their activity. Some barriers are financial (investment in capital equipment, etc.) and discriminate between firms, but they also take other forms, such as requiring operators to join an association.

Independent operators are looking for low-cost complementary technical solutions to reduce their investment overheads. These inventive systems offer a solution to a large share of the urban population, but in technical terms they often fall short of national and international standards, which would require too high an investment. To launch or expand their business the vast majority of these entrepreneurs invest their own assets or borrow from members of their family.

It proved very difficult to explain the price system applied by small private operators in the area covered by our survey. Several factors specific to their business may explain their prices: the availability of water resources and their distance, the distance to the water network, seasonal variations in availability and so on. But other factors are specific to the operators themselves: the net earnings decided by the operator, the time limit for recouping the investment, among others [CON 04]. Despite these factors, our impression is that in a market without much competition the small private operators achieve comfortable profit margins. In so far as households do not really have any choice of operator they have no option but to accept the prices charged by the operators.

Another characteristic of the informal operators is their flexible approach to payments, which may be made in a large number of different ways: payment with each purchase, payment with credit and pre-paid purchases. We did not observe such diversity in the towns under study. Apart from exceptional sales to a household, for which payment is immediate, the tanker companies and resellers bill their customers once a month. Furthermore, a large proportion of bills are paid.

To limit their exposure to risks private operators adopt policies to minimize investment and recoup their initial outlay as quickly as possible. They adapt services in order to reduce overheads and achieve the highest possible profit margin. Furthermore, through corruption of officials and policy makers, private operators can extend their customer base and maintain high tariffs.

4.4 CONCLUSION

For a long time it was thought that the universally superior, valid norm in an urban environment was access to a network via a single public or private-sector operator. But in towns in developing countries it is proving increasingly difficult to generalize this norm.

There is a very real gap between the targets set by governments and the means available to achieve them. The goal set by town councils to use the network to provide an adequate service available to the entire population seems unrealistic.

The fragmentation and differentiation of the service are two key trends in the water supply of the small and medium-sized towns covered by the study. The fragmentation of the built environment in Indian towns affects the water service in terms of quality and quantity. Access via a differentiated service (with several sources and players) could offer a solution enabling an overall service to be extended to peri-urban territories.

The local authorities[22] in India tend to disregard the part played by small private operators, but their service is tolerated. As noted by McGranahan et al. even a system involving well-run small companies may be seen as a setback for government, having failed to supply water via the network [MCG 06]. Although these forms of supply are not optimal, they may under certain conditions secure a minimum level of access to the resource. To operate on the assumption that such operators are fundamentally inadequate, would mean missing a major opportunity to improve the conditions of access to water. But at the same time it is problematic to suppose that selling water is fundamentally desirable [KJE 06].

The variety of supply companies and the persistence of customary access confirm the idea that there is not a single model for water supply in towns in developing countries. This powerful trend is likely to persist in the years to come.

NOTES

1. Bombay changed its name to Mumbai in 1995, when the Shiv Sena party took over the state government. Throughout this chapter we shall use the term Mumbai, regardless of the historical context.
2. 'Degenerated peripheralization' is characterized by a largely underprivileged population, a lack of infrastructure for urban services and facilities, the presence of heavy and/or polluting industry outside the city centre and a degraded environment [KUN 02].
3. This form of peri-urbanization is characterized by the stark contrasts and increased segmentation of peri-urban spaces, and by the emergence in these spaces of new forms of segregation, social extremes and even fragmentation [DUP 04].
4. Municipal Corporations (MCo) are the administrative bodies in cities with over 5,00,000 inhabitants. Smaller towns (population 20,000 to 5,00,000) are run by Municipal Councils (MC). A gram panchayat is the administrative body at the village level.
5. A district is an administrative division of the territory. In India states are divided into districts, then *tahsil*, which in turn comprise towns and villages.
6. With more than 1,00,000 inhabitants per sq km the city of Mumbai has reached saturation. In 1991 a third of the population of the MMR was already living off the island.
7. This chapter presents the findings of a field study of certain peri-urban territories near Mumbai between January and October 2005. To carry out this work we received a grant from the French Foreign Ministry (November 2004 to October 2005). We were based at the Centre for Human Sciences (CSH) in New Delhi, which provided logistics and financial support for the field surveys. Our project also received funding from the Franco-Indian ARCUS programme (2005-8) sponsored by the French Foreign Ministry and the Rhône-Alpes Regional Council.
8. This law, which was passed in 1976, set a cap on land property in large towns in the state. It applies to Mumbai, Thane and Kalyan, but the legal details are so complex and contradictory that it proved completely unworkable, its sole effect being to make the property market even more obscure and segmented [MIL 01].
9. The Water and Sanitation Department, Urban Development Department, Infrastructure Development Corporations and Public Health Engineering Department.
10. The government standard for mains losses is set at 15 per cent.
11. Regularized neighbourhoods have been planned by the relevant authority as part of urban development, whereas non-regularized neighbourhoods come about through illegal occupation and construction.
12. The survey of households we carried out indicates levels of supply much lower than the amount 'supplied' by the municipalities and spanning a much shorter period.

13. 1" = 1 inch = 2.54 cm.
14. *Pucca*: A structure in which the ground, walls and ceiling are made of solid materials (stone, concrete, brick, etc.).
15. *Semi-pucca*: A structure in which either the ground, walls and ceiling are not made of solid materials.
16. *Katcha*: A structure in which neither the ground, walls nor ceiling are made of solid materials but of temporary materials (wood, leaves, plastic, etc.).
17. Some writers furnish urban studies, others summarize research work covering a large number of countries: [WHI 91], [WHI 93], [CRA 94], [WEG 99], [KJE 00], [MCI 03], [CON 04], [NJI 04a], [NJI 04b], [TRI 06], [KJE 06], [MCG 06].
18. The work of Zérah, Llorente, Raghupathi and Maria for Delhi [ZER 00], [LLO 02], [LLO 03], [RAG 03], [MAR 06]; Choe et al. (1996), for Dehra Dun [CHO 96]; Allen et al. and Ruet et al. for Chennai [ALL 06], [RUE 07].
19. Only engineers from the Vasai water and sanitation department take occasional samples to check the quality of water in privately owned wells and bore-holes used for domestic consumption.
20. The Maharashtra Jeevan Pratikaran (MJP), equivalent to the state water board, plans and builds water supply schemes.
21. The City and Industrial Development Corporation (CIDCO) is the town-planning agency for the Vasai-Virar area.
22. The city of Chennai seems to be an exceptional case. At the start of the 2000s the local authorities started contracting the supply and distribution of water in the city to small private operators.

5

Access to Drinking Water in Chennai
An Analysis of Institutional Failure

LINGAPPAM VENKATACHALAM AND SIVARAMAN VANATHY

5.1 INTRODUCTION

Rapid population growth and the development of activities that consume water have led to a considerable increase in water demand in the Chennai urban agglomeration. One of the major issues related to the development of the city over recent years has been how to meet this additional demand. A significant proportion of the population of Chennai is poor, and access to water has become a vital aspect of urban poverty alleviation. The risk is that, overall, water supplies will not be able to keep pace with ever increasing demand. The potential improvements to quality of life that can be expected from a rapidly developing urban economy might thus be cancelled out by the negative effects of water shortages.

Despite efforts from government agencies, public policies designed to provide Chennai consumers with adequate supplies of good quality water have so far failed to achieve their objectives. Although there are several dimensions to this failure of government policy, our discussion will focus on the economic aspects. Water scarcity is caused by negative externalities that affect water resources destined for urban areas. Water is used inefficiently, in particular because of the lack of incentive and disincentive mechanisms to encourage reasonable use of resources. The institutions and institutional arrangements that might regulate the opportunistic behaviour of economic agents involved in the water sector are sadly lacking. Government agents act inappropriately, sometimes being overzealous and at other times not intervening sufficiently in water-related matters. This behaviour has a negative impact on the running of water supply development programmes. Guidelines that might encourage economic agents to actively participate in government programmes are non-existent or poorly defined, standing in the way of a win-win outcome. Inadequate public policies encourage economic agents to behave opportunistically, which raises the cost of supplying water. Policies also remain path-dependent while the behaviour of economic agents can change rapidly. Finally, a herd mentality can encourage authorities to adopt water supply policies simply on the grounds that they have been successfully implemented elsewhere by funding agencies.

We shall examine the various aspects of policy failure within an economic theoretical framework. This type of analysis, currently lacking in the literature on urban water supply issues, can help identify ways of strengthening institutions and policies through the introduction of instruments that can enable urban water supply systems to be organized efficiently, equitably and sustainably.

In this chapter, we use a theoretical framework based on environmental economics and new institutional economics to examine some of the main problems encountered by the Chennai water supply authorities. The city's water supply problems are considered to stem from institutional failures, which include both government shortcomings and market failure. After a brief description of the city of Chennai, we will look at the main characteristics of the city's water supply system. We will then go on to analyse the different organizational aspects and areas of governance that have clearly been affected by institutional shortcomings. Finally, we suggest a few changes that might be made to current institutions in order to rectify the shortcomings.

5.2 THEORETICAL APPROACHES TO URBAN WATER SUPPLY

The various problems of delivering water to urban populations, particularly those in developing countries, have given rise to an abundance of literature. On the basis of this literature, the problems facing water authorities can be divided into three broad categories, depending on whether they stem from lack of natural resources, lack of financial resources, or lack of institutional resources (or institutional failure) or governance shortcomings, which impact in one way or another on the objectives of policies aimed at maximizing social welfare. These problems of scarcity can be interpreted theoretically in terms of market or government failure and institutional limits, by referring to environmental economics and new institutional economics.

The theory of government failure suggests that the discrepancy between the maximum welfare that is targeted and the actual benefits brought by a particular water supply regime is caused by two factors: lack of government intervention in matters where such intervention is necessary, and intervention in matters that should not concern the government. Theoretical explanations can be proposed for governments' behaviour, although such explanations have not been tested empirically in the context of urban water supply. The theory of public choice [BUC 62] maintains that government failure stems from the strategies adopted by politicians and bureaucrats who devise water policies in such a way as to maximize their own personal interests and minimize social welfare. This is because government agents behave like rational economic agents, their main goal being to maximize their personal gain, which they do through rent-seeking behaviour. Being part of the government, these agents can create greater opportunities to maximize their personal advantages, compared with ordinary individuals whose opportunities are limited within their own sphere of influence. The theory of public choice considers that government agents act with unbounded rationality, in the sense that they can use any available strategy to achieve their own ends. Thus, deliberately creating water scarcity becomes a dominant rent-seeking strategy for these agents. Government policies are then doomed to failure. The reasons for government policy failure have also been explained by other theoretical approaches. Thus, followers of the Austrian school of economic thought suggest that individuals and households have a huge variety of mental representations that policy makers cannot take into account, with the result, for example, that water management policies do not fulfil social objectives. Water demand forecasts, pricing, determination of the type and level of service, etc., decided in the context of urban water supply programmes are clearly affected by the inability of 'planners' to understand these various user preferences, and the result is a negative impact on the outcome of water policies [VEN 05]. Recent theoretical developments in behavioural economics applied to environment policies suggest that generally speaking individuals experience cognitive difficulties when making empirical decisions, and decisions of government agents – the individuals with bounded rationality – can lead to failure of water sector policies [SHO 08].

The theory of market failure is based on Pigou's analysis of welfare and examines how markets create disparities between private benefits and social benefits, with the former taking precedence over the latter. Extended to the urban water sector, this approach suggests that while water supply markets can maximize private benefits from water supply they generally fail to minimize the social costs of third-party effects [COL 00]. Private sale of water in urban areas is supposedly guided by the principle of profit maximization. This market-based sector has its negative impacts, including overexploitation of aquifers, and it also imposes considerable social costs on third parties. But the cost of extracting water does not reflect this social cost, and volumes extracted are systematically in excess of the optimum level, which is the level reached when the social marginal benefit is equal to the social marginal cost of extracting the water. The water price reflects only the private cost, so demand from buyers is also higher than the optimum level of demand [MOE 02]. This type of situation results in over-use and therefore waste of water. The social cost resulting from this waste of resources is not accounted for in the prevailing price in a private market. Finding ways to include it thus becomes a major problem in an unregulated private market. However, certain advocates of private water markets maintain that such systems can help reduce another type of social cost in urban areas, which without these markets would be considerable. Water scarcity imposes costs on society in terms of lost income due to water-related diseases, increased health care costs, reduced productivity, the extra cost of obtaining water elsewhere, and so on. Private water markets reduce these costs by reducing scarcity. Furthermore, proponents maintain that the negative externalities or third party effects supposedly created by these markets are in fact the result of poor government policy and not the markets as such. Market failure, therefore, is a result of government failure.

In recent years, new institutional economics has sought to demonstrate the role of institutions in the broad sense of the term, both formal and informal, in achieving water supply objectives in urban areas in developing countries. Some of these institutions are efficient, others are not, but in theory only the efficient institutions should be able to survive. If inefficient institutions are always replaced by efficient institutions, then ultimately there would only be efficient institutions, and a Pareto optimal outcome would ensue. The most important points in this institutional analysis of urban water supply concern questions about the ongoing phenomenon of water scarcity in urban areas and the reasons why different levels of efficiency can be observed at a particular time. An institution may operate efficiently from one particular point of view, but may be inefficient in other respects. Efficient institutions and inefficient institutions can co-exist in an economy. An efficient institution cannot always produce an optimal solution. An efficient institution that generates social benefits for one group may at the same time generate significant social costs for another. In a pure market configuration, an institution's efficiency is judged in terms of its ability to minimize the transaction costs of exchange. An analysis of urban water sector institutions should start with the observation that existing institutions are not able to supply water in an efficient, equitable and sustainable manner, with the result that the social benefits are not maximized. In other words, new institutions or institutional arrangements are needed to facilitate the emergence of social benefits through appropriate water supply services. These institutional changes in the urban water sector are costly: 'they evolve incrementally, connecting the past with the present and the future' [NOR 91, p. 97]. Changing the path of institutions in a desirable manner will result in increased transaction costs. Rodrik and Fernandez note that inertia on the part of institutions or a *status quo* bias caused by uncertainty about the future can affect institutional reforms which would in fact be advantageous if carried out [ROD

91]. One of the overall aims of reforms is therefore to eliminate institutional inertia. This can be a costly challenge, increasing the transaction costs, at least during the initial period. But it would seem to be an important aspect of urban water sector reform, since classic institutions have been seen to hamper reform efforts. For example, bureaucrats lobby against market-based reforms in the sector, fearing these reforms will gradually diminish the power they exercise in the top-down system. The complexity and uncertainty that characterize the present institutional framework are likely to hinder the emergence of new efficient institutions in the urban sector. The various social codifications (representations, customs and regulations) affect outcomes in the urban water sector. The bounded rationality of the various stakeholders leads to incomplete institutional arrangements [WIL 00], which also increases transaction costs. It is important to identify and analyse the institutional shortcomings in the urban water sector before initiating any reforms.

5.3 CHENNAI CITY

Chennai (also known by its former name of Madras) is the capital of Tamil Nadu state. Chennai is India's fourth largest metropolitan city in terms of population. The Chennai Metropolitan Area covers some 1,189 sq km and comprises Chennai City Corporation, 16 other municipalities, 20 Town Panchayats,[1] one cantonment, and 214 Village Panchayats[2] scattered over 10 Panchayat Unions in the neighbouring districts of Thiruvallur and Kancheepuram.

Chennai City itself covers an area of 176 sq km and according to the 2001 census has a population of 43,40,000 people. This figure was expected to reach 5.4 million in 2008. The ten-year population growth rate for 1981-91 was 17.24 per cent, while for the following 10-year period it was 9.76 per cent. The city covered an area of 68 sq km in 1901, with a population of 5,40,000. From 1941, the population has increased rapidly. Population growth in the city and the other parts of the metropolitan area from 1971 onwards is shown in Table 5.1. Current population density is estimated at 24,231 inhabitants per sq km. Population density is correlated with

TABLE 5.1: TEN-YEAR POPULATION GROWTH RATES FOR CHENNAI METROPOLITAN AREA

Geographical areas	Population (in millions)				Annual rate of growth (%)		
	1971	1981	1991	2001	1971-81	1981-91	1991-2001
City of Chennai	2.64	3.28	3.84	4.34	2.20	1.58	1.23
Municipalities	0.48	0.81	1.18	1.58	5.24	3.80	2.91
Town Panchayats	0.11	0.16	0.27	0.38	4.43	4.94	3.62
Village Panchayats	0.26	0.33	0.52	0.73	2.40	4.38	3.58
Chennai Metropolitan Area	3.50	4.60	5.81	7.04	2.76	2.37	1.93

Source: Census of India, 2001, and Chennai Metropolitan Development Authority (CMDA)

negative externalities arising from congestion, noise pollution and the accumulation of solid waste and waste water.

According to statistics from the Chennai Metropolitan Development Authority (CMDA) the population of the Chennai metropolitan area has doubled in thirty years, increasing from 3.5 million in 1971 to 7 million in 2001. This is the overall growth rate for the metropolitan area, but rates vary according to the different types of locality. For example, the municipalities and town panchayats have grown at a much faster rate than the city proper. But for the metropolitan area as a whole, the annual population growth rate fell slightly from 2.76 per cent for the period 1971-81 to 2.37 per cent for the period 1981-91, with a further decline of 1.93 per cent for the period 1991-2001. Furthermore, 1,079,414 inhabitants of Chennai live in slums. This represents 25.60 per cent of the total population, making Chennai the city with the highest proportion of slum dwellers in the state of Tamil Nadu. Improvements in water supply will clearly make an important contribution to alleviating poverty. Since the slum population is poor, their capacity to pay for services is limited. The financial viability of projects, the level of service provided, the democratization of financing, etc., are thus vital aspects to be addressed in the context of urban water supply programmes.

An analysis of the demographic profile of the metropolitan area reveals huge internal migration, which poses major problems in terms of supplying public facilities and services. The extremely cosmopolitan nature of the city of Chennai attracts migrants from all over India. About 74.5 per cent of migrants arriving in Chennai come from other parts of Tamil Nadu state, while 23.8 per cent come from other regions of India and 1.7 per cent from other countries (2001 census). Although the proportion of migrants living in the City of Chennai fell from 37.24 per cent of the total population in 1961 to 21.6 per cent in 2001, migrants still account for a large share of total inhabitants, which places increased pressure on basic amenities. Various push-pull factors are responsible for the high levels of urban migration. Failing agriculture and an improved level of education among rural populations are among the factors that push people to move to the city. Better job opportunities for skilled and unskilled workers, availability of better education, including higher education, and the attraction for potential migrants of the increased social capital among settled migrants are just a few of the 'pull' factors that motivate migration to the city.

Migration to the city has a huge impact on demand for environmental amenities, water supply and health care, and on the management of negative externalities. The effects of internal migratory flows will vary depending on where the migrants settle and what institutions are available in those areas. Thus, the social capital built-up by previous migrants and available for new migrants acts as a magnet [WOO 00]. If a significant proportion of settled migrants live in slum areas, this social capital will attract more potential migrants to these areas, generating higher marginal costs related to the externalities.

The extent of the problem of migration stems to a large degree from the failure of the authorities to control migration into the city, and more particularly to address the factors that make people want to leave rural areas. There are a number of measures that could be introduced to help stem this migratory movement: develop and

TABLE 5.2: MIGRATION TO CITY OF CHENNAI (IN THOUSANDS)

Year	Total population of City of Chennai	Distribution of total migrants according to origin			Total migrant population	% of migrant population in total population of city
		Other parts of Tamil Nadu	Other parts of India (excluding Tamil Nadu)	Other countries		
1961	1,729	447 (69.45)	171 (26.60)	25 (3.90)	644	37.24
1971	2,469	551 (70.61)	200 (25.63)	29 (3.76)	780	31.59
1981	3,284	719 (71.28)	255 (25.31)	34 (3.41)	1008	30.70
1991	3,843	644 (70.51)	242 (26.47)	28 (3.01)	918	23.90
2001	4,344	698 (74.49)	223 (23.80)	16 (1.71)	937	21.57

Source: Census Reports; percentages shown in brackets.

decentralize industrial activities outside large urban centres, promote urbanization and develop better amenities in other parts of the state, build better road and rail links between Chennai and other towns in the state, relocate certain industrial activities and services to neighbouring towns, create an attractive environment in neighbouring towns and satellite towns so as to encourage new business activities and services. Instead of adopting a regional development strategy of this kind, policy makers are focusing on improving resources to meet the increased demand for facilities from the urban population. As mentioned earlier, a policy of this kind can make the city even more attractive to potential migrants. The alternative options for stemming urban migration should be examined by the authorities on the basis of cost-benefit analyses with a view to reaching more informed decisions about investment in amenities in Chennai or in the state in general.

The population of the metropolitan area is expected to reach 12.6 million by 2026, including 5.8 million in Chennai city alone.

It is clear from these figures that planners and public policy makers will be faced with the enormous task of supplying additional water to meet the needs of the growing population in the years to come. Several questions therefore need to be addressed: what are the present physical and institutional constraints affecting the future development of the water supply system? What are the different options open to the city? What would be the cost of these options? What kind of problems will have to be addressed in improving water supply services? In the next section, we try to shed some light on these questions.

5.4 GENERAL SITUATION REGARDING WATER SUPPLY IN CHENNAI

The Chennai Metropolitan Water Supply and Sewerage Board (CMWSSB, known as Metrowater) was created in 1978 by Tamil Nadu Act 28. Metrowater is the statutory body responsible for supplying good quality water in sufficient quantities as well as sewage services for the population of Chennai metropolitan area. In order to provide water on a reliable and equitable basis, the CMWSSB (the Board) drew up a Master Plan in 1978, which it updated in 1991, with the aim of meeting the water and sewerage needs of the current population as well as the population up to 2021. For water distribution purposes the Board has divided the city into 16 zones. Each zone has its own subsystem comprising a distribution station, underground and above-ground storage facilitites, pumping stations and wells. The distribution stations are supplied with treated water via water mains from the water treatment plants.

The Board collects water from surface and groundwater sources. Surface water comes from a number of different sources in the metropolitan area as well as outside: Poondi, Cholavaram, Redhills, Chembarambakkam, Rettai Eri and Porur Lake. Veeranam Lake is situated 240 km to the south of Chennai. The New Veeranam Project was set up in 2003 at a cost of Rs.7,200 million (approx. €150 million) to supply 180 mld to the city of Chennai. The Kandaleru reservoir in Andhra Pradesh is also another major source of water for the metropolitan area, provided under the Krishna Water Supply

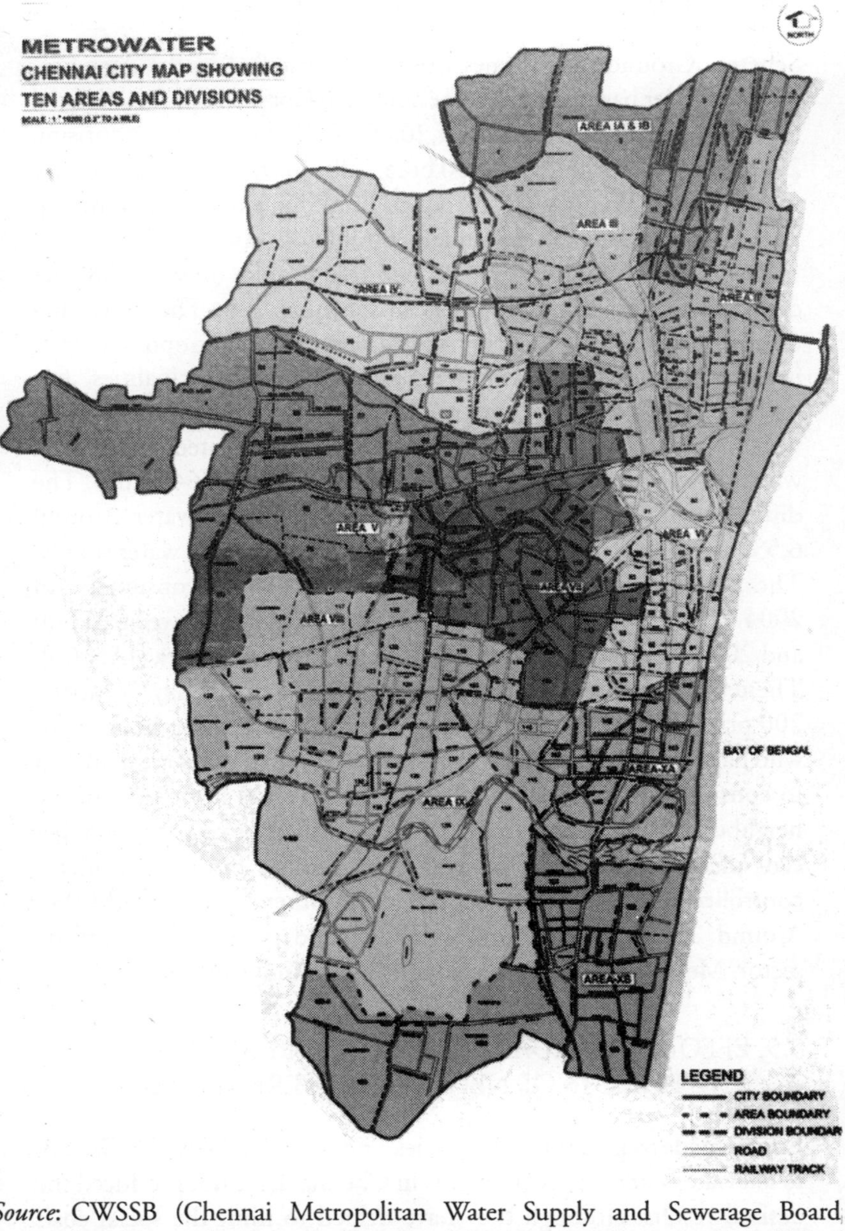

Source: CWSSB (Chennai Metropolitan Water Supply and Sewerage Board http://www.chennaimetrowater.com/ph%20on%20Operation/area.JPG

FIGURE 5.1: MAP SHOWING THE AREAS COVERED BY THE URBAN WATER SUPPLY SYSTEM OF CHENNAI

Scheme. Groundwater comes from wells installed in the Araniyar-Kortaliar river basin and from the Southern Coastal Aquifers. Official estimates suggest that there are 4,20,000 wells in the city, comprising 27,000 open wells and 3,90,000 bore wells. In addition, three reverse osmosis desalination plants produce drinking water from seawater. Together the plants can desalinate 200 mld of seawater.

At present, the Board supplies 645 to 650 mld, of which 585 are delivered to domestic consumers in Chennai City. The remaining 60 to 65 mld are supplied to other users in the metropolitan area: industry, the 'bulk consumers', 10 peripheral municipalities, five town panchayats, two village panchayats, and the cantonment. Total water demand from the present population is estimated at 848 mld, which is well above current supply from the Board (645 mld). The difference of 200 mld comes principally from groundwater. Around 6,530 wells have been dug by the government for daily water supply. The Board rents tanker-trucks to deliver water to consumers. In 2004, about 6,000 tanker-trucks with a capacity of between 10,000 and 20,000 litres delivered water in the metropolitan area [JAN 06]. These tanker-trucks make an average of 1,300 trips a day. A further 700 private tanker-truck trips are made to carry water to households who pay for this additional water. An estimated 125 mld are delivered to consumers by tanker-trucks. This water comes from wells in the neighbouring agricultural areas [LAK 07]. Approximately 65 per cent of water consumed by households comes from government-controlled sources, and 35 per cent from other sources [GAM 03]. Around 25 per cent of total water demand is met by the private sector. Most of this water is drawn from groundwater sources.

5.5 EFFORTS TO ADAPT WATER SUPPLY AND THE EFFECTS OF NEGATIVE EXTERNALITIES

Efforts made by government agencies, and particularly the CMWSSB, to alleviate water supply problems in Chennai have not produced the desired results, although they have helped to limit the social costs of inadequate water supply. Clearly there is still a large gap between the amount of water that the Board can supply and the total water demand from households. A vital question remains unanswered with respect to policy: Why, despite all the efforts made by government agencies over a long period of time, is there still this substantial gap between supply and demand? One of the main reasons behind the creation of the Board by the Chennai Metropolitan Water Supply and Sewerage Act in 1978 had been to promote and guarantee the planned development of water supply and sewerage services for the population of the metropolitan area. So what has happened to this planned development? And how have the government policies failed? Why did things not go according to plan? Why did successive planners not learn from past experience in their approaches, benefiting from feedback and correcting past mistakes when drawing up their own plans? Is the city's problem of water scarcity attributable to the strategic behaviour of government officials seeking to achieve their own ends, as suggested by the theory of public choice? Or is the problem due to the inability of government agents to forecast needs on the basis of the different preferences of the various populations? Is the bounded rationality of government agents to be blamed? While it is impossible to provide rigorous answers to all of these questions, we shall attempt to examine the main consequences of government policy failure.

Thus, as new institutional economics attempts to demonstrate, the inefficiency of governments opens the way to private water markets and private sector participation in water supply management. The efficiency ascribed to the private markets that have sprung up in the city seems to suggest that private markets can capitalize on government inefficiency – even in the case of quasi-public goods such as water, which historically falls entirely within the realm of the public sector. Thus, the argument that inefficient institutions would be replaced, at least in part, by efficient institutions holds true, at least as far as Chennai's water supply sector is concerned. So why are private operators, organized informally, able to gain a strong foothold in the water sector and maintain that position over time if a strong government organization is already in place? In addition to government inefficiency being cited as a possible reason for the emergence of private markets, mention is frequently made in the literature of the private sector's ability to provide consumers with access to water supplies that is both differentiated and reliable.

And since consumers generally give priority to reliability of supply, spontaneous order emerges to promote private water markets. Since households are willing to pay more for a reliable supply which they value highly [ANA 01], the private sector emerges as an efficient institution that can meet needs. The private sector thus has every opportunity to maximize its profits.

Just as failure to meet demand is a common occurrence in the water sector because of an inherent scarcity of the resource, private markets are also becoming a common feature. But the problem here is that even if efficient private markets have enabled supply to better match demand, these improvements have come at a cost. In private markets, those who benefit from additional supplies pay more for a more reliable supply. In other words, if the public utility itself had made available sufficient quantities of water, beneficiaries of this water in urban areas would have found themselves in a Pareto-optimal situation while at the same time enjoying a substantially higher consumer surplus.

Water extraction generates social costs for society as a whole. When water is extracted without control, in particular from groundwater sources, a negative externality is created in the form of the depletion and degradation of the resource, with significant third-party effects and social costs. In the conventional literature on negative externalities, private agents behaving opportunistically are generally blamed for negative externalities. It is then up to the government to compensate for the social problem by taxing harmful activities or seeking a market solution by creating property rights. However, the negative externalities and third-party effects observed in and around Chennai have clearly been caused not only by private operators but also by governments.

The first negative externality we shall look at is groundwater depletion. Laksmi and Janakarajan reported that in many of the areas where the water board extracts raw water, the groundwater table is getting lower and lower [LAK 07]. For example, at Poondi, groundwater was at a depth of about 10 m in January 1999 but by January 2003 it had dropped to about 20 m. A similar case was observed in Tamaraipakkham, where the water table dropped from a depth of about 6 m in January 1999 to about 20 m in January 2003.

Similarly, there has been a gradual fall in the hydrostatic level in many parts of the city. For example, a study conducted by the State Ground and Surface Water Resources Data Centre revealed that the groundwater level had dropped from a depth of 3.8 m in the first quarter of 2006 to 4.2 m in the first quarter of 2007 [HIN 07].

The effect of negative externalities on third parties should not be neglected. Depletion of groundwater resources due to uncontrolled extraction of water in peri-urban and rural areas in order to meet the demands of the urban population imposes a social cost on the populations of all these areas [GAM 03]. First, increased water demand from the city of Chennai and the emergence of private markets have resulted in what has been termed a 'tragedy of the commons', a phenomenon that usually affects common property resources such as groundwater. The picture painted in the theoretical literature is one of selfish agents seeking to maximize their personal gain through use of a common-pool resource, giving little thought to its depletion or degradation. But in peri-urban and rural areas not all economic agents behave in this way, but just a handful of wealthy farmers and tanker-truck owners who privatize groundwater resources by investing significant amounts of money in groundwater extraction activities.

It is sometimes said that these agents are led by the 'invisible hand' and consider that it makes more economic sense to sell water to urban areas than use it for agricultural purposes. Yet their selfish approach not only imposes costs on themselves but also raises the costs of water extraction for other farmers who rely on groundwater to irrigate their crops. This is a direct consequence of the externality. An indirect impact is that the decrease in agricultural output and jobs linked to the reduction in the amount of groundwater devoted to farming causes particular hardship for marginal farmers and landless farm labourers. In addition to selling water of their own free will, some farmers may also be forced to sell the water from their wells. For example, the agricultural sector in Tamil Nadu state has been undergoing a crisis over the past few years because farmers have stopped cultivating their land for a variety of reasons: lack of work force, their children have left in search of white collar work in urban centres, distortions in market prices of produce, insufficient rainwater or crop damage caused by out-of-season rainfall, to name just a few. But farmers also stop farming their land because there is insufficient water for their crops, and this scarcity is due to the depletion of groundwater resources. Struggling farmers then sell water for non-agricultural uses as an alternative source of income. Furthermore, governments provide farmers in the state with free electricity, which lowers the relative cost of extracting water. The combined effect of all these different factors encourages farmers to sell their water to urban users, thereby creating cumulative third-party effects.

Another negative externality stems from water quality degradation. Unremitting exploitation of groundwater in the coastal areas of Chennai and neighbouring areas caused severe problems of sea-water intrusion at the end of the 1990s. Although the problem resulted from the ongoing extraction of groundwater by both the public and private sectors, it was widely believed that the increasing number of private operators played a decisive role in this major crisis. As a result of overexploitation, the aquifers in the metropolitan area started to attract sea water from the Bay of Bengal, which increased the Total Dissolved Solids (TDS) in the groundwater. Numerous consumers who were dependent on groundwater for their daily requirements had to turn to other (costly) sources. Water extracted from groundwater sources in distant areas was delivered to consumers by tanker-truck. Although no attempt has ever been made to measure the social costs of this salt-water intrusion crisis, the nature and extent of the problem suggest that these costs must have been very high, especially in the Chennai metropolitan area. A detailed scientific study would be needed to determine the true social cost and to identify appropriate strategies for dealing with salt-water intrusion. It would also be useful to look into ways of mitigating the harmful effects of an incident of this kind with a view to ensuring that the situation does not worsen in the future.

5.6 INSTITUTIONAL ARRANGEMENTS

The main institutional response to the question of water supply has been government intervention aimed at reducing the negative externalities arising from overexploitation of resources. What is the theoretical basis for such intervention? In the context of Coase's theory [COA 60], a negative externality problem occurs because of the high transaction costs of dealing initially with the externality. In other words, if the transaction costs involved in controlling the negative externality had been low, the externality would have already been dealt with. Since transaction costs determine the nature of economic activities, according to Coase's theory it should be possible to reduce the negative externality through strategic action to modify the transaction costs related to harmful economic activities. Chennai Metropolitan Area Ground Water (Regulation) Act of 1987 prohibiting the exploitation of the groundwater was a strategic intervention of this kind on the part of the Tamil Nadu state government and fits in with Coase's theory on transaction costs. The 1987 Act gave the Board sole authority over digging wells and extracting and transporting water in certain designated areas. This government intervention increased the marginal cost of extracting water in these areas on account of the increase in transaction costs imposed by the Act. For example, various additional costs were incurred in seeking permission to dig wells, 'persuading' officials, paying for the services of intermediaries in order to obtain licences, plus the actual cost of obtaining the licence, the opportunity cost incurred in waiting for the official decision to grant the licence, and other costs in the event of refusal of a licence.

Although this government intervention restricted the activities of a great many water vendors, some private operators in vulnerable areas still continue to extract and sell water without the necessary permission [JAN 06]. So why do these operators break the law? Conventional microeconomic theory suggests that these people are acting rationally when they make such decisions in that they consider that the benefits obtained from breaking the law are greater than the penalty for doing so.

The likelihood of being punished is positively correlated with the degree of monitoring to ensure that legislation is respected. Thus, offenders may consider that if there is only a slight possibility of being prosecuted, the risk of contravening the law can be taken. And given that the law is difficult to enforce in the Chennai metropolitan area, vendors continue to take their chance and extract and sell water.

Also, the cost incurred in breaking the law is linked to three other factors: the commitment of the officials responsible for monitoring, the amount of the bribe needed to win over officials and the amount of the fine. If government officials are rent-seeking and intent on maximizing their own personal benefits, potential law-breakers may consider it more advantageous to pay a bribe than a fine. Thus, through an effective bargaining system, water vendors and officials can reach a Pareto-optimal situation. In a legal regime, if law-abiding individuals are outnumbered by utility-maximizing, self-interested vendors and officials, then, all other things being equal, violation of legislation will become the dominant strategy. The probability of maintaining legal standards is very low in a weak regime of this kind and monetary and comparative cost considerations can lead rational players into the utility-maximizing behaviour of overexploitating water resources. In this case, other stakeholders are penalized.

Another effect of the 1987 Act has been to boost the packaged water industry in the city. While many water vendors unwilling to take risks have disappeared from the market, other private operators have used the opportunity to create a packaged water market. Bottled and packaged water can be purchased at various locations in the city. Lack of precise information on the number of sales points, the volumes of water extracted and sold, the nature of the networks and value chains in the system, the related transaction costs, and so on, make it impossible to carry out a detailed analysis of this market. Suffice it to say that bottled water has become a major industry in Chennai and one that is considered to be a result of government intervention through the 1987 Act. It would appear that the higher transaction cost imposed on individual private operators (i.e. tanker-truck owners) following the introduction of the Act led to a reduction in the relative transaction cost for other private operators, namely packaged water vendors. It can thus be seen that an institutional intervention targeting a specific activity can have cascading effects on the transaction cost of related activities. The ultimate results of an institutional intervention will depend on the changes affecting the components of the transaction costs in all of the institutions concerned.

At the beginning of the 1990s, the government introduced a mandatory rainwater harvesting measure to further alleviate the negative externality in the Chennai metropolitan area. All the buildings owned by households, as well as commercial, industrial and government premises, had to be equipped with specially designed structures to direct rainwater falling on the roofs into the ground, thereby contributing to groundwater recharge. Owners incurred significant costs in adapting their buildings. In the case of the government, it was able to transfer a substantial share of the cost of recharging the groundwater, including transaction costs, onto the beneficiaries themselves. This measure had positive effects on groundwater recharge. Information based on 60 wells scattered across the city suggests that the groundwater level has improved considerably, the average depth in 2007 being 3.45 m compared with 6.18 m in 2004 (*Times of India*, 30 July 2008). Another study conducted by the Board found that the groundwater table had risen a further 2.5 m between 2007 and 2008.[3] It has been shown that rainwater harvesting also helps improve the quality of groundwater. For example, a report reveals that the TDS (which provides an indication of mineral content) measured in water from wells in the northern part of the city fell from 5,000 ppm (parts per million) in 2004 to 300 ppm in 2007. However, information about water quality collected by the Board shows that improvements must still be made in many other parts of the city.

So does economic analysis provide a better understanding of the real impacts of policy initiatives in the groundwater sector? Conventional cost-benefit analysis indicates that the social benefits stemming from overexploitation of water resources are generally assumed to become social costs once the situation is reversed and exploitation is restricted. Similarly, the social costs caused by overexploitation are assumed to become social benefits when the situation is reversed. But this has not always been shown to be true empirically. The *ex-ante* and *ex-post* social benefits and costs of public intervention are not necessarily equal. This is one of the problems of cost-benefit analyses. The problem cannot be viewed as a static one; the effects of public policy on behaviour and institutions must be taken into account. When a long-time frame is involved, as in the case of overexploitation of water resources requiring changes in the institutions involved to reverse the trend, differences between *ex-ante* and *ex-post* benefits and costs can be considerable.

The problem of salt-water intrusion in Chennai gave rise to the creation of private water markets in just about every part of the city. A great many households purchase packaged water, mainly for drinking, from these vendors. Although salt-water intrusion had a negative impact on certain households by reducing water availability, the welfare of households that depend on packaged water may be improved since they are using better quality water than that available before the crisis. Although this water is costly, consumer surplus may be increased because of changes in the factors influencing demand for good quality water (such as income). If we take into account the behaviour of the population, measures to deal with salt-water intrusion may not bring the benefits present before the crisis. The reason for this is a *status quo* bias that may discourage consumers from switching back from private supply to the public service. Another aspect to this issue revealed by numerous cost-benefit analyses conducted in developing countries and in India in particular is that households that obtain relatively poor quality water from existing (mainly public) sources are willing to pay more for better quality water. Thus, households that were willing to pay for better water before the onset of salt-water intrusion have been able to benefit from the better quality water offered by the private sector. Since cost-benefit analysis does not really take into account the transaction cost (which changes as the institutions evolve between the two periods of time), *ex-ante* and *ex-post* outcomes may be different. Any measure to restore the ecological characteristics of the groundwater should take into account the reactions of the institutions (which also evolve in response to changes in public policy) as well as the ultimate benefits to the population in order to anticipate the full impact.

5.7 OUTLOOK

It is important to identify the options available to public agencies in general and to the Board in particular in addressing the problem of water scarcity in Chennai in the coming years. Solutions can be found on the supply side and on the demand side. The Board considers that there are no longer any new water supply sources able to meet further increases in demand. However, it does have plans to restore thousands of water supply structures (e.g. the traditional irrigation tanks) in and around the city. If they are put back into service, these structures, which have become unusable because of lack of maintenance, could satisfy future water requirements [JAN 06]. Some of Chennai's big lakes (such as Pallikaranai Lake) that have enormous potential for supplying surface water for the urban population are under severe stress due to pollution from urban wastewater. One of the best options open to the Board would be to renovate existing surface water structures. While this seems to be a sensible choice, there would be significant implications with respect to ensuring the proper management of these water sources after renovation. An important question that should be asked is why these extensive and vital bodies of water, supposedly a precious resource for the economic agents that depend on them, have been allowed to fall into total disuse. These bodies of water, that once supplied water for irrigation among other things, had previously been managed efficiently by economic agents who obtained fairly substantial revenues from these resources. But subsequently, as the areas of farmed land began to shrink because of problems in the agricultural sector and groundwater started to be used increasingly, these benefits decreased considerably and the structures gradually fell into disrepair. As long as this situation remains unchanged, these traditional water resources can only be successfully revitalized if a response is found to an important institutional question, namely how the structures will be managed.

The willingness of economic agents to manage these systems is influenced mainly by the incentives and disincentives stemming from the institutional arrangements. However, the neglected state of these water reserves suggests that existing institutions have been unable to come up with the necessary incentives. A solution would be alternative innovative arrangements, such as the creation of a market-type environment in which economic agents managing the structures would receive compensation or payment commensurate with the services received by the beneficiaries. This type of arrangement, known as Payment for Environmental Services (PES) [WUN 05], has proved itself in the field in both developed and developing countries as a promising instrument for managing environmental resources, including water [WUN 08], and the Government of Tamil Nadu and the Board could explore this option.

On the demand side, there are many possibilities for improving efficiency of water use among the population. One possibility would be to revise the pricing structure, replacing the arbitrary way of determining tariffs with a system based on user preferences. In most cases, there is a big difference between what consumers would like and what policymakers decide [VEN 05]. Numerous empirical studies have shown that users are willing to pay more for a better, more reliable water supply. Decision-makers should take note, and determine who is willing to pay and how much they are willing to pay. This information can then be used to create an equitable and efficient price structure. Furthermore, this structure should be designed in such a way as to encourage users to recycle a large amount of wastewater.

Another possibility would be to allow formal markets to provide certain water supply services on the basis of comparative benefits and transaction costs. For example, a public private partnership (PPP) is considered a viable option for the efficient provision of water supply services since the private sector can minimize the transaction cost of certain activities and limit unaccounted-for water, leading to gains in overall efficiency. However, introducing a PPP is no easy task. Behavioural inertia plays a role in preventing the entry of private operators. Furthermore, private sector participation is often assumed to mean privatization of water, which is a public good.

But a PPP arrangement is not privatization. It merely gives the private sector partial or full responsibility for certain activities related to water supply, treatment or distribution. Urban water supply can be considered to a certain extent to be divisible. Using simple technology, users in certain categories can be excluded from various services. It is possible, for example, to establish property rights over individual connections in private homes for groups that are willing to pay. And since such connections are costly, those who cannot afford the additional payment will be denied the possibility of acquiring such property rights. Similarly, guaranteeing property rights over a particular level of water supply services for low-income groups (essentially water supplied from public taps) suggests that the higher income groups can be excluded from such services. Even under a public regime, urban water supply services still retain their characteristics of 'private good'. The presence of private operators in this sector can be justified on the grounds that they can reduce transaction costs and thereby improve the overall efficiency of the water supply service.

5.8 CONCLUSION

Water supply is one of the keys to the economic well-being of urban populations, and especially poor urban populations. But ensuring well-being by improving water supply to urban communities is limited by a certain number of institutional shortcomings entrenched in this sector. In the case of Chennai and its surrounding areas, these shortcomings can be found in all aspects of the water sector. When an institution fails for reasons of inefficiency, another institution should replace it; this is known as the evolutionary approach to institutional dynamics. However, a new institution might improve the efficiency of one particular aspect but create inefficiencies elsewhere. For example, private operators might enhance efficiency by providing a more reliable service for users, but inefficiencies can appear in the form of third-party effects. In other words, even if an institution succeeds in reducing transaction costs in certain activities, this reduction may lead to an increase in the transaction cost of another activity. This suggests that no institution can operate efficiently in all aspects. The inefficiency caused in different water sector institutions infiltrates other activities without really being addressed and then becomes heightened in the entire supply and distribution system. There is a high level of uncertainty and complexity as regards the institutional dynamics of the urban water sector. Any institutional reform of the urban water sector designed to tackle problems of scarcity, negative externalities and third-party effects must be based on an in-depth analysis of the interactions between institutions and of the institutional failures of each institution in a particular environment. In this chapter, we have examined such interactions in the context of Chennai's urban water sector, using a theoretical framework provided by new institutional economics. Other studies of this type are necessary if we are to fill the enormous gap in knowledge about this sector.

NOTES

1. Town panchayats are communities that have the recognized status of town in terms both of urban criteria and tax revenues [OLI 04], p. 72.
2. A village panchayat is a community that does not have sufficient tax revenues to be classified as a town but has the necessary urban characteristics (over 5,000 inhabitants, over 400 h/sq km, over 75 per cent of working population employed in non-agricultural activities) [OLI 04], p. 74.
3. These results appear to conflict with the results mentioned in our earlier discussion about groundwater exploitation. There may be a number of reasons for this: agencies may take measurements at different places and the difference in the depth of the water table between these locations can lead to variations in results. Differences in the frequency of measurement can also give conflicting results. For example, studies that measure variations from one year to another may show a rise in the water table, whereas studies that take measurements over a longer period might show a drop in the groundwater level. To obtain a really accurate picture, further details need to be included from available information on geographical locations, rainfall amounts, extraction rates, and so on.

6

Sectorization and Territorialization of Water Demand in Megalopolises

MAHFOUD BOUDIS AND YVES SAILLARD

6.1 INTRODUCTION

The various cases we described in the previous chapters have highlighted the importance of the organization and management of water supplies in satisfying the needs of populations in megalopolises. We also showed the constraints involved, but a widely held view is that these could partly be overcome with more efficient institutions. In this chapter and those that follow, we will endeavour to explain this with particular emphasis on defining urban and peri-urban water demand and the factors that compose it. The complexity of water demand in megalopolises is such that we need to describe the various components involved. We will highlight two main aspects: the diversity of usage (or sectorization) and the spatial aspect (or territorialization). In this chapter we suggest a model that attempts to define water demand in megalopolises according to these aspects and to explain the medium-term factors in its evolution.

We will refer to a model that has already been developed to simulate urban water demand in European Mediterranean cities, namely G-EAU [BOU 05]. This model used a sector-based approach to demand that provided an estimate of water requirements for an entire urban territory. Variations of G-EAU have simulated water demand in a variety of contexts (the cities of Grenoble, Naples, Barcelona and Marrakech). The WATER_UP simulation model we propose here is an extension of this methodology. One extension consists of marking out the city space by distinguishing the city proper, which is relatively well circumscribed, from the peri-urban space, which has a more blurred and fluctuating boundary. This is particularly useful for studying cities in developing countries, especially Indian megalopolises. Another extension consists of introducing the impact of governance on the evolution and viability of urban water supply systems. From a methodological point of view, this means having a general modelling framework that is specified for each urban reality studied, and not just a collection of successive variations of the model. In this way we hope to benefit from experiences observed in some cities and test their impact on others.

Extending the definition of water demand to peri-urban territories consists of more than simply altering the spatial aspect. It must also take into account the complementary and competitive relationships between the two types of territory with regard to the distribution of a shared resource. Furthermore, the peri-urban areas themselves are very diverse. Each megalopolis, and certainly each of the Indian cities studied here, has developed specific urban territories. The question then arises about the unity of water supply management over the entire urban territories of the same city. This may take the form of a shared governance for the set of urban and peri-urban territories, a segmented management of urban and peri-urban areas, or a separation of the central city and the 'small cities' in the peri-urban areas.

The aim of the simulation tool described in this chapter is to simplify the analysis of possible evolutions in urban water supply systems based on structural data specific to each town, but also on experiences observed elsewhere. A common sector system was devised whereby each city is distinguished according to the distribution between its different water usage possibilities. A common minimal spatial structure distinguishes the urban territories from the peri-urban ones. The simulations of evolutions in water demand are the result of hypotheses about the structural parameters and the management methods used.

We shall begin this chapter by presenting the general methodological approach and the modelling characteristics. We will mainly refer to the G-EAU model. The simulation tool is then extended to include its sectorization and territorialization aspects. The structure of this new model, WATER-UP, and the description of its simulations will be found in the next part. We will conclude with the types of scenarios that may be tested. The tool will be deployed in the following chapter and will provide the basis for a discussion on possible evolutions in urban water supply systems.

6.2 THE PRINCIPLES OF AN APPROACH TO URBAN WATER DEMAND: THE G-EAU[1] PRECEDENT

A number of methods and models have been devised for studying the management and planning of water resources [LOU 05]. Our approach refers more to the family of analytical and determinist models used to simulate water demand on different territorial scales and for different economic sectors. It is the extension of several models, such as MADH2O [GAR 93], which focused on the prospective demands on the Algerian water basins, especially for industry. Similarly the DELTA model, conceived for France and also applied to Greece, described the evolution of water requirements for agriculture and livestock [ARR 93]. More recently, the demand for urban water in the Euro-Mediterranean cities was explored in depth using the G-EAU [BOU 05] model. Since that will serve as our starting point, we will provide a reminder of how it works.

The G-EAU model described the evolution of determining factors in water demand in urban agglomerations of various sizes and in different regions such as the Rhône-Alpes region of France, the Roman Campagna in Italy, Catalonia in Spain and the Marrakech Haouz in Morocco, whether or not existing supplies are good. A model of urban water demand was created that could be adapted to each case. One of the original features of this tool was its three-dimensional representation of water consumption according to sector, time and space, with the time step selected by the user [ARR 00]. In this section we will describe how the G-EAU method deals with these aspects.

6.2.1 *The G-EAU Approach and the Sectorization of Demand for Urban Water*

The sectorization of demand describes the diversity of uses for water. We consider that usage depends on the techniques of supply and demand, the actors involved, the management and means used. There are several levels of demand satisfaction depending on observed practice and the evolution scenarios envisaged. A given use may have a range of environmental impacts and result in either water wastage or preservation, and contribute – or not – to pollution. Satisfaction levels are related to the management method (or methods) adapted to several complementary forms, be they legal, economic or institutional (see Figure 6.1). The interactions between demand satisfaction methods and management methods indicate various types of water usage.

Having specified the water usage, the G-EAU model enables us to simulate urban water demand for a given period, according to the most appropriate geographic entities.

Up to now the applications of the G-EAU model have largely been quantitative, simulating demand levels for comparison with available resources. Matching available supply with demand requires an analytical and hierarchical model, whose structure, according to

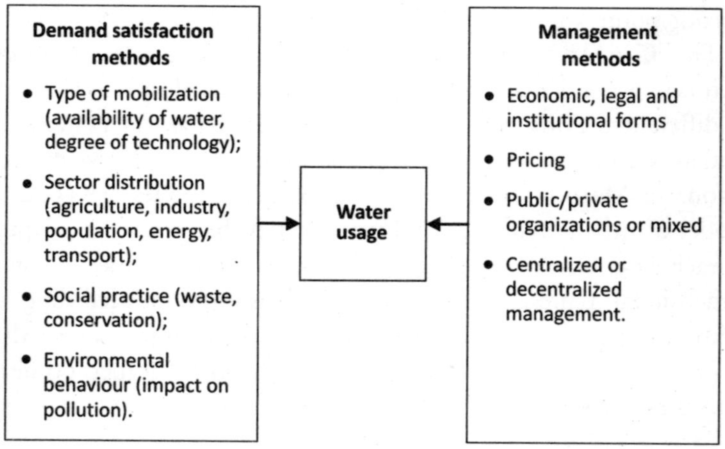

FIGURE 6.1: WATER USAGE

different variables related to the urban water supply and demand and the dependency between these variables, is shown for the Euro-Mediterranean case in Figure 6.2.

Water resources for cities may be above or below ground (dams, lakes, rivers *versus* wells, bores and springs). In some cases, other types of resources such as harvested rainwater or desalinated seawater may also be used. City water supplies consist of the volume produced after deduction of leakage and loss, largely as a result of the quality of the utility's network, which varies according to the urban area in question.

Sector nomenclature, which is useful for evaluating demand satisfaction, was defined in the application of the G-EAU model (as shown in Figure 6.2) according to the sector-based uses of water in the Mediterranean region [ARR 02]. It is presumed to be homogeneous

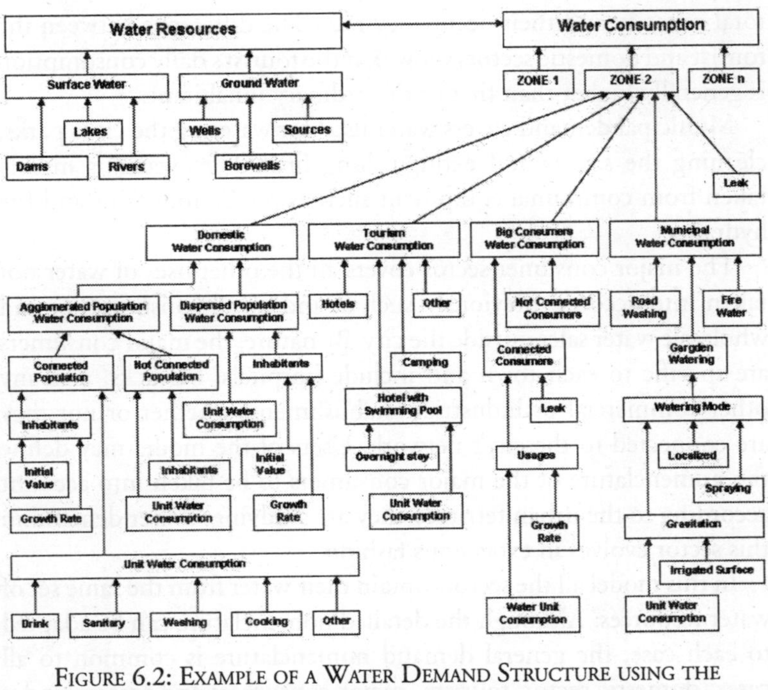

FIGURE 6.2: EXAMPLE OF A WATER DEMAND STRUCTURE USING THE G-EAU METHOD: THE EURO-MEDITERRANEAN APPLICATION

and invariable in relation to the various zones of the city, and should be adapted in the case of other urban contexts.

The model distinguishes between several major sectors of urban water consumption, namely the domestic sector (the population demand in Figure 6.2), tourism, major industrial consumers and municipal use.

In the domestic sector, we distinguish between the population connected to the water supply network and the segment that is not. Consumption in this sector depends on population numbers (weighted by the network connection rate) and the unit consumption per inhabitant. Collective usage is then added to this consumption. The evolution of these exogenous variables enables us to simulate long-term domestic water demand.

Water demand for the tourist industry depends on the type of tourist infrastructures in the city (hotels, hotels with swimming pools, campsites, etc.), their connection to the distribution network, their total capacity and their occupancy rate. The difference between the tourist and domestic sectors show that the tourist's daily consumption is generally higher than that of the ordinary inhabitant.

Municipal demand covers water used for watering the city's parks, cleaning the streets and extinguishing fires. That water is mainly taken from communal equipment such as public fountains and fire hydrants.

The major consumer sector covers all the other uses of water not taken into account previously such as industrial consumption and wholesale water sales outside the city. By nature, the major consumers are specific to each town and include hospitals, barracks, and any other commercial or industrial establishment, whether or not they are connected to the city's network. Users of the model may define the nomenclature of the major consumers to be taken into account according to the urban territory they are studying. Water demand in this sector evolves in exogenous fashion.

In this model all the sectors obtain their water from the same set of water resources. Although the detailed nomenclature can be adapted to each case, the general demand nomenclature is common to all cases (domestic sector, tourism, major consumers and sectors under state or municipal control). However, each sector definition must be explained. There can be two objectives for reconstructing demand in this way: to reconstruct actual demand from elementary data, or to evaluate the consequences of normative objectives, such as the daily per capita consumption. In fact, both uses are complementary and enable us to construct public policy objectives.

6.2.2 *The G-EAU Approach and the Territorial Aspect of Urban Water Demand*

In the G-EAU model, water consumption is estimated according to different geographic divisions (districts, municipalities, etc.). There is no pre-defined geographic scale. For each spatial unit in the network we evaluate the water requirements of the various sectors (inhabitants, tourism, major consumers, municipal water) as well as water losses in the distribution network.

The sector nomenclature of the G-EAU model should be adapted to the various urban territories and the model's objectives. In Grenoble, the G-EAU application emphasized the economic management of the resource. The data were defined in detail on the billing group scale. A billing group corresponded to a set of streets in which the water meters are read and bills sent to consumers in the same period. The spatial entity used by the Grenoble water management authority does not correspond to any geographic, administrative or territorial management logic [BRI 02]. Generally speaking the G-EAU method does not impose a definition of a geographic zone with different coherent hierarchical levels [MAT 01]. The spatial divisions that serve to reconstruct water demand are specific, heterogeneous and particular to each city.

The spatial structure must therefore be selected according to the optimum way of managing water demand for each territory. This will depend on the objectives set and the scenarios under consideration. For regional planning purposes, for instance, the administrative structures might be stressed, while an assessment of distribution methods and inequalities in water access may justify smaller geographical divisions. Macro-economic management of water resources and waterworks would require observation of the basins and sub-basins providing them. In the G-EAU system, urban water demand may be spatialized to a very precise degree on the condition that homogeneous data is available for each spatial unit in the network. In the case of Grenoble, the G-EAU model used disaggregation and aggregation procedures such as those suggested for geographic information systems [PUM 97], as well as a heuristic approach [BRI 02]. Several organizational levels relating to water management were identified and the city's urban territory was structured in such a way as to identify the criteria for a sustainable water management system.

The WATER-UP approach for urban water supply systems suggested here will be both more limited and more ambitious. Geographic zoning is limited to the distinction between the urban area (the city proper) and the peri-urban one. However, these territories are not defined exogenously but will evolve over time independently.

6.3 MODELLING URBAN AND PERI-URBAN WATER DEMAND WITH WATER-UP

Using G-EAU as a starting point, we suggest developing a demand simulation model that will allow a prospective and comparative analysis of urban water supply systems to be extended to peri-urban contexts. To do so, models originally drawn up for Euro-Mediterranean cities must be extended to include the characteristics of water demand in megalopolises.

The model we suggest, WATER-UP (Water Access for Territories Urban and Peri-urban), is an exploratory one. It pursues the general objective of providing an overall representation of water demand in the cities in question in the broadest sense, that is to say by regrouping the urban and peri-urban territories, distribution and supply management, whether or not the supply follows the extension of the peri-urban territories (more frequently not, in the case of megalopolises). The spatial management of water demand must be able to take into account the specificity of the urban and peri-urban territories, as we will see when we present the cases of Bengaluru, Chennai and Mumbai. The various water consumption sectors are treated as in G-EAU, but with a combined nomenclature for this pilot version and appropriate indicators. The time frame is a medium-term one, to enable us to simulate the evolution of demand, the organization of resources, and management methods. The simulations use available data and explicit hypotheses to test the implications of alternative scenarios. Like G-EAU, WATER-UP is an analytical and deterministic discrete time simulation model.

We have seen in previous chapters the broad diversity of supply methods for fresh water and problems in satisfying needs according to the cities we have studied (Grenoble, and the three Indian cities of Mumbai, Bengaluru and Chennai). However, in presenting these different cases we also demonstrate the usefulness of identifying the dynamics of the urban and peri-urban territories, of showing their interdependence and of integrating them in the same water supply approach.

In WATER-UP the emphasis is on two main questions. The first is of a demographic and spatial nature: at what pace are the cities expanding, and over which territories? The city's expansion territory is understood in terms of economic activity, types of habitat and existing natural resources. The second question concerns the continuity of water supply services to these new territories, the distribution network and the organization of supplies, as well as governance and management.

6.3.1 *A Preliminary Condition: Urban and Peri-urban Spatial Dynamics*

As we have seen in the previous chapters, Indian cities have seen a massive growth of peripheral urban territories. These usually have poor basic infrastructure and require considerable investment, notably to ensure water supplies for a rapidly growing population. The speed with which the urban and peri-urban territories have grown oblige us to reason in terms of spatial dynamics. The territorial dimensions, together with their distribution and content, evolve in a relatively short time frame.

However, integrating the spatial dynamics of cities in representations of the evolution of urban water demand poses a few problems. There is usually a discrepancy in the administrative limits set up by the managing institutions in relation to the spread of demand. Water resources are divided between those available for the urban space in its strictest definition (mainly the existing network), those that can be allocated to all the territories (by extending the network or adding complementary means of distribution), and the resources exploited locally by the peri-urban population. These resources are deducted from competing activities, notably agricultural ones.

Figure 6.3 is a representation of the principal characteristics of these spatial dynamics. The urban zone covers a population that mainly depends on the urban water supply for its water. The peri-urban zone includes all the peripheral territories, whether or not they have an administrative organization. The population in that zone may be using the urban utility network but is mainly using complementary (and often private) resources. The borders between the urban and peri-urban areas are hazy and fluctuating. They are only really revealed when water supply problems occur. In WATER-UP we consider that the sectorization of demand can be carried out over all these territories. The distribution between the various sectors, like the territorial aspects, governs the evolution of water demand.

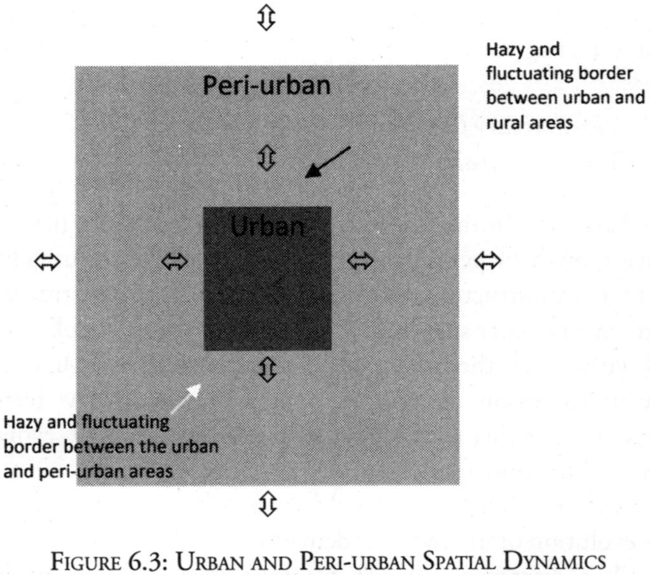

FIGURE 6.3: URBAN AND PERI-URBAN SPATIAL DYNAMICS

Unity of management, which is already difficult to implement in a case like Grenoble, is definitively broken when we take into account the peri-urbanization of megalopolises. The management of water supplies is traditionally provided at city level in its strict, historic sense. However, several possibilities may be found in the peri-urban territories: a relative dependence on urban water management, local management by administrative districts, overall management (both urban and peri-urban), and the absence of local water regulations. In the following chapter we will show how the various cases we have studied illustrate the diversity of these management methods.

6.3.2 *Sectorization of Water Demand*

We define as 'sectors' the groups or categories of consumers with the same water uses where the distinction is relevant for water management, and for which data is available whether from regular statistics, censuses, or surveys. Our analysis of available water consumption data for the four cities we have studied, allows us to distinguish between two major sectors, which may be broken down further according to the city:

- The domestic sector, covering households whose supplies may come from very diverse sources. They may be connected individually or collectively to a public distribution network, resort to the private sector, have their own resources or depend on the informal sector. Part of their needs may also be covered by public municipal fountains.
- The non-domestic sector, which is the demand for water generated by the various market and non-market sectors including commerce, industry and government. Part of this sector is supplied by the public network while another buys water from private distributors or has its own resources. This sector also includes municipal water for various communal uses (watering parks, fire hydrants, street cleaning, etc.).

Here our analysis focuses on the domestic sector. In addition to consumption by users connected to the public utility network, the model looks at network losses and the volume of water sold outside each zone. During the simulation, the sector nomenclature we have used is presumed to be invariable over time, even though the relative weight of a sector may vary according to the simulation scenarios we examine. Water demand sectorization is estimated for each urban and peri-urban territory.

6.3.3 *The Time Aspect*

WATER-UP is a discrete time continuous simulation model. We have preferred to use quinquennium steps rather than annual simulations. The model mainly simulates trends and the impact of public decisions is felt after a period of several years. Our horizon is 2025, using 2000 as the base year. The model retrospectively simulates water demand from 2000 to 2005. Its flexibility is mainly due to the alternative hypotheses about the respective evolutions of the urban and peri-urban territories. The rapid transformation of the cities we studied may, however, be affected by important changes in the cities' spatial dynamics ([PUM 92], [SAN 93], [SAN 98]) and/or by major economic transformations.

At each simulation stage, overall demand is the sum of estimated demand for each sector and each zone.

According to the urban management method in use, the assessment of the balance between available supply and demand is carried out at different levels and for different spaces. The available quantities of water resources are estimated exogenously. We apply supply system and distribution efficiency rates to these volumes. Water resources may also be bought and sold outside the urban space in question. The efficiency rates take into account network leakage as well as illegally tapped water and, more broadly, non-revenue water.

We may observe both the overall and local balance in water supply and demand, sector by sector. The scenarios tested may then change the parameters or the reference hypotheses to alter these projections and analyse their impact on other sectors. One of the advantages of the model is that it factors in the interdependence of all the sectors and the various territories in the distribution of a shared resource.

The WATER-UP model describes production flows, as well as the distribution and consumption of water resources. It produces diagnoses on the satisfaction of water requirements and assesses the water balance. It is then up to public policy to select the appropriate scenarios and to provide the means for managing them.

6.3.4 *Formulating the WATER-UP Model*

The WATER-UP model's water demand is given in Figure 6.4:

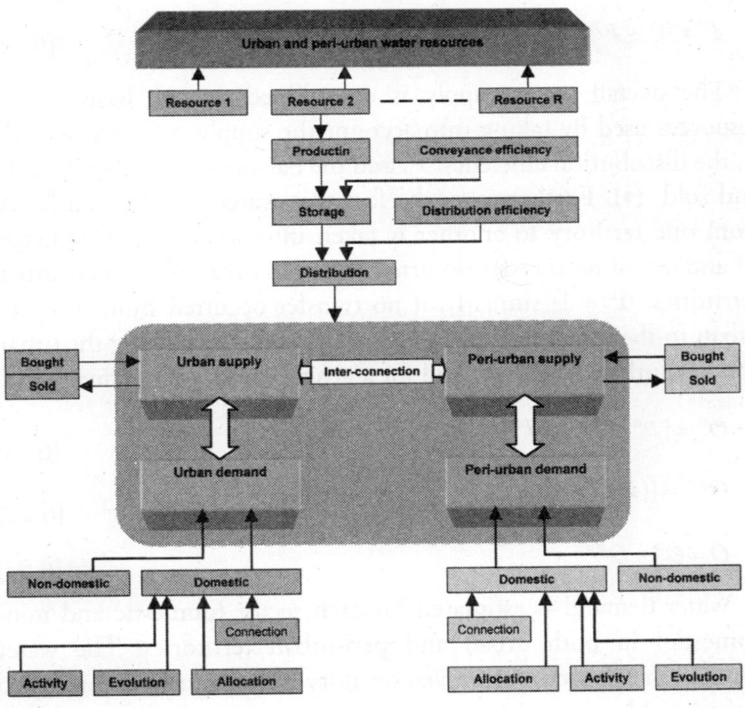

FIGURE 6.4: SECTORIZATION AND TERRITORIALIZATION OF WATER DEMAND IN WATER-UP

6.3.4.1 Supply and Demand

We consider that a set of water resources ($r = 1, \ldots, R$) can supply a city's urban and peri-urban territory. The overall volume of water resources used over a given period corresponds to the sum of the volumes used by the type of resource, which constitute the exogenous data. By identifying the resources present in the urban and peri-urban territories the overall resource is shown as follows:[2]

$$P^u = \sum_{r=1,R} P_r^u \qquad [6.1a]$$

$$P^{pu} = \sum_{r=1,R} P_r^{pu} \qquad [6.1b]$$

$$P = P^u + P^{pu} \qquad [6.1c]$$

The overall water supply is determined on the basis of the resources used by taking into account the supply system efficiency, r_a, the distribution efficiency, r_d, and the balance of the water bought and sold, (•). Furthermore, the fact that water may be transferred from one territory to another is taken into account in parameters α^u and α^{pu} (if no transfer occurred from the urban to the peri-urban territories, $\alpha^u = 1$; similarly, if no transfer occurred from the peri-urban to the urban territories, $\alpha^{pu} = 1$). By distinguishing the urban and peri-urban territories, still for a given period, we obtain:

$$O^u = [P^u \alpha^u r_a^u + P^{pu}(1-\alpha^{pu}) r_a^{pu} + \Delta^u] r_d^u \qquad [6.2a]$$

$$O^{pu} = [(P^u(1-\alpha^u) r_a^u + P^{pu} \alpha^{pu} r_a^{pu} + \Delta^{pu}] r_d^{pu} \qquad [6.2b]$$

$$O = O^u + O^{pu} \qquad [6.2c]$$

Water demand is estimated for each sector (domestic and non-domestic) in both urban and peri-urban territories. The water demand in one sector of a given territory is determined according to three variables: water consumption by the sector's consumption unit for the reference year, d_s, the original level of sector activity, A_s, and the growth rate for these activities in the territory, $\bullet_s$. This parameter, which expresses the hypotheses for demographic change in the domestic sector, is a determining one. It also indicates the sector component transformations of urban and peri-urban territories. By distinguishing the urban and peri-urban territories, and any territory that may have several water consuming sectors, we obtain the following:

$$D_s^u = A_s^u(1+\eta_s^u)d_s^u \quad [6.3a]$$

$$D_s^{pu} = A_s^{pu}(1+\eta_s^{pu})d_s^{pu} \quad [6.3b]$$

And overall, for the entire urban and peri-urban territory:

$$D = D^u + D^{pu} \quad [6.4c]$$

According to the scenario hypotheses, demand flows may be based on the continuation of observed demand or be normative and voluntarist.

6.3.4.2 Management Levels and Balancing Resources with Demand

When the unity of water supply management is broken we cannot simply match supply to overall demand. Several standard ways of balancing supply and demand are possible *a priori*. Below are some standard and extreme cases.

- The full sharing of available resources at overall level for both urban and peri-urban territories.

  $$O \leftrightarrow D \quad [6.5a]$$

  This model for balancing supply and demand assumes overall water supply governance and interconnecting networks between the urban and peri-urban territories.
- Strict separation of urban and peri-urban territories.

  $$O^u \leftrightarrow D^u \text{ et } O^{pu} \leftrightarrow D^{pu} \quad [6.5b]$$

  This extreme case assumes, for instance, that the distribution network remains confined to the city proper and that the urban territories need to resort to new resources or do not draw on the quota of existing resources allocated to the city. Two parallel organizations handle the water supply.
- The urban territories alone supply all the urban and peri-urban territories.

  $$O^u \leftrightarrow (D^u + D^{pu}) \quad [6.5c]$$

  This situation corresponds to an absence of own resources in the peri-urban territories, with the risk of depletion for the urban territories as well as a reduction in quality. It also indicates the absence of organization in the peri-urban territories.

One might of course imagine all the intermediary situations between the overall mode of balancing, the separation of territories or the onus of the supply solely on the city proper. One of these might correspond to a 'reasoned' sharing, whereby the city only shares any excess water it might have:

$$(O^{u} - D^{u}) + O^{pu} \leftrightarrow D^{pu} \qquad [6.5d]$$

The choice between the various ways of balancing water supply and demand should be specified according to the city studied and should form part of the choice of scenarios. Depending on the level of balancing required, the retroactive effects triggered by the assessment of the state of resources and consumption may differ in terms of investment, the search for new resources, and the control of demand.

6.3.4.3 Parameters of Urban Water Policies

The model's hypotheses concern the data for the exogenous variables and the values of the parameters.

For a given organization of the territory, predefined sectors, a fixed time frame and fixed time steps, the exogenous variables and parameters to be defined concern either the urban economic activities or the city's water supply system.

Water consuming activities in a city may be specified by initializing three activity indicators:

- The initial activity indicator for each sector in each zone:

  $\overline{A_s^u}$ and $\overline{A_s^{pu}}$

- the rate of evolution of the activities in each sector and each zone:

  $\overline{\eta_s^u}$, $\overline{\eta_s^{pu}}$

- per unit water allocation in each zone:

  $\overline{d_s^u}$ and $\overline{d_s^{pu}}$

The per unit water allocation represents public control of water consumption. The managing authorities observe levels and set objectives to vary these according to the consumption differentials in urban and peri-urban territories, and according to the consumption observed elsewhere in the world or the standards recommended by international organizations. The city's water supply may be characterized by the instantiation of three types of technical parameters:

– the production capacity of each type of water resource:
  P_r^u and P_r^{pu} , $r = 1,\dots R$
– the water supply system efficiency:
  r_a^u and r_a^{pu}
– the distribution network efficiency
  r_d^u and r_d^{pu}

Technical efficiency reflects losses and leakage in the network. Public policies aim to become aligned with rates shown for other cities or those set as national, regional or international objectives. Adjustments require long-term investment and policies.

6.3.4.4 Scenarios for Simulating Water Demand and 'Reasoned' Projections

The WATER-UP model was conceived to introduce complementary reactive hypotheses during projections. Public water distribution may lead to situations with poor quality water and/or insufficient quantities that need to be dealt with. It may then be necessary to buy water to offset supply shortages in the public network, either explicitly or by developing informal sectors or practices to serve as adjustment measures.

The simulations show what additional supplies may be necessary for particular territories, and the extent of investment required. They also show which efficiency gains would lead to a balanced management of resources. The share of non-revenue water consumption[3] is a determining indicator for a water management system in developing cities. It depends on the age of the network, technological constraints, and the institutional and financial resources that can be mobilized.

However, it is also a means of adjustment for indirectly satisfying demand from consumers with insufficient income to pay for water.

As for the available water resources, we believe that uncontrolled growth and urbanization, as well as the prospects of climate change, will deplete both surface and ground water. Conversely, recycling and seawater desalination techniques can increase the supply by means of non-conventional resources. Other resources may also be mobilized, for example through rainwater harvesting and wastewater treatment.

WATER-UP is an analytical model that makes it possible to access the water supply organization and the entire set of demand determinants. It is possible to alter the tree diagram (Figure 6.4) at a specific point (including in case of conflicts in resource allocation between users) and then check the impact of a given measure on overall demand. By iteration we can therefore construct successive scenarios and analyse their results.

We can illustrate the potential use of the WATER-UP model to simulate water demand in urban and peri-urban territories by proposing several standard scenarios:

- Economic growth scenarios to determine the volume of water necessary to support an economic activity that will promote the development of that territory;
- Urban planning policy scenarios to analyse the evolution of demand for water spatialized according to a selected breakdown;
- Water policy scenarios to identify the instruments required for rationalizing the water supply by acting on the network efficiency, recycling, desalination, and the deployment of new waterworks;
- Environmental policy scenarios to measure the impact of water purification and recycling plants on supply and demand, and encourage the population to use water-saving equipment.

With these scenarios the model can be used for projection purposes by carrying out direct simulations for answering analytical questions such as what would happen if a given water supply or demand strategy were implemented. The iterative examination of several direct simulation scenarios would also provide decision-making uses for the model by testing alternative actions aiming to achieve a balance between available resources and consumption.

The simulations we suggest in the following chapter provide an illustration of WATER-UP modelling. They will mainly indicate the characteristics of the evolution of water demand and the conditions for balancing supply and demand in the urban and peri-urban territories of the Indian megalopolises.

NOTES

1. This section summarizes the more detailed presentation of the G-EAU method to be found in the article by Boudis et al. [BOU 05]. We have not described all the technical characteristics of the model, such as the integration of knowledge bases, the graphic interface and that of the simulator, or the algorithm for solving the hierarchical model [BOU 97], [BOU 03], [PAG 99a].
2. To simplify the equations, time periods are not shown in the notations. When the equations represent time changes, they are expressed as though the projection only covered a single period.
3. Non-revenue water includes: leaks in the network, stolen water, free water supplied to certain consumers, service water for cleaning reservoirs and pipes, and water accounted for in meters but not billed at the time, etc.

7

Elements in Water Demand Forecasting for Indian Megalopolises

MAHFOUD BOUDIS, YVES SAILLARD AND
GUNDAPPA SATHYANARAYANA SASTRY

7.1 INTRODUCTION

The aim of the WATER-UP model described in the previous chapter was to help identify the systems of urban and peri-urban water supply and demand. In this chapter we use the cases of Bengaluru, Chennai and Mumbai, to show how this tool enables us to carry out a prospective analysis of water supplies in the large cities of developing countries.

In this first part we will start by detailing our general analytical framework with the stylized observations from the previous chapters devoted to urban water supply systems. In the second part we will describe elements of these systems' dynamics with WATER-UP, by defining the standard trajectories according to the most decisive hypotheses. We will conclude the chapter with diagnostic elements and the anticipated extensions to the WATER-UP method.

7.2 GENERAL CHARACTERISTICS OF WATER SUPPLIES IN THE MAJOR INDIAN CITIES

Figure 7.1 is a diagram of our observations on the cases of Bengaluru, Chennai and Mumbai. It shows three different types of territorializations: of demand, of management and of the water itself. One of the complexities of urban water supply systems is the

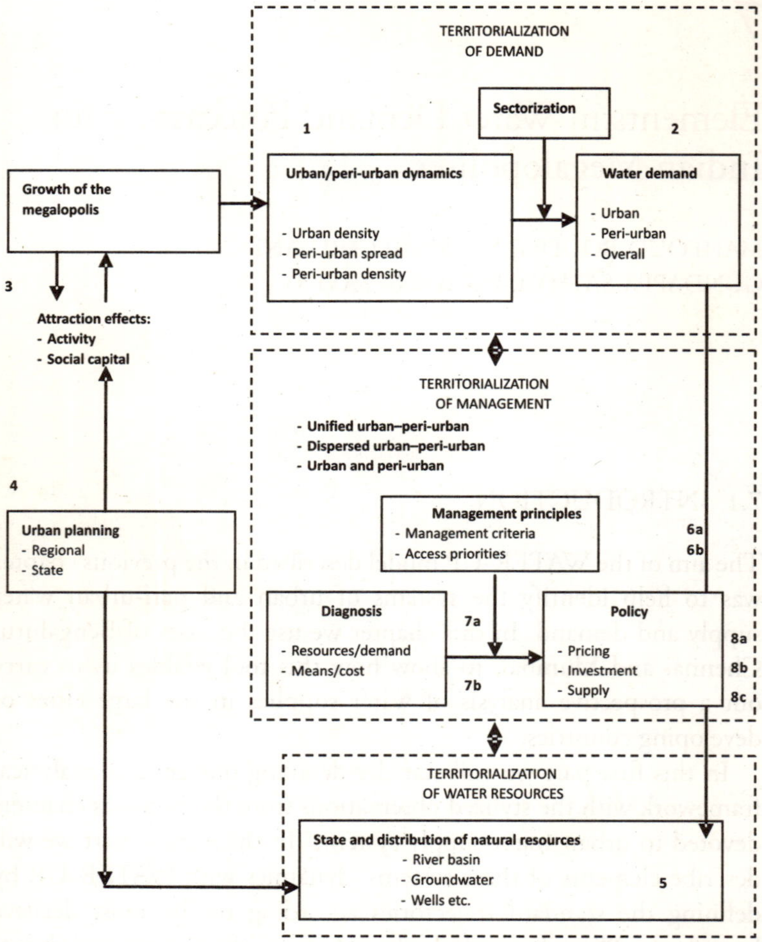

FIGURE 7.1: TERRITORIALIZATION AND REPRESENTATION OF URBAN WATER MANAGEMENT ACCORDING TO WATER-UP

fact that these territorial aspects are quite distinct. To put it simply, the territorialization of demand is the result of an economic and demographic process that is not directly related to water policy but rather to urban planning and development. This is beyond the remit of municipalities and lies more in state or even central government policies. While the territorialization of resources can be improved, it is largely imposed by the natural environment. However, management territorialization must act in numerous areas. It must adapt to spaces determined by the city's central administrative authority, the local authorities concerned and the structures in place for coordinating between the urban and peri-urban units. The borders between the urban and peri-urban areas fluctuate considerably as a result of demographic growth and a range of economic and social dynamics. We consider an urban management territory as being endogenous, or a 'compromise territory' which itself is unstable.

Because of the instability and endogenous nature of the 'management territory', the balance between the water supply and consumption may be established in different areas, on which both diagnoses and policies depend. To simplify matters, we have distinguished three types of demarcation of management territories in Figure 7.1: an overall one that integrates both the urban and peri-urban areas, a segmented one between the urban and homogeneous peri-urban areas, and a segmented one between a homogeneous urban area and a peri-urban one spread between several local managements. Doubtless the third configuration is the most widespread. Because of the rapid growth rate of the peri-urban areas and their diversity, the first two configurations, in which the peri-urban area can be managed as an entity, are problematic. The usual situation is that of a scattered configuration where attempts are made to evolve towards a coherent and/or integrated management system.

In developing countries, a determining characteristic of urban water supply systems in the major cities is the level of uncertainty they face in demand and in natural water resources. The impact of peri-urbanization and its destabilizing effects have been described elsewhere. But the uncertainty also weighs on choices concerning natural resources, including between states, on the effects of climate change, or the impact of water usage on pollution. We consider that these various unknown quantities currently impact domestic consumption and the conditions for household access to drinking water.

Under these complex conditions, water management methods mainly try to act on the demand with measures governing the supply network, pricing and incentives. Resource management is largely a matter of investment to ensure that new resources are harnessed and existing ones treated. Such measures commit the authorities in the medium or long term, with results appearing later.

Table 7.1 summarizes the various observations we developed in Chapters 3, 4 and 5.

TABLE 7.1: OBSERVATIONS ABOUT THE REPRESENTATION OF URBAN AND PERI-URBAN WATER MANAGEMENT

Observations on the territorialization of demand

1. *Urban/peri-urban dynamics*
   - Peri-urbanization diversity (spread, density, fragmentation);
   - Imbalance in the urban and peri-urban infrastructures;
   - Industrial districts of the city transformed into residential ones;
   - Water services split between the urban and peri-urban areas;
   - Poverty and water issues connected.
2. *Demand*
   - Major portion to the domestic sector;
   - Growing demand as a result of the transformation of the urban population.

Observations on the growth of megalopolises – Urban planning policies

3. *Loop*
   - Rapid demographic shifts;
   - Migratory flows from the region, other Indian states or abroad;
   - Population pushed out from the centre to the outskirts: property prices, transport costs, etc.;
   - Social capital acquired by the migrants
4. *Urban planning policy*
   - Rapid industrialization;
   - Failure of agriculture and education policies in the rural areas of the state, greater social capital conferred on migrants, which in turn attracts more migrants to the city;
   - Sharing of resources to be negotiated between states;
   - State regulations governing the use of ground water.

Observations on the territorialization of water resources

5. *State of the resources*
   - Ground water in danger;
   - Greater distance, deeper extraction levels, and very high losses;
   - Ageing equipment, faster obsolescence, time required for programmes to be implemented;
   - Uncontrolled extraction, impact of deterioration and social costs;
   - Privatization of rural water for urban supplies and impact on agriculture;
   - Cases of sea water intrusion;
   - Capacity of public authorities to implement regulations governing the use of resources
   - Indirect effects of regulations, according to their implementation, on the private supplies of packaged water.

Observations on the territorialization of management

6. ***Management principles***

6a. Management criteria

- Independent management body;
- Management of water according to river basin;
- The no losses/no profits principle;
- Public service management, municipal water company, delegation;
- Integration of the distribution and purification functions;
- Revenue collection and pricing according to projected costs;
- Corruption;
- User representation;
- Coordination between institutions, etc.

6b. Priorities

- Priorities for accessing drinking water;
- Incentives for households to be connected to the network;
- Predominance of the lowest water consumption segments, with an increase in medium consumption segments, and a gradual move by the highest consumption segments towards private supplies.

7. ***Diagnoses***

7a. Resources/demand

- Shortages severely aggravated by water losses;
- Controlled water is quality water;
- Maximum population threshold that can be served by the harnessed resources.

7b. Means/costs

- Exponential growth of production costs.

8. ***Policies***

8a. Pricing

- Relationship between the price and consumption/set price;
- Price differentiation, redistribution between households and between households and major consumers;
- Instability and review of prices paid according to the lowest consumption segments.

8b. Investment

- Heavy investment required to increase available resources;
- Importance of unauthorized connections.

8c. Supply

- Alternate, intermittent and unequal supply, according to the urban zone;
- Use of private sources, well digging, the development of an informal sector;
- Self-production initiatives, rainwater harvesting;
- Losses as adapting to shortage;
- Transfers with rural areas.

7.3 THE DYNAMICS OF URBAN AND PERI-URBAN WATER MANAGEMENT SYSTEMS

We will demonstrate the dynamics of the urban water management systems starting with an initial situation in which the balance achieved between water resources and individual consumption may be below the recognized needs perceived as 'normal' – at least for a portion of the population.

The increase of available resources is slowing down. Water resources have already been harnessed to a considerable extent in order to satisfy the sharp increase in demand that has followed the development of the major Indian metropolises over the past 30 years. Underground resources are in danger of drying up and additional ones are increasingly far away. Water from desalination or rainwater harvesting will take time to develop, and is becoming increasingly capital-intensive.

While demographic growth is sustained overall, it is tending towards lower levels. However, growth in overall consumption remains exponential due both to demographic growth and to a higher level of individual consumption.

At the beginning of the period water 'losses' were in the region of 50 per cent. However, there are two different types of losses, true ones resulting from network inefficiency, and unaccounted-for water, consumed but not billed due to a lack of meters and/or illegal consumption. If the networks were renewed, we believe that real losses could stabilize to levels observed elsewhere in the world (around 20 per cent). The remaining 'losses' should be returned to the population's water consumption, and then incidentally be transformed into revenue water to augment the finances of the water management bodies. With this hypothesis, it is considered that the reduction of loss levels from 50 to 20 per cent (for example) does not alter the real level of consumption or the pressure on resources. However, it does correspond to a transformation of demand. We consider that unaccounted-for water consumption is directly constrained by the available water supply and opportunities for obtaining new resources. Accounted-for water is mainly channelled through network connections and follows a different demand model.

To make water 'billable' does not necessarily simply mean installing individual meters. The costs of managing information, installation and maintenance costs and the returns on consumption billing should be compared [BAR 01].

Figure 7.2 illustrates our reference trend for resources using the following hypotheses:

- average 5 per cent annual growth of available water resources over the period 2005-10, losing 1 per cent average annual growth over each five-year period to reach 1 per cent between 2020 and 2025;
- annual demographic growth of 3 per cent throughout the forecast period;
- losses reduced to 20 per cent at the end of the period, with unaccounted-for water gradually transformed into accounted-for water throughout the period.

D consumption in the graph in Figure 7.2, shows the change in domestic demand in relation to demographic growth alone. Distributed water covers all water uses, whether accounted for or not, with or without losses. 'Accounted-for consumption' is what the water management bodies have accounted for in consumed and billable water. We assume that at the end of the period there will no longer be any unaccounted-for water, but only true water losses. The area between the 'real consumption' curve and the 'accounted-

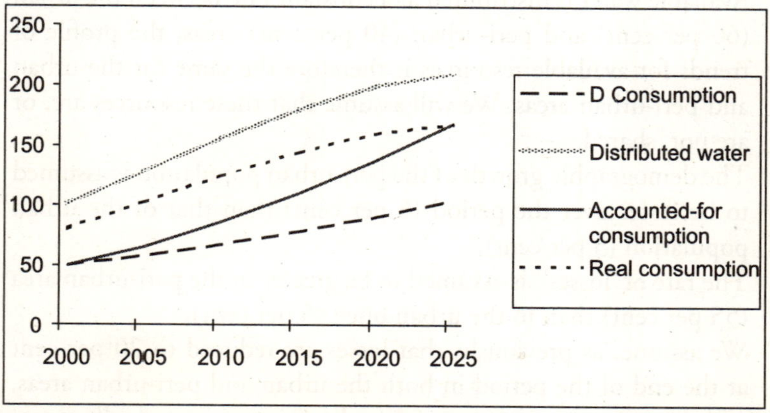

FIGURE 7.2: REFERENCE TREND FOR RESOURCES AND OVERALL CONSUMPTION

for consumption' curve corresponds to the integration of part of the population into the distribution network and billing system. In WATER-UP this transfer of consumption model is conveyed by the shift from consumption according to water supply opportunities to consumption requested according to usage of accounted-for water.

Given the determining contribution of the domestic sector, changes in accounted-for water consumption depend on the demographic growth of the urban and peri-urban areas. The rate of demographic growth includes the population transfers between the urban and peri-urban areas as well as those between rural areas (or those outside the city) and the urban and peri-urban areas. In our forecasts, we also take into account the hierarchy of usage in the urban and peri-urban territories.

Several hierarchies are possible:

- the urban area takes precedence over the peri-urban one;
- the peri-urban takes precedence over the urban one;
- the urban and peri-urban areas are managed together.

The following provide additional hypotheses for the graphs below:

- As previously, the annual average growth of available water resources is established at 5 per cent over the period 2005-10, and 1 per cent average annual growth for each five-year period thereafter, to reach 1 per cent between 2020 and 2025;
- Available water is distributed at a constant rate between the urban (60 per cent) and peri-urban (40 per cent) areas; the profile of trends for available resources is therefore the same for the urban and peri-urban areas. We will assume that these resources are, or are not, shared.
- The demographic growth of the peri-urban population is assumed to be faster over the period (6 per cent) than that of the urban population (3 per cent);
- The rate of 'losses'[1] is assumed to be greater in the peri-urban area (55 per cent) than in the urban one (45 per cent);
- We assume, as previously, that losses are reduced to 20 per cent at the end of the period in both the urban and peri-urban areas, and that non-revenue (unaccounted-for) water is gradually transformed into revenue (accounted-for) water over the period.

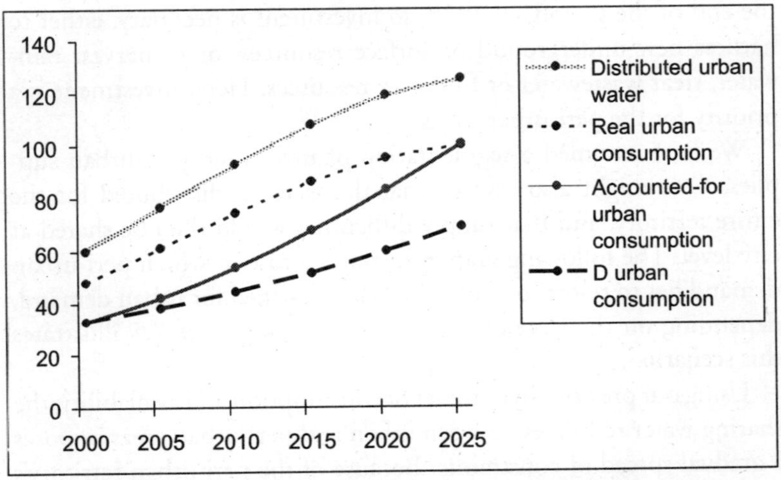

FIGURE 7.3: TRENDS FOR AVAILABLE WATER RESOURCES AND URBAN CONSUMPTION

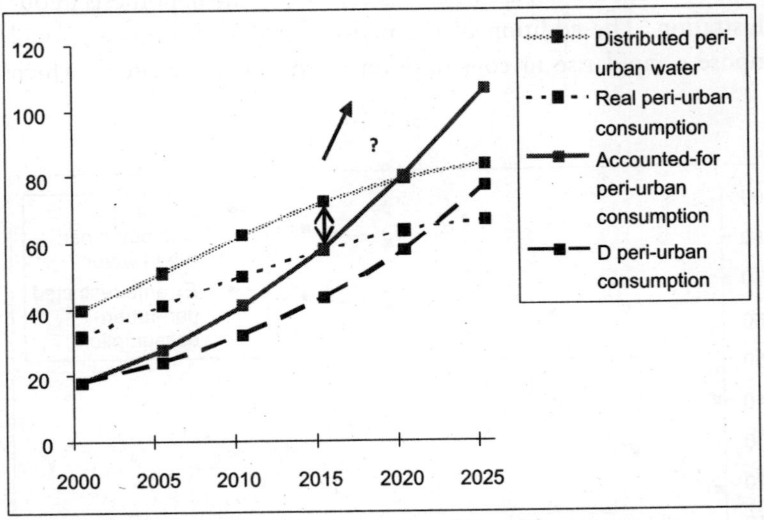

FIGURE 7.4: TRENDS FOR AVAILABLE WATER RESOURCES AND URBAN CONSUMPTION

In this case, the peri-urban water supply becomes insufficient as early as 2015, even with the ambitious 20 per cent loss reduction objective. Moreover, the urban territories also reach their limits at the end of the period, in 2025, so investment is necessary, either to harness new underground or surface resources, or to harvest rain-water, treat wastewater or find new resources. Here, investment is a priority for the peri-urban areas.

We have assumed a segmentation of urban and peri-urban supplies. One might also assume that the water is distributed for the entire territory, and that supply difficulties would then be shared at city level. The following graph illustrates a case in which peri-urban demand has to resort to a supply usually destined for urban demand, depending on the state of available resources. Figure 7.5 illustrates this scenario.

Using our previous hypotheses of consumption and availability, the sharing water resources between urban and peri-urban areas imposes a gradual spread of constraints. Because of the peri-urban territory's rapid demographic growth and the considerable supply constraints, this will be the first area to be hit by water shortages. Consumption in this area should fall after 2015 according to the hypothesis in our illustration. The addition of the peri-urban demand in excess will impose a rapid rise in consumption in the urban territory, which

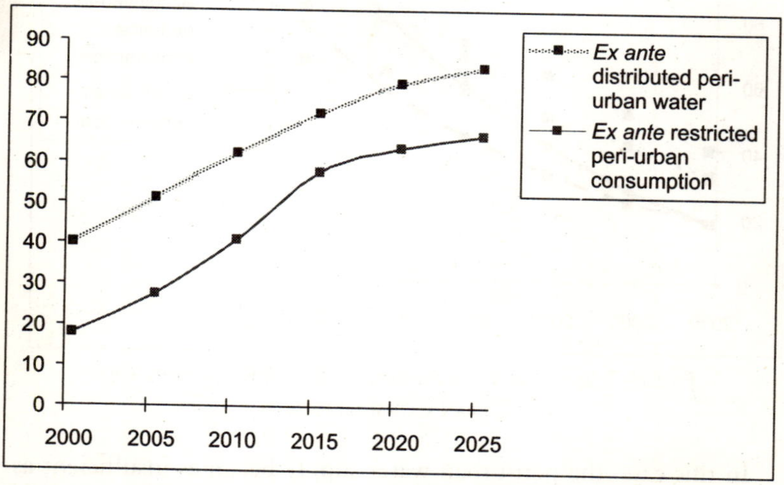

FIGURE 7.5A: EX ANTE LIMITS OF PERI-URBAN CONSUMPTION BEFORE SHARING WATER RESOURCES

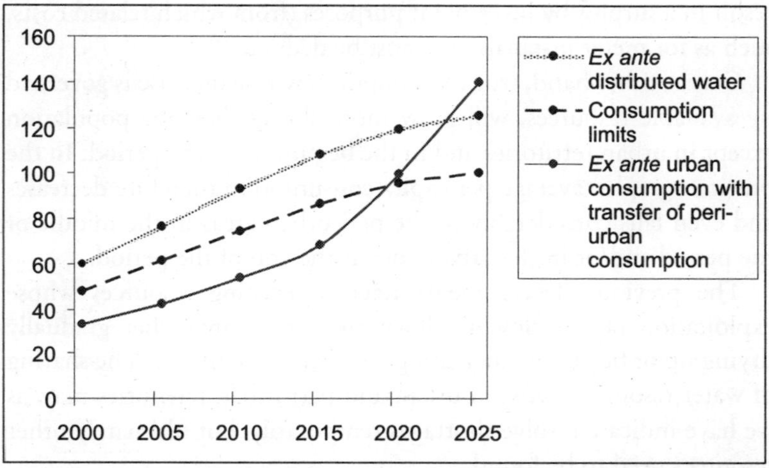

FIGURE 7.5B. URBAN CONSUMPTION WITH THE TRANSFER OF EXCESS PERI-URBAN CONSUMPTION RELATIVE TO AVAILABLE WATER RESOURCES

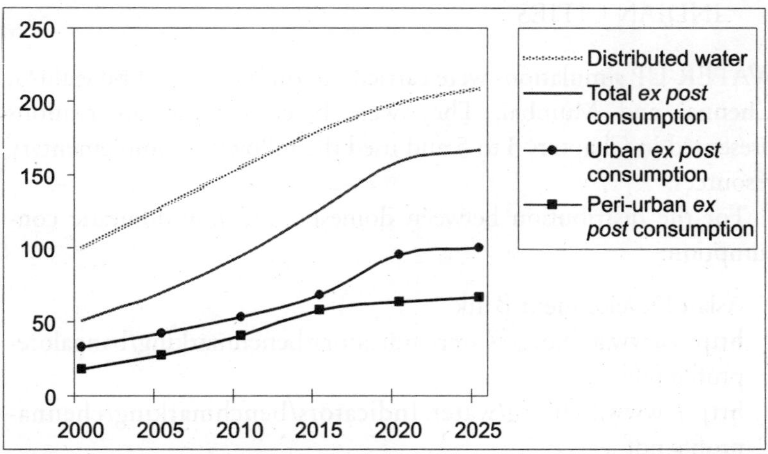

FIGURE 7.5C. TRENDS FOR URBAN, PERI-URBAN AND TOTAL CONSUMPTION WITH SHARED WATER RESOURCES

should also fall starting from 2020. The overall urban and peri-urban consumption curves trace these changes.

All the preceding graphs assume that there will be no increase in individual consumption, only that there will be a transfer of 'invisible' consumption to an accounted-for and billed consumption. This will result in a surplus by investment purposes (from which related costs, such as for meter installations, must be deducted).

On the other hand, true consumption, whose increase is governed by available resources, will grow more slowly than the population except in urban territories and in the beginning of the period. In the previous graphs, average per capita consumption therefore decreases and even falls considerably in the peri-urban areas in the middle of the period and/or in the urban ones at the end of the period.

The previous developments refer to existing resources whose exploitation rate is slowing down since they are either gradually drying up or becoming increasingly expensive to utilize. The sharing of water resources between urban and peri-urban territories may, as we have indicated, solve shortages temporarily, but ultimately other resources need to be found.

7.4 APPLYING THE WATER-UP MODEL TO INDIAN CITIES

WATER-UP simulations were carried out on the cities of Bengaluru, Chennai and Mumbai. They were based on the observations presented in Chapters 3 to 5 and used the following complementary resources:

For the distribution between domestic and non-domestic consumption:

- Asian Development Bank
  http://www.adb.org/Water/Indicators/benchmarking/bangalore-profile.pdf
  http://www.adb.org/water/Indicators/benchmarking/chenna-profile.pdf
  http://www.adb.org/Water/Indicators/benchmarking/mumbai-profile.pdf

For projections of resources and equipment projects in Mumbai:

- The Bombay Community Public Trust
  http://www.bcpt.org.in/Publications/pubdetails.asp?[8]

For projections of resources and equipment projects in Chennai:

- Draft Master Plan – II for Chennai Metropolitan Area, [A short version of the main report]
  http://www.hindu.com/nic/draftmasterplanii_short.pdf

Table 7.2 shows the main population characteristics of the three Indian cities used in the model, with both urban and peri-urban population numbers.

TABLE 7.2: POPULATION SIZE IN 2001 OR THE CLOSEST YEAR

BENGALURU	
Urban population	4,313,248
Peri-urban population	1,306,891
Total population	5,620,139
CHENNAI	
Urban population	4,343,000
Peri-urban population	2,698,000
Total population	7,041,000
MUMBAI	
Urban population	11,978,450
Peri-urban population	4,455,936
Total population	16,434,386

Source: *Census of India*, 2001.

The three cities differ in their overall size and the distribution of their urban and peri-urban territories. Chennai has a larger peri-urban area, which accounts for nearly 40 per cent of the population, whereas in Bengaluru and Mumbai the peri-urban area accounts for approximately one quarter of the population.

Our hypotheses for the trends in distributed water use different time profiles but fairly similar average annual growth rates, namely 2.3 per cent in Bengaluru, 2.8 per cent in Chennai and 3.8 per cent in Mumbai.

The dynamics of change in demand are focused on the domestic sector. However, domestic and non-domestic sector distribution varies according to the city and the urban and peri-urban areas. The domestic sector prevails in urban consumption, especially in Chennai and to a lesser extent in Bengaluru and Mumbai.

Initial projections assumed that average per capita consumption would be sustained, without any improvement in access to clean water. This was established as follows, in litres per person per day: 78 litres in Bengaluru, 87 litres in Chennai, and 100 litres in Mumbai. Per capita consumption tends to overestimate real consumption, especially in peri-urban areas.

Domestic consumption increases according to demographic hypotheses. We have two main hypotheses for each city: faster peri-urban demographic growth than urban, and a slowdown in demographic growth in each of these territories (except in Chennai's peri-urban area where a slight increase in demographic growth is expected). The average annual growth hypotheses are summarized in Table 7.3.

Consumption in both domestic and non-domestic sectors is better balanced in the peri-urban areas because of the industrial activities carried out there, notably in Mumbai. Non-domestic consumption is predominant in Bengaluru's peri-urban area. The city's demand for non-domestic water (for industrial, commercial and municipal use) evolves according to the pace of its economic and industrial growth. This currently represents approximately 10 per cent of overall consumption but we believe this will rise to around 30 per cent in the long term. Industrialization, like demographic

TABLE 7.3. EXPECTED DEMOGRAPHIC GROWTH FOR THE CITIES OF BENGALURU, CHENNAI AND MUMBAI (IN ANNUAL AVERAGE GROWTH RATE, IN PERCENTAGE)

Cities	Demographic growth at the start of the period (2000-5)	Demographic growth at the end of the period (2020-5)
Bengaluru		
Urban	2.7%	2.2%
Peri-urban	5.2%	3.3%
Chennai		
Urban	1.2%	1.1%
Peri-urban	3.7%	3.9%
Mumbai		
Urban	2.0%	1.0%
Peri-urban	8.3%	5.5%

growth, occurs faster in peri-urban areas, where agricultural areas are frequently transformed into industrial ones, rather than in the urban areas where industries are usually encouraged to move out to the peripheral areas and give way to trade and service activities. In Bengaluru, the projected annual average growth rate for non-domestic consumption is 0.6 per cent for the urban area and 2.9 per cent for the peri-urban one. Non-domestic consumption is increasing more rapidly in Chennai (with rates of 2.5 per cent and 3.7 per cent respectively) and in Mumbai (with rates of 1.4 per cent and 6.7 per cent respectively).

Estimates of the percentage of unaccounted-for water are from available official sources, which tend to minimize these. The 17 per cent loss rate for Chennai is certainly very underestimated. That is also true for Mumbai (see Chapter 4) where the urban (25 per cent) and peri-urban (33 per cent) rates are distinguished. Bengaluru's urban and peri-urban areas total 43 per cent. These indicative parameters for unaccounted-for water are doubtless where the greatest uncertainties lie and where testing various assumptions may shed light on alternative scenarios.

The simulation results are presented in three parts: the general trends in water supply and consumption, the distribution of consumption between the urban and peri-urban areas, and the adjustments of supply to demand. The former two are based on the existing situation, notably in terms of average consumption per inhabitant, and on trend extensions. The third discusses several possible variations in past trends and transformations that lead to alternative scenarios for changes in supply and consumption.

7.4.1 *General Trends in Water Supply and Consumption*

The following graphs (Figures 7.6a, b, and c) trace the projections of overall supply and consumption (both urban and peri-urban) for each of the three Indian cities. We distinguish between domestic and non-domestic consumption. Both supply and consumption are expressed in millions of cu m.

As in the previous section, we assumed a gradual integration of unaccounted-for water into accounted-for water, on the hypothesis

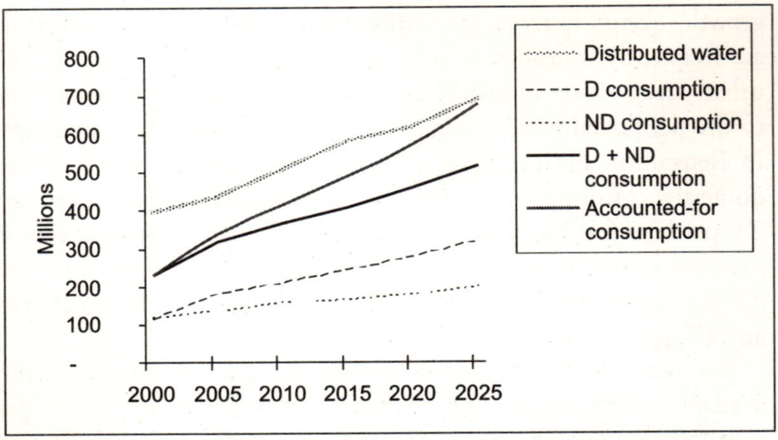

FIGURE 7.6A: WATER-UP SIMULATIONS OF WATER SUPPLY AND CONSUMPTION IN BANGALURU, IN M CU M

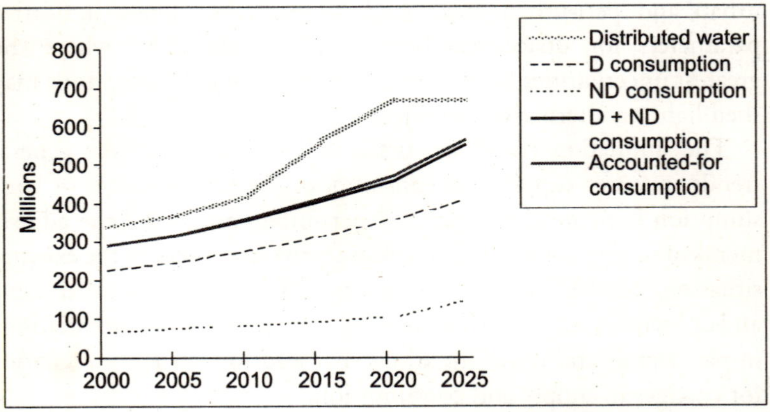

FIGURE 7.6B: WATER-UP SIMULATIONS OF WATER SUPPLY AND CONSUMPTION IN CHENNAI, IN M CU M

that some of the losses will not be able to be reduced further. The 'accounted-for' water curve does not correspond to improved average access to drinking water, but rather to a transfer of water usage from an unaccounted-for and non-billed form to another that is both accounted-for and billable.

At this overall level we observe fairly different configurations of water usage projected to 2025, for instance between comparable domestic and non-domestic consumptions (Mumbai), and a

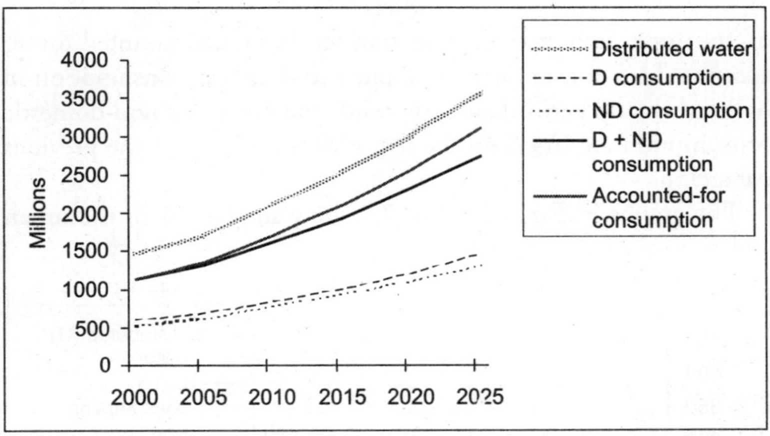

FIGURE 7.6C: WATER-UP SIMULATIONS OF WATER SUPPLY AND CONSUMPTION IN MUMBAI, IN M CU M

predominance of domestic usage (in Bengaluru, and especially in Chennai). Expected consumption, in terms of accounted-for consumption and given our hypotheses about the transformation of domestic consumption, will double in Chennai and increase three-fold in both Bengaluru and Mumbai. Water consumption volumes will be in the region of 0.5 billion cu m (Chennai), 0.7 billion cu m (Bengaluru) and 3 billion cu m (Mumbai) by 2025.

The distributed water capacity appears able to follow the rise in consumption in Mumbai and Chennai. However, if we take the irreducible losses into account, the limit will be reached from the middle of the projection period in Bengaluru.

These projections are carried out on the basis of average per capita consumption being maintained at the levels shown in statistics for the beginning of the period, which doubtless overestimates real consumption.

7.4.2 *Urban and Peri-urban Access to Water*

The following projections distinguish between the urban and peri-urban territories of each city. The water resources change at both urban and peri-urban levels as they do at the overall city level. The distribution of resources is that observed in 2000 at the beginning of the projection period. The transfer from unaccounted-for to accounted-for consumption is applied to domestic consumption in both urban and peri-urban areas, while the trends for non-domestic consumption are based on the hypotheses outlined in the previous paragraph.

The graphs in Figures 7.7 to 7.9 show similarities in the urban and peri-urban situations.

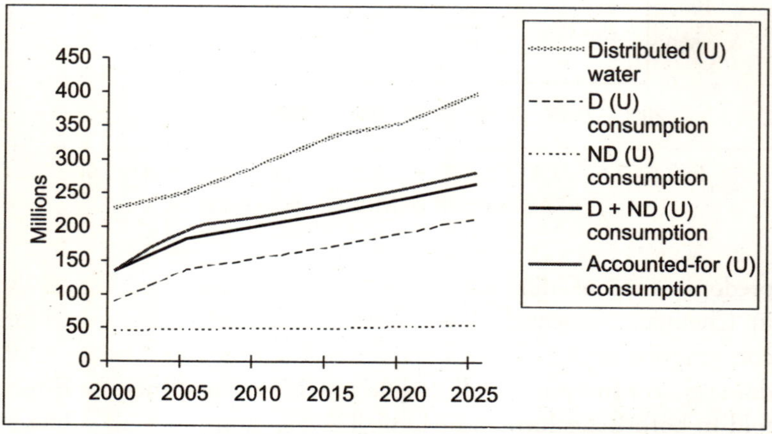

FIGURE 7.7A: WATER-UP SIMULATIONS OF WATER SUPPLY AND CONSUMPTION IN URBAN BENGALURU, IN M CU M

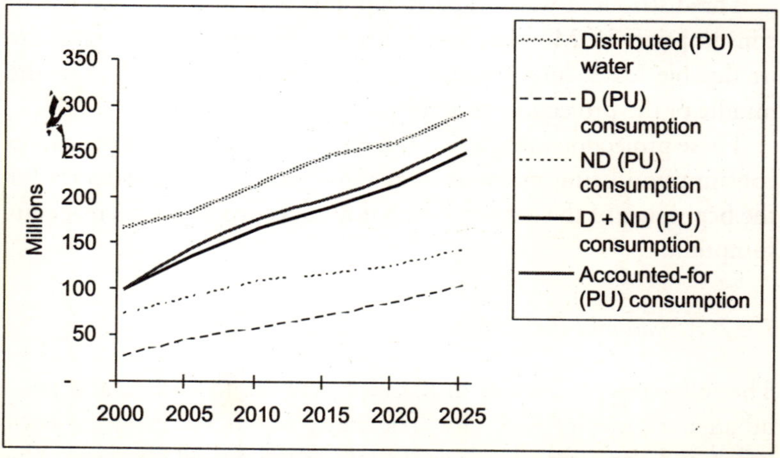

FIGURE 7.7B: WATER-UP SIMULATIONS OF WATER SUPPLY AND CONSUMPTION IN PERI-URBAN BENGALURU, IN M CU M

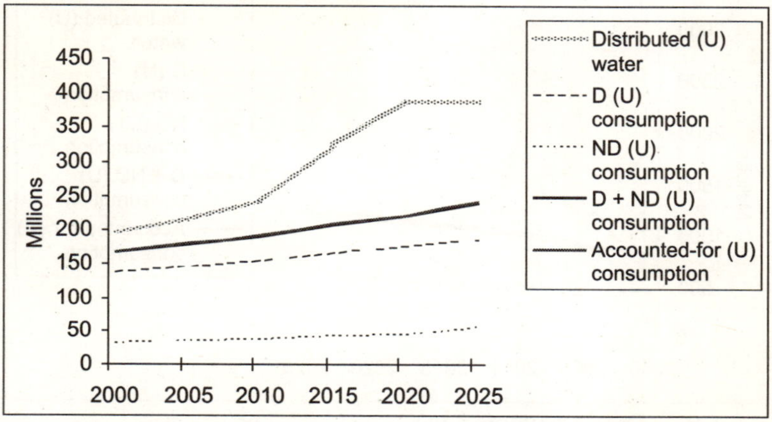

FIGURE 7.8A: WATER-UP SIMULATIONS OF WATER SUPPLY AND CONSUMPTION IN URBAN CHENNAI, IN M CU M

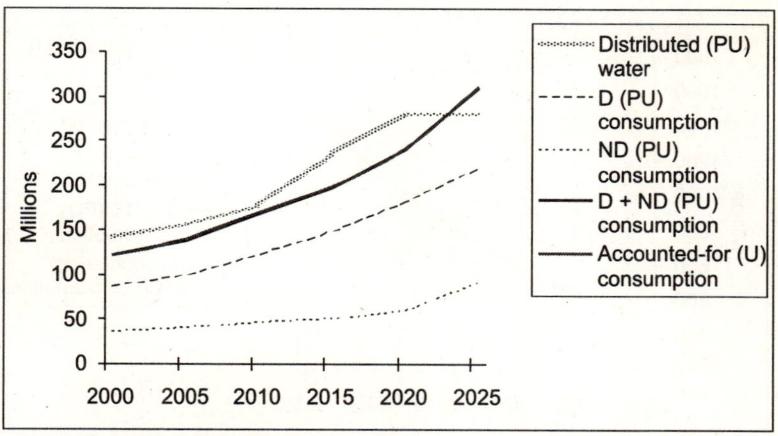

FIGURE 7.8B: WATER-UP SIMULATIONS OF WATER SUPPLY AND CONSUMPTION IN PERI-URBAN CHENNAI, IN M CU M

7.4.3 *Adjustments Between Territories*

The limitations on water access are greatest in the peri-urban areas of all three Indian cities. The situation is especially serious in Chennai and Mumbai where the water resources have already reached their limits at the beginning of the projection period. Mumbai has had rapid population growth together with an increase in water-consuming economic activities.

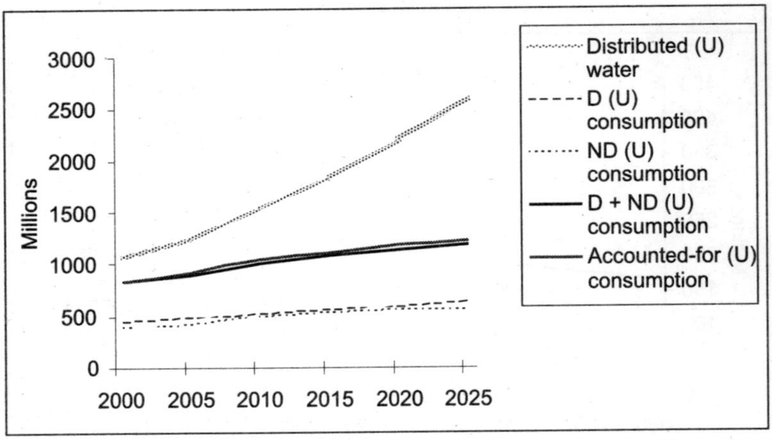

FIGURE 7.9A. WATER-UP SIMULATIONS OF WATER SUPPLY AND CONSUMPTION IN URBAN MUMBAI, IN M CU M

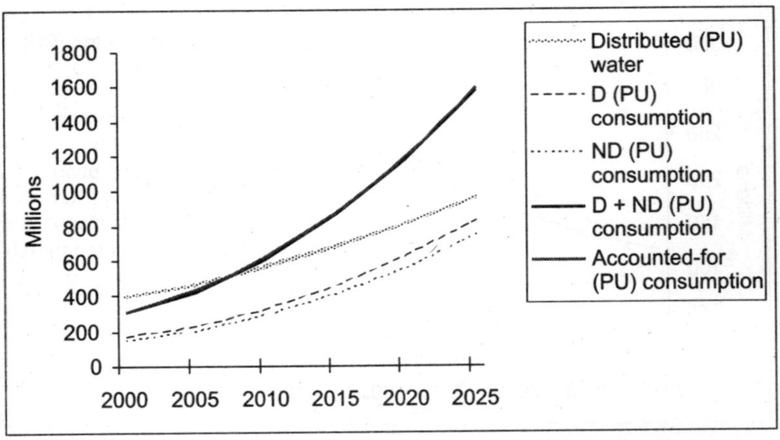

FIGURE 7.9B: WATER-UP SIMULATIONS OF WATER SUPPLY AND CONSUMPTION IN PERI-URBAN MUMBAI, IN M CU M

If Bengaluru, Chennai and Mumbai do not mutualize and integrate the management of these resources at the megalopolis level, their peri-urban territories will, under different conditions, be subject to serious shortages. Using the reasoning we developed in the previous paragraph, the transfer of resources within the megalopolises could alleviate these problems of water access, albeit without solving them.

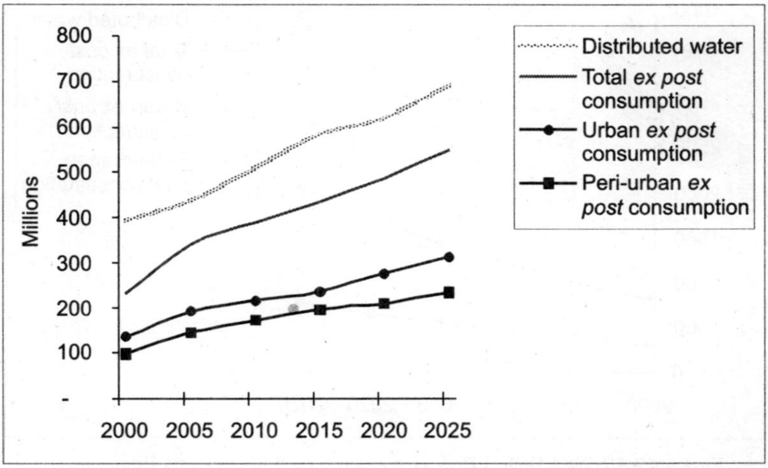

FIGURE 7.10: WATER-UP SIMULATIONS OF URBAN AND PERI-URBAN CONSUMPTION WITH SHARED RESOURCES IN BENGALURU, IN M CU M

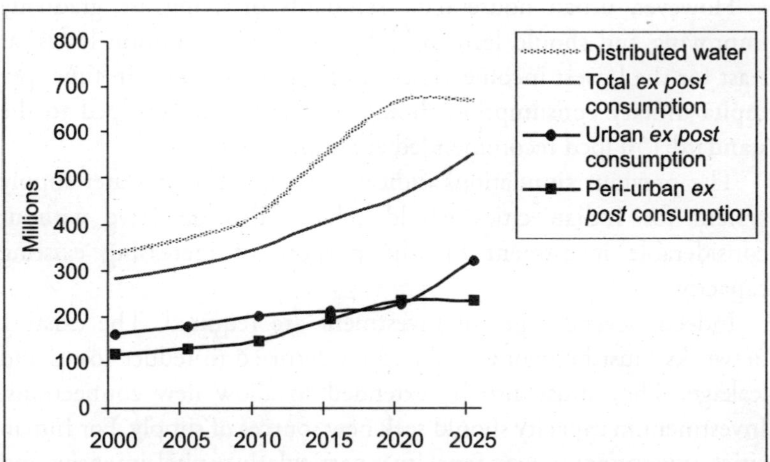

FIGURE 7.11: WATER-UP SIMULATIONS OF URBAN AND PERI-URBAN CONSUMPTION WITH SHARED RESOURCES IN CHENNAI, IN M CU M

The sharing of water resources to the benefit of the peri-urban areas, would, at best,[2] allow individual consumption levels to be maintained (Chennai), or reduced by only 10 per cent (Mumbai) and 20 per cent (Bengaluru).

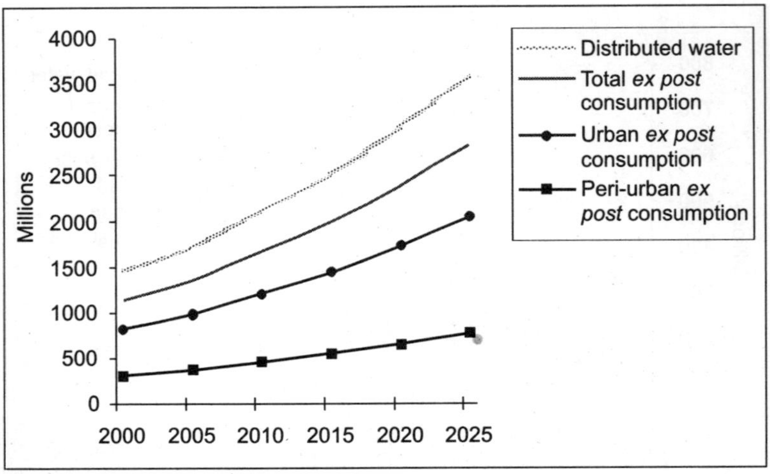

FIGURE 7.12: WATER-UP SIMULATIONS OF URBAN AND PERI-URBAN CONSUMPTION WITH SHARED RESOURCES IN MUMBAI, IN M CU M

However, urban households' standards of living are gradually improving and should lead to higher water consumption levels, at least for the lowest income segment of the population. In time, per capita unitary consumption should increase from 100 lpcd to the standard 150 lpcd recommended at national level.

The previous simulations indicate that no current water supply system for Indian cities would achieve this objective without considerable investment for the purpose of increasing existing capacity.

Indeed, several types of investment are required. The existing networks must be maintained and modernized to reduce losses and leakage. They must also be extended to allow new connections. Investment in capacity should seek new sources of supply. For Indian cities, investment in new capacity is particularly capital-intensive and implies alternative resources such as treating wastewater, rainwater harvesting and seawater desalination. The extent of the investment required to attain the individual consumption objectives is such that merely improving management or billing methods is not enough. Public financing based on economic development and international support is needed. For instance, according to estimates made in

Mumbai for work to extend the water supply capacity, some Rs.7 billion to Rs.14 billion would be required to deliver an additional 10 litres of water per person per day.[3]

To go further in forecasting water requirements it would be necessary to establish a dynamic assessment of the water resources. This cannot be carried out by experts alone but must be the result of interactions with all the actors concerned. To continue using a model such as WATER-UP would therefore mean including a negotiation process between institutional representatives. This differs from the standard approach where, to escape from a centralized management system, each consumer becomes an investor.[4]

In France, the drinking water community (CEP) was instituted in 2007 to help coordinate the numerous actors in the sector (see Chapter 2). In the Grenoble urban area this body has contributed to the urban development master plan (SCOT) carrying out a quantitative and qualitative diagnosis of water resources and identify the actions necessary to secure long-term drinking water supplies for the urban area [CEP 08]. We have outlined the guidelines here as an example of the procedures that may be used.

The purpose was to establish, interactively, an agreement supported by all citizens and elected representatives.[5] The work was carried out simultaneously on several critical aspects, for the purpose of inspiring future policy. First an updated and a medium-term (2025) assessment of resources was established. That is how the simulations we presented in this chapter for the three Indian cities were used. Then an evaluation was made of the vulnerability of the resources in terms of quality and exposure to pollution risks. That is what we have begun to do here, but should also include quality factors and be adapted to the various residential zones. Lastly an action plan was suggested to the various partners based on the identification of critical water access issues, which assumes that a priority will be established between the actions to be taken. These can be of different types, for instance preventative, relating to network interconnections, or investment. Following the dissemination of these proposals, a collective process is required to select the final objectives, the means for implementing them, and the timing.

NOTES

1. Included in what we previously described as 'losses' are the true losses related to the quality of the water distribution equipment *and* consumed unaccounted-for water.
2. We assume that the cuts in consumption required for respecting the anticipated limits on available resources will affect both domestic and non-domestic consumption.
3. According to the Water Sector Initiatives of the Municipal Corporation of Greater Mumbai, the Bhatsa Dam project will cost Rs.739 crore (or Rs.7.39 billion) for an additional capacity of 355 mld. The Vaiterna project would cost Rs.1,329 crore (or Rs.13.29 billion) for an additional capacity of 300 mld. To make things simpler, our estimates are based on a water-using population of 30 million inhabitants.
4. [SRI 08].
5. 'The Drinking Water Community (CEP, "*Communauté de l'Eau Potable*" for the Grenoble Urban Region (RUG, *Région Urbaine de Grenoble*) coordinates the action of water utility producers and/or distributors, local authorities (through municipal companies or intermunicipal bodies) with authority over drinking water, and local water commissions CLE, *Commissions Locales de l'Eau*), set up as part of the local Water Development and Management Scheme (SAGE, *Schémas d'Aménagement et de Gestion des Eaux)*. The CEP works alongside the Urban Development Master Plan (SCOT, *Schéma de Cohérence Territoriale*) currently being drafted for the Grenoble area and which will cover 243 localities and approximately 720,000 people' [CEP 08], p. 11.

8

Defining Public Policies Concerning Access to Drinking Water

YVES SAILLARD AND LINGAPPAM VENKATACHALAM

8.1 INTRODUCTION

Albeit to varying degrees, India's metropolises are dealing with the problem of drinking water shortages. This situation stems from three principal factors: the demographic and economic changes taking place in these cities, the significant relative cost of investments needed to modernize water supply networks, and management methods that are reputed to be inefficient.

The population of India's cities is increasing very rapidly, spurred on by industrial development and the growth of services. The country's large metropolitan centres are attracting migrants from neighbouring areas as well as migrants from other states. In the absence of public regional development policies to encourage rural populations to remain where they are, the exodus to cities is gaining momentum, and urban and peri-urban areas are now enormous. A huge proportion of the population lives in extreme poverty.

India's megalopolises are having to meet rapidly increasing requirements for water, while many supply networks are in disrepair due to severe budgetary restraints. Furthermore, rapid growth in demand for drinking water means that water has to be extracted from places farther away from cities, making it increasingly costly to bring this water to the consumer. Unfortunately, cities have nowhere near the financial resources that are needed to meet investment needs.

There are many factors that contribute to inefficient management of urban water supply and distribution systems. First, there is the question of how responsibility is shared between city authorities and peri-urban areas, which may be disorganized or organized under the responsibility of numerous administrative units. Sometimes agreements must be reached with other public authorities and between states in order to share water resources that are further and further away from the place of use. Employees of water authorities may be tempted by corrupt practices, resulting in services no longer being fairly distributed. And a major problem is that of unaccounted-for – or 'lost' – water, where differences of up to 50 per cent have been observed between the actual amounts of water fed into distribution systems and the amounts metered and invoiced.

Faced with this situation, urban and peri-urban populations have had to develop a variety of strategies to deal with restrictions on drinking water supplies. Urban dwellers are obliged to adapt to an intermittent supply, which most often means that access to water is restricted to three or four hours a day on certain days of the week. The poorest population use public standpipes, obtain water illegally or purchase water from individual resellers or from owners of private wells. They also resort to buying bottled water.

Initially, public authorities responded to the threat of drinking water shortages by pursuing huge investment programmes financed by subsidies and price rises. Generally speaking, this type of policy was not successful in guaranteeing access to drinking water for entire urban and peri-urban populations in a way that enabled international consumption standards per capita per day to be met. Measures such as these were also considered to accentuate inequalities among different categories of the population. This type of supply-driven approach[1] is also known to limit innovation in terms of demand management, in particular where water conservation is concerned.

There has now been a shift in public policy toward demand-oriented management, an approach which in the short term will help limit investment expenditures and the resulting burden of debt. The savings made will enable supply and distribution costs to be better covered. Another objective of demand-driven policies is to reduce disparities in drinking water access stemming from differences in income levels, not only by introducing suitable pricing policies, but also through incentives to encourage better-off households to save water. From a wider perspective, public policies favouring an approach based on demand management are aimed at using a whole series of instruments to enable more efficient use of water.[2]

In addition to highlighting the need to reform public policy, analyses of shortcomings have encouraged authorities to look into alternative policies, in particular the development of public-private partnerships and reform of pricing and payment systems for water services. Trends in public policy toward demand-oriented management and the encouragement of greater private sector participation are converging towards a new water management model that is based on an internationally recognized representation of what are deemed 'best practices' with regard to water management.

These trends will be described in greater detail in the following sections, along with a more detailed discussion of the limits of public-private partnerships.

8.2 DIAGNOSIS OF PUBLIC POLICY WITH REGARD TO WATER RESOURCES AND INTERNATIONAL REPRESENTATION OF BEST PRACTICES FOR WATER MANAGEMENT

The survey of water resource management models and methods published by UNESCO in 2005 provides fairly clear evidence of agreement at the international level with regard to best practices in water management [LOU 05]. This book uses a pedagogical approach to present methods and advice on water management and planning techniques: simulation methods, models, database, etc. The main points covered are summarized below:

1. Water resources cannot be managed purely in terms of cost-benefit results and equitable distribution; ecological and environmental objectives must also play a part. More generally, questions concerning water supply cannot be resolved without calling on the skills of scientific and technical experts and examining the many related economic and social factors.

2. There are many issues to be addressed when drawing up water

management policy, and objectives may sometimes be conflicting. The two general approaches to planning and management are the top-down approach and the bottom-up approach, either of which can be adopted to produce a single plan and management policy. The top-down approach to management has been the domain of professionals and is based on the assumption that certain institutions, usually public agencies, will take charge of all planning and management activities. Stakeholders generally have no part in drawing up measures. In contrast, in the case of bottom-up management, stakeholders are involved in creating management plans and programmes from the outset and they work together to reach a consensus. The shift from a top-down towards a bottom-up approach is presented as something that is seen as desirable by populations.[3] Although separate from the trend towards demand-oriented management, this shift in approach reinforces the movement away from state responsibility and towards consumer responsibility. Public regulations provide a framework in which self-organization of water management mechanisms can develop, without the public authorities having a supervisory role. Integrated Resource Water Management (IRWM), as defined in the Dublin principles of 1992, combines these two approaches.

3. Water is an economic good, as stated in the fourth principle of the Dublin Statement. There are two aspects to this definition of the economic nature of water. First, water is scarce (in other words it is not a 'free good') and as such it has an economic value; it must be used in an optimum manner, in such a way as to maximize the net benefits. Second, water must be managed like all other economic goods, and the investment and operating costs involved in managing the resource must be covered by generating appropriate funds. This can be interpreted in two different ways: one might simply say that funds must be generated to cover costs, or one could go a step further and introduce a principle of management autonomy, which means that those managing the resource must organize their own financing, which is usually through recovering costs from consumers. The second interpretation would seem to be the overriding one.[4] But this principle of covering costs must take into account first of all the needs of the poorest consumers, who may be unable to pay full cost-recovery prices and, second, cost

recovery may have to be limited to recovering operating costs. It may be noted in passing that the price given to water, according to standard economic approaches, acts for the consumer as the only indicator of the real cost of supplying the water, as if the population needed the price to make them aware of the scarcity of the resource. Observations of problems of access to water in India's large cities, as in other developing countries, and of the experience of reform programmes suggest a dual approach: the real construction of market processes and the projection of virtual markets in alternative water resource management models. Real market processes provide a way of adapting to shortages. Virtual markets are largely inspired by best practices developed by international agencies and concern access to drinking water as well as other basic services to the community such as health care and education. Given the distinct approaches of these market construction dynamics, there is no certainty that the virtual markets, resulting from a 'top-down approach', and the real markets will converge virtuously towards market models. Considerable confusion could result from the assumption that virtual markets inscribed in reforms could be implemented and work spontaneously in a different way from the market processes already in place. In the following section, this question is examined in relation to the public-private partnership (PPP), which has emerged as a reference model for reforming public water services.

8.3 LESSONS TO BE LEARNED FROM AN INSTITUTIONAL INNOVATION: PUBLIC-PRIVATE PARTNERSHIPS

8.3.1 *The Emergence of the PPP as an Institutional Innovation*

Dealing with the problem of 'institutional scarcity' poses considerable challenge, in particular for developing countries, when it comes to supplying urban populations with water in an equitable, efficient and sustainable manner. Institutional failure has been a dominant feature in the urban water sector in a large number of countries. This failure essentially stems from lack of information, unsuitable information processes, information asymmetry linked with the opportunist behaviour of economic agents, and apathy on the part of institutions resulting from certain behavioural anomalies of consumers (such as inconsistencies in preferences and choice of processes). In an attempt to tackle these problems, institutional reforms were introduced in this sector by numerous developing countries at the beginning of the 1990s. These reforms focussed for the most part on introducing PPPs, presented as an alternative model that was free of some of the constraints on existing institutions. This was a condition for obtaining good results. However, recent literature on institutions in the urban water sector suggests that the first generation PPP model introduced in the 1990s suffered high failure rates [BRA 05]. While empirical studies have been carried out to determine the improvements in well-being resulting from the very few successful PPPs [GAL 05], no studies have attempted to use a standard methodology to assess the loss of well-being caused by PPPs in different parts of the world that have failed in their objectives. It is hugely difficult to estimate loss of welfare because relevant information is unequally distributed. However, two things are clear. First, in terms of supply, the transaction cost incurred by the public sector in order to create a favourable environment in a PPP system would have been economically non-productive because of the substantial administrative charges. Second, in terms of demand, consumers would have ended up with a less reliable water supply after the reforms, resulting in increased opportunity costs. Generally speaking, when the PPP model has failed, it is because, from an economic standpoint, the undesirable social costs have tended to outweigh any desirable social benefits.

Aside from the economic impact, the failure of the PPP model, designed and enthusiastically implemented by those in the administrative echelons, has left decision-makers and contributors with little room to manoeuvre with respect to institutions in the water sector. Yet institutional aspects are vital in a context where it is urgent to implement water-related development objectives, including that of alleviating urban poverty. This new kind of challenge involves two types of problems that must be taken into account in the institutional context: (a) Why has the PPP, which was considered a viable institutional alternative for ensuring an efficient water supply system, met with failure? and (b) Given the limited institutional options, what alternative institution might be able to overcome the present shortcomings and supply water to urban populations in an efficient, equitable and sustainable manner? These two questions will be examined in the next part of this chapter with reference to existing literature and a case study.

8.3.2 *Lessons to be Learned from Experiments with PPPs*

Empirical studies suggest that PPPs created in the urban water supply sector have met with mixed success. Overall, negative effects tend to outweigh positive aspects,[5] with failures far outnumbering so-called success stories.

In cases where PPPs have been deemed successful, the private sector has clearly generated additional social benefits compared with the previous public monopoly. In a certain number of countries one of the real benefits generated by the private sector was a reduction in the price of water such that even the poorest segment of the population was able to have access to improved water services. For example, in Manila, in the Philippines, when the private sector started to provide a service that facilitated drinking water access for a large number of households, including those in poor neighbourhoods, the price of water fell by 67 per cent [DUM 00]. Similarly, the cost of water estimated at Rs.1,000/kilolitre and charged by water vendors in the informal private sector in Tirupur, an industrial town in southern India, was reduced to Rs.5/kilolitre when a PPP took over management [VYA 04]. Although certain errors can be found in the results reported in these studies, they do not appear to affect the general conclusion that in certain areas the creation of PPPs has led to substantial reductions in water prices. Besides improving access to water supply, price reductions also bring additional social benefits to households. For example, it was shown that in 30 per cent of municipalities in Argentina where the private sector provided improved water services, average infant mortality related to waterborne diseases fell by 8 per cent. The effect was greatest for the poor population, with a reduction of 26 per cent. All of these direct and indirect economic impacts were attributed to the advantages of private-sector participation. For example, the efficiency of water services was improved by introducing various measures to drastically reduce the proportion of unaccounted-for water (including improvements to systems and the installation of meters). The above examples show that, even though water remains a public good, the private sector as well as the public sector can play a role in providing improved services at a lower cost creating both economic and social benefits for the communities involved.

However, in numerous other countries, prices for water services increased with the entry of the private sector, with the poor segments of the population being the most affected. For example, in Aguascalientes, Mexico, the price of water rose by 60 per cent with private management, and every day 300 households had their water supply cut-off because of non-payment [MOR 05]. In a great many countries, the 'initial bids' made by water companies prior to awarding of the contract would be fixed higher than the level of investment necessary to improve the delivery of water and the quality of the service, leading to suspicions of collusion among some of the large companies in the water sector. In fact, collusion between companies and the authorities can also happen as a result of rent-seeking, a common strategy among 'rational' government officials in developing countries. In most cases, the actual transaction cost resulting from the rent-seeking behaviour is never known, but private companies operating in the water sector have in fact included such costs in their prices after contracts have been signed. In other countries, the initial price of water was reduced slightly so as to attract more customers; it was then gradually increased as private sector participation expanded. The steep increase in price was then blamed on increased production costs, attributed mainly to external factors specific to the region, such as general inflation or unfavourable exchange rates. Aside from these 'strategic factors', new institutional economics provides us with substantial theoretical literature suggesting that the bounded rationality with which private operators anticipate future costs and profits, and the problem of asymmetry of information about the efficiency of existing arrangements, also explain why the initial price of water rises significantly with private-sector management. Unfortunately, water pricing in the private sector has not yet been sufficiently researched using a bounded rationality framework.

Price increases, especially in areas where there are no alternative water resources, have impacted on the poor, who make up a significant proportion of urban populations in developing countries. Since governments have to take into account equity issues in cases of private management they have to take on new roles and responsibilities that are economically costly. For example, in Santiago de Chile, the government had to introduce special 'water stamps' to help the poor [GLE 02]. This initiative resulted in a win-win situation for the private sector and the poor, but the extent to which these measures increased public sector charges is not known. In certain cases, when contractual terms prevent prices from being raised repeatedly, private companies under obligation to provide water services to the poor population have to seek subsidies from the public authorities to make up for growing deficits brought about by rising costs. These problems related to water prices and the need for measures to help the poor show that the transaction costs for implementing these measures are far from negligible. Rather than being minimized with the introduction of PPP arrangements, which in theory this is what is supposed to happen, the costs seem to be transferred elsewhere in the economy. Yet despite all these costly measures, by the end of the 1990s, the private sector had seemingly satisfied only 3 per cent of the total urban population in poor countries [BUD 03].

Apart from the indicators mentioned above, there is no empirical evidence on important questions concerning the participation of private companies in the urban water sector. For example, no real studies have been carried out into ways in which the private sector is able to respond when water becomes increasingly scarce in certain areas. If it responds by trying to improve efficiency, then beneficial results can ensue. On the other hand, if it responds by increasing prices, then the social cost will rise due to the redistribution of user resources in reaction to the new price structure. Similarly, little research has been done on the net economic effect of the reaction of previously existing institutions (such as informal water markets, civil society, etc.) to the introduction of a new formal private market. Fernandez and Rodrik drew up a theoretical framework for studying how an institutional response such as 'resistance to reform' could result in a bias towards the *status quo* among users, which would lead to inefficient institutions remaining in place. However, no empirical studies are available on the possible transaction costs in the urban water sector caused by a *status quo* bias. In certain urban areas in developing countries, intransigent resistance to water sector reform has prevented the implementation of reforms that were very costly to draw up. Introducing appropriate institutional arrangements to overcome resistance caused by uncertainty about reforms involves additional transaction costs. These charges have to be carefully estimated so that decisions can be reached on whether or not to implement reforms. No doubt influenced by the various factors for and against private involvement in water supply services, private investment in the sector had fallen by 30 per cent by the end of the 1990s. Although there are considerable gaps in the existing literature, it would be fair to conclude that the private sector was unable to sustain its involvement in meeting urban water supply requirements.

8.3.3 *Reasons for the Shortcomings of PPPs*

There are many reasons, both theoretical and empirical, for the shortcomings of PPPs. These include the tendency of political decision makers to impose an 'outside' institution to correct the shortcoming of a government institution, the tendency to deal with macroeconomic crises by privatizing even social sectors such as water supply services, attempting to treat the symptoms rather than the underlying causes of water sector problems, tackling problems without having a proper theoretical understanding, and so on. A number of these questions will be examined in detail below.

8.3.3.1 FAILURE OF INSTITUTIONS IN THE URBAN WATER SECTOR

The negative consequences of the inability of traditional institutions to supply a given amount of water to a maximum number of households were what justified the institutional reforms such as the experiments with PPPs in the urban water sector. Among the conventional institutions, the public authorities played a decisive role, while informal private markets and the tertiary sector, that is non-government organizations and community associations, played only a peripheral supporting role. Since public organizations have had a decisive part to play in water supply services, failure on their part and the resulting negative effects on well-being have necessarily been given much attention in the urban water sector. The fact that in 2005 an estimated 1.1 billion people did not have access to safe drinking water[6] shows the extreme gravity of this failure. Among the factors that in the past have contributed to failure of the public sector are corruption in the water supply sector, general inefficiency of the system due to the vicious circle of dwindling and deteriorating groundwater stocks, lack of flexibility in rules and regulations of water sector policies, inability to incorporate demand factors in water supply policies, arbitrary pricing policies, and lack of accountability and inadequate monitoring.

The persistent gap between water availability and demand caused by institutional inertia opened the way for the creation of powerful informal water markets in many urban areas. This situation has led in various ways to an inequitable distribution of economic resources. Thus, even though informal private markets seem to have helped alleviate the problem of water scarcity at a microeconomic level, they still come under fire for a variety of reasons. First, they deprive the poor of coverage or they oblige the poor to pay charges that extract a larger part of consumer surplus which otherwise could have gone toward enhancing their economic welfare. In other words, informal markets create a maximum of benefits for a very small number of households and a loss of benefits for a substantial number of poorer households. Private markets are also criticized for the negative externalities that they generate as a result of groundwater over-use in areas where water resources are already scarce, creating conflicts between the economic interests of the different stakeholders. It has been clearly demonstrated in certain parts of southern India, for example, how an informal water market led to over-exploitation of aquifers, causing problems such as seawater intrusion. Furthermore, by delivering poor quality water to households, informal water suppliers often share some of the responsibility for serious health problems among their customers. Yet these informal water markets continue to prosper in numerous urban areas despite their negative consequences, and the reason for this, as affirmed by economists, is that these are efficient institutions that can remain economically efficient despite the nature of their results. In the event of a decline in well-being due to the simultaneous failure of the public sector and markets, spontaneous order will supposedly produce collective action among the agents in a community so as to minimize the social cost of water shortages. However, the community is bound to be ineffective given the negative externalities, the problems of freeriding, the effects of elite capture, higher transaction costs related to fulfilling social objectives, over-dependence on external players to support community services, and the inability to expand services to satisfy larger communities. Furthermore, community management has played a minimal role in urban water supply systems compared with other urban institutions throughout the world. It follows that institutions are totally incapable of identifying the successful aspects of public systems and private markets in the water sector and combining them in such a way as to maximize the comparative economic and social advantages of each. The PPP was presented as a model in the field of development, but the negative aspects were not given serious consideration, and it is these aspects that led to the failure of the PPP.

8.3.3.2 MACROECONOMIC CRISES, HERD MENTALITY AND PRIVATIZATION OF WATER

The introduction of PPPs in the water sector was also prompted by the economic crises affecting numerous developing countries at the end of the 1980s and the beginning of the 1990s [BRA 05], [SAL 04]. These crises were characterized essentially by huge fiscal deficits and led to the privatization of a great many services which had until then been delivered by the public sector, including in particular urban water supply. For example, Argentina took the risk of privatizing urban water services within the context of a broader programme of structural adjustment measures designed to halt its macroeconomic crisis [GAL 05]. But many countries embarked on the privatization of public sector services that had hitherto been operated efficiently. Similarly, the large deficit in the water sector, caused by the vicious circle mentioned earlier, had resulted in very low levels of investment. Thus, in the 1980s, only 0.45 per cent of the PIB of developing countries was invested in water supply and sanitation projects. As a result of this situation, governments wanted to boost investment by involving the private sector. The hope was that the private sector would bring the additional investment required and reduce the gap between water supply and demand through efficiency gains, better distribution networks, and so on. But these 'rational expectations' on the part of the public authorities were not properly met since private investment in the water sector turned out to be far lower than desired [OWE 05].

Another reason why the PPP model failed is related to the herd mentality of countries that adopted a uniform approach to privatization of water services. As previously mentioned, the economic crisis caused by the fiscal deficit was the main driver for the privatization effort [MEN 99]. It was believed that responsibility for the fiscal deficit lay with the 'mammoth', the public sector companies – and this included public utilities – which were making a loss and were receiving hefty subsidies from governments. Since water supply was one such sector benefiting from huge subsidies, the countries, with the help of international funding agencies, started to introduce PPPs. But each country followed exactly the same model without making adjustments to allow for specific local factors, whether social, economic, political or institutional. Yet these are the factors that have the greatest influence on the success of newly-created institutions, such as water-sector PPPs. With no blueprint that could be adapted to local conditions, the various countries followed a uniform approach based on supply-side factors. In short, the countries were unable to recognize that something which works well in one place may not work well in another, or that something that works well at one particular time may not have the same success at a later date [BAS 05].

8.3.3.3 WATER AS AN ECONOMIC GOOD

A gradual shift – especially in political circles – from the conventional approach whereby water was treated as a 'freely available' good also contributed to the idea that water supply services should be transferred to the private sector. Many non-economists support the opinion that households have good reason to demand a 'basic right to water' and that it is the responsibility of public institutions to ensure that this right is respected with non-market arrangements, laid down in legislation or in the constitution. A counter-argument to this idea of a basic right to water is put forward by certain economists who prefer to focus on the importance of 'water rights' [THO 98], such that the market mechanism can ensure efficient use of scarce water, based on purchasers' willingness to pay and the principle that sellers can receive payment for the water supplied. According to the schema advanced by Coase, if rights to water are given to households then it must be possible to attribute costs to these rights, corresponding to the payment for acquiring the rights. Water rights as far as vendors are concerned means that sellers such as farmers can sell water to purchasers with high use values, based on the opportunity cost of the use of the water. As suggested in economic theory, the market establishes a balance between water demand and supply, regardless of who initially holds the property rights, provided that a favourable competitive environment is created to minimize transaction costs. Thus, the concept of water rights recognizes fundamentally that the acquisition of property rights over water involves considerable opportunity costs measured in terms of the alternative uses to which the resource could otherwise be put. Any change in the quantity or quality of water stocks resulting from the transfers will involve both negative and positive externalities that affect the distribution of welfare in society. Thus, if it is agreed that the 'basic right to water' is to be guaranteed, there will be a significant economic cost. Economists would therefore tend to treat water as an economic good [ROG 02], and subscribe to the user-pays principle whereby costs are covered by users thereby ensuring the financial sustainability of water services. While there might be consensus on the notion of water as an economic good, debate continues among economists over the institutional organization of water supply, whether it should be a public good or a private good. Certain economists suggest that, because of the very nature of the benefits and social costs associated with water supply, decentralized markets cannot provide adequate water services since they have to contend with classic problems such as market shrinking by private operators, the problem of freeriding linked to the use of social benefits, and so on. [SAM 54]. This school of thought strongly defends the principle that water supply should be organized by a central authority in order to maximize social welfare [HAN 06]. However, the counter-arguments in favour of private-sector involvement in water supply are varied. These are discussed below.

By applying the Big Bills[7] theory to the urban water sector, certain economists consider that significant sums of money in potential payments are not collected in urban areas of developing countries and are waiting to be collected by those who supply high-quality water services to households. These 'big bills' can be seen at the level of households in two different forms. First, in the form of 'defensive expenditures' incurred in terms of the increased opportunity cost of the time taken to collect water that is of good quality but which comes from sources that are far away, additional expenditures related to buying water from private vendors, and additional medical costs to treat diseases caused by poor quality water – all expenditures supported in existing inefficient water supply systems. Second, these 'big bills' also appear in the form of householders' willingness to pay for access to better quality water in an improved supply system. In the case of defensive expenditures, it has been shown for example that the 'direct cost' incurred by households that bought all their water from private vendors amounted to a maximum of 56 per cent of the total income of households in Onitsha, Nigeria [WHI 91]. The implication of this policy is that these 'big bills' could be collected appropriately and efficiently by the private sector, which is assumed to operate according to the principle of 'unbounded rationality'. But an important question here is whether households would wish to transfer all of their expenditures on water to the formal private sector, and, even if they did, how would they maximize their welfare since they would gain no consumer surplus from this transfer. The answer is that if households can agree to pay more in the existing system, for poor quality water, then they would agree *a fortiori* to pay even more, as suggested by the principle of rationality, for good quality water supplied by a private system, thus benefiting from a significant consumer surplus. It is here that expenditures of the 'willingness to pay' type come into play. Numerous contingent valuation (CV) surveys conducted in urban areas in developing countries have found, for example, that households are indeed prepared to pay an additional amount (of the order of 5 to 12 per cent of their income) in order to have access to improved water services [WHI 91]. The Big Bills argument applied to the water sector would therefore seem to be strengthened by CV surveys, providing encouragement to decision-makers to forge ahead and collect these sums of money by involving the private sector more. But two points should be emphasized: first, the ability of the private sector to amass the defensive expenditures incurred by the population depends on a multitude of considerations related to the private management method, such as how the population perceive the formal private market, representations of institutions that are supposed to deliver water, the reliability of supply, etc. Given that uncertainties still persist regarding all of these considerations, it is not possible to validate predictions of population behaviour that are based on 'rational expectations' concerning privately managed water services. And the results of numerous economic studies, particularly CV surveys, have been affected by biases and by errors that invalidate the economic valuations presented and give little credibility to their results. It is hardly surprising that the PPP model, developed on the basis of erroneous forecasts and incorrect estimates, met with little success.

8.3.3.4 INAPPROPRIATE PRICING

Since the private sector is guided by the principle of rationality and profit, water pricing plays a decisive role in the introduction of a PPP in any given area. However, setting the price of drinking water has proved in practice to be a real challenge. We must remember that determining prices on the basis of costs has dominated the water supply sector for a long time. But this mechanism does not take into account individual preferences, which creates a few problems from a demand-side point of view. Furthermore, setting the price on the basis of opportunity cost, as suggested by certain economists, creates a host of other practical problems. In the case of the water sector, the opportunity cost does not depend solely on the value of the water in its present use but must also include its value in the next-best choice. This does not include merely the value related to water quantities, but also quality, more specifically the 'externality cost' of water use in an alternative use. It is very difficult to estimate the value of water in alternative uses if these alternative uses are non-market in nature. Moreover, environmental economists have identified five types of value generated by environmental resources such as water: direct use value (for example, water for drinking or irrigation), indirect use value (for example, water used for biodiversity protection), option value (a person's willingness to pay for protecting resources for future use), quasi-option (a person's willingness to pay to maintain the *status quo* until more detailed information on the available alternatives becomes available), and existence value (a person's willingness to pay in order to protect water for its intrinsic and specific benefits) [FRE 93]. It is a costly business trying to estimate all the economic values that must be included when determining opportunity cost pricing. But, most important, the economic valuation of water-related services is itself a controversial exercise. For example, the estimated value can vary depending on the economic valuation technique used [VEN 03]. The use of two different techniques to evaluate two different types of benefit leads to aggregation or additivity problems. Furthermore, when two valuation techniques are used to estimate one particular benefit, several values can be obtained, posing the dilemma for decision-makers of choosing between them. Value judgements thus play a big role in reaching normative decisions about water pricing policies. Since the private sector is generally motivated by profit, ethical value judgements are largely absent from water pricing practices.

A major problem posed by PPPs is how to find a pricing structure that will satisfy the social, economic and environmental objectives of the water sector. At the moment, there would appear to be no consensus on how to determine drinking water prices in urban areas. Generally speaking, in numerous urban water pricing systems, prices are determined on the basis of costs. At the moment, the current method for setting prices is aimed at full recovery of costs, with costs defined in the strict sense. The full-cost pricing mechanism is supposed to cover the total average cost of supplying water to households, including infrastructure depreciation costs and operating and maintenance costs. However, in economics, full-cost pricing refers to the opportunity cost of water, which includes direct costs (infrastructure, operating and maintenance costs), but also indirect costs (waste water treatment), and the other elements of opportunity cost (use value in next best alternative use) [ROG 02] and the cost of reduction of non-use values (values given by individuals to the existence of the water resource and its preservation for future use). This means that unless the price reflects the full economic value of the water supplied, the social cost of providing water cannot be properly taken into account in water management. If the private sector adopts the principle of full-cost pricing for water, then equity becomes the main problem. Water pricing by the private sector has not enabled the reality of world environmental problems encountered in the water sector to be addressed. Furthermore, the private sector, which was expected to make up for the public sector's inability to set appropriate prices, has generally failed to do so. The private sector has thus fallen short in terms of efficiency as well as failing to reach the objectives of equity and environmental sustainability.

8.3.3.5 MILLENNIUM DEVELOPMENT GOALS AND OTHER CONSIDERATIONS

Aside from the reasons mentioned above, the emergence of the Millennium Development Goals (MDG) in national political debate at the beginning of the 1990s and the professed urgency to achieve these goals (in particular target 10 of MDG 7 concerning access to water) have helped focus the spotlight on the private sector as an alternative institution. However, MDG 7 only states what is to be achieved and not the way in which this should be done. In other words, the institutions needed to reach the water supply targets were not really called into question by the United Nations Organization and in the end the political decision makers seized upon the PPP as a possible solution to their problems. Furthermore, water shortages caused by rapid urban growth, the deterioration of traditional storage systems and the pollution of water resources also focused policies more on the private sector. Rather than tackling the underlying causes of these problems and introducing some standard solutions, such as control of migration from rural to urban areas or pollution control measures, governments placed their hopes on the PPP. For example, the scarcity of water – which is by nature both absolute and relative – gave substance to the idea, albeit an ambiguous one, that water had an exchange value. This idea began to spread, opening up the possibility of buying and selling water in a marketplace, in particular one with private operators. Rather than looking to the market for solutions, public authorities should have looked to improve water conservation measures, for example through rainwater harvesting schemes or the rehabilitation of water storage facilities.

8.3.4 *An Alternative Option*

The institutional shortcomings in the urban water sector discussed above show the path dependency of institutional change. Replacing a failing institution with a new institution which also ends up by failing will merely increase social costs rather than reduce them. This was clearly demonstrated by the failure of the PPP. Public decision-makers have the choice of either creating new institutions or trying to breathe new life into the old ones. The limits of our rationality reduce our capacity to introduce new institutions in the water supply sector, as indicated by the PPP experience. Reactivating existing institutions through the introduction of innovative policies appears to be one of the best solutions available. From this point of view, we consider here that the public sector can itself play an effective role and organize sustainable water supply services, provided that the policies in force are adjusted to take proper account of supply and demand factors. This approach can be presented as 'new wine in old bottles' and might be criticized as taking a backward step and one which could again end in public sector failure. But a clearer understanding of past shortcomings shows us that it is not the public sector as an institution that failed, but rather it is the policies of this institution that did not succeed in attaining the objectives set by the water sector. This can be illustrated by an empirical study conducted in the peri-urban context of Tamil Nadu that identified a disparity between public policies and the preferences of the population with respect to water supply programmes. It showed that simple innovative measures could be used to better achieve water supply objectives [VEN 05]. It also showed, for example, that the long delay on the part of the authorities in implementing a long-promised new water supply programme raised social costs in two ways. First, numerous households had to pay considerable sums to buy water from the private sector, expenditures that could have been minimized if the project had been completed on time. Second, because of the delay, many households decided not to participate in the new programme, which affected the potential revenue of the water authority, jeopardizing the viability of the scheme. Many households continued to use costly resources such as private water markets until the programme was implemented, which had a detrimental effect on allocation of household income. Households that wanted individual connections were prepared to pay an average of Rs.2,500 as an advance payment, but the authorities remained intransigent, insisting on an advance payment of Rs.4,000 for each individual connection. As far as monthly rates were concerned, households were prepared to pay an average of Rs.35 for their water consumption, but the authority's policy was to set this rate at Rs.60 a month. The empirical study revealed that if the advance payment and monthly tariff had been reduced to Rs.2,500 and Rs.35 respectively, 82 per cent additional households would have opted for individual connections. This would have increased the town's water revenues significantly. Furthermore, according to the public service policy, water supplied under any new programme would be delivered via new pipes and not existing ones. Households with old individual connections, which used existing pipes, found the financial cost heavy, since they would have had to pay an additional Rs.2,000, bringing the initial payment to Rs.6,000 for an individual connection. In fact, 47 per cent of households that were unable to pay a Rs.6,000 advance payment in a single sum were willing to pay in instalments. However, the public service did not have sufficient funds to support this method of payment. As part of the new programme, the public authority decided to distribute an additional 40 lpcd[8] of water to households, increasing available water from the current 40 to 80 lpcd. But households did not want this amount of 'good quality' water. They preferred a 'small' quantity of drinking water and non-drinking quality water from already available local sources for other uses. Citizens would then not have had to pay additional sums for water that they did not want, and furthermore conservation of good quality water would have been enhanced. Similarly, the problem of equitable distribution could have been solved if the public water authority had installed more public taps in the poorer districts rather than adhering to a strict uniform policy of providing only two public water taps in each residential district irrespective of income levels. Furthermore, those households that were in favour of more public taps were also willing to pay for them, so as to have rights of ownership over them, which would also encourage responsibility.

An important lesson to be learned from the above-mentioned study is that at a microeconomic level it is possible to identify simple ways in which water supply policies can be adapted to take explicitly into account demand behaviour and thus considerably change policy outcome. However, top-down management combined with policies that are difficult to apply makes it harder to appropriately adapt local policies. This is another reason for failure. If it is difficult to get the public sector to back-pedal and there is strong political will to introduce alternative institutions such as the PPP, then it is important that demand requirements be systematically taken into account in reform projects. This would also help limit threats to the sustainability of the new institutional arrangements. The success of an innovation depends on how institutions can effectively adapt to changes in individual preferences, and how they can help coordinate stakeholders on the social and political questions that they come up against.

8.3.5 *Lessons to be Learned from the PPP Experiment*

Urban water supply institutions have a vital role to play in attaining major development goals, including alleviation of poverty. However, institutional shortcomings have been path-dependent, with the main institutions in this sector already failing in the past to produce expected results. To overcome the failure of conventional institutions in the urban water supply sector, an alternative institution, the PPP, was introduced in various developing countries in the 1990s. However, PPPs also failed to reach their objectives, for a variety of reasons. First of all, when measures were taken to introduce this type of partnership, the fundamental principles of economic theory were not observed. For example, water became a private commodity rather than a public good, water prices were determined arbitrarily rather than on the basis of economic values, and so on. Similarly, measures taken to introduce PPPs in urban water sectors did not properly take into account demand-side or behavioural factors in the specific social, economic and institutional contexts. In terms of alternative solutions, we have shown through a case study conducted in a suburban context that a simple reorientation of local public water supply policies can result in the provision of efficient and sustainable services. These corrections require greater adherence to fundamental economic principles, particularly where public goods are concerned, and greater emphasis on the preferences of individuals and households. The success of water-sector institutions thus depends essentially on the underlying economic framework adopted and the extent to which this framework can take into account the preferences of all those affected by these policies.

8.4 INTEGRATED MANAGEMENT AND DEVELOPMENT

Observations concerning access to safe water in large cities in developing countries have shown that the issues faced are not simply about optimum prices[9] or how efficiently the resource is managed but involve a whole range of economic and social factors.

The recent UNESCO report places particular emphasis on how questions concerning water are related to development strategy choices, to the involvement of different actors in civil society and to a whole range of economic and social dynamics [UNE 09]. The risk of a global water crisis is due to the inadequacy of public policies, insufficient coordination among stakeholders and lack of investment. But the diagnosis on the state of access to drinking water, particularly in developing countries, is clearly linked to the world economy and the global crisis, demographic dynamics, climate change, cultural transformations, and so on. Many of the observations on water resources stem from factors outside the water sector. With economic growth, water uses change and are influenced by policies on international trade, education, public health, employment and technological innovation.

While the question of water resources must be examined in a context of economic and social determinants, it must also be recognized that water has its own economic value. Water resources are increasingly being seen as part of a 'common natural heritage' [PET 09]. Large international organizations, the ecological movement and general concern about protecting natural resources have helped over recent years to create this representation of water. There are several implications attached to this vision of water as a heritage resource: recognition of its economic value, the idea that water is a good to be transmitted from one generation to the next, and the need to maintain and look after this resource. However, the examination of the ways in which the populations of large Indian cities access drinking water, along with analyses of future trends, reveal the institutional limits to incorporating these ideas in policy and encourage us to approach the issues related to water supply in terms of social power.[10]

As discussed in the first part of this chapter, the difficulties encountered by public sector management of water supply systems have led to the promotion of principles of decentralized management and user participation in the restructuring of water services. However, approaching the issue in terms of 'common heritage' involves more than striving for economic efficiency in the strict sense [PET 09]. This type of approach requires first of all the involvement of all the stakeholders, who must negotiate on an ongoing basis in order to adapt to changing constraints and ensure the collective management of water resources. It also means promoting security of supply as well as equitable access to water. If water is a heritage resource in this sense, then it cannot be managed simply in terms of market relations; there is also a need for non-market approaches.

If we approach the problem from this angle, water supply reform in megalopolises must give full recognition to the importance of interactions between users and managers and to the need for consultation with groups representing the interests of users. As mentioned in Chapter 2, arrangements of this kind are involved in water management in France at different levels: the Water Development and Management Scheme (SAGE, *Schéma d'Aménagement et de Gestion des Eaux*) which covers a particular territory within the larger area covered by a river basin, the Master Plan for Water Development and Management (SDAGE, *Schéma Directeur d'Aménagement et de Gestion des Eaux*), and local water commissions (CLE, *Commissions Locales de l'Eau*), which liaise with other public institutions on questions of water. However, if coordinated management of a common heritage such as water is to succeed, there must be territorial anchoring and a feeling of community belonging. This is also what creates the common heritage. From this angle, we can consider that periurban areas, in their commonly accepted definition of demographic aggregations on the periphery of a major centre, are in fact groups of micro-communities rather than a fixed social entity.

The various problems of water supply cannot be solved simply by ensuring coordination among individual actors. The issues observed in the context of water supply services in large cities in the developing world point to the need for an integrated approach to water management, but an integrated approach in a much stronger sense than that mentioned in the introduction to this chapter and which is based more on objectives of decentralization and governance through demand-oriented management. To understand the water supply problems of megalopolises in developing countries and the need for appropriate public policies we must also understand the dynamics of the institutions that manage water resources as well as the modes of economic and social development of these cities.

Water governance is structured through a whole combination of more or less coherent arrangements of institutions and rules based on a wide variety of factors such as property rights over water, use and exploitation rights and public intervention instruments. This so-called environment of rules places constraints on the behaviour of users and in part determines the ways in which they access water. The impact and effectiveness of public policies must be assessed in relation to these arrangements: how can policies change the way in which water is used, how can policies contribute to the development of these institutions. With this in mind, the notion of the Institutional Resource Regime has been developed in order to take into account institutional resource economics and analysis of policy design [VAR 08].

These considerations appear to be crucial in light of the observations made for the three Indian cities of Bengaluru, Chennai and Mumbai. In fact, institutional regimes for water can comprise more or less efficient institutions, with or without a regulative system. These arrangements determine not only the organization of public supply and distribution networks, but also the capacity for water privatization, the commodification of water uses, the space occupied by informal sectors, and the monitoring of water quality and uses that lead to the deterioration of water resources. These institutional arrangements go far beyond simply organizing water services; to a certain extent they represent the context. The rapid development of Indian megalopolises, and especially peri-urban areas, is an important factor that has contributed to the destabilization and incoherence of water sector institutions. These institutions must therefore also develop so that they can ensure better access to water and more equitable use of this resource.

With this type of approach, water governance is no longer a question of public policy in the strict hierarchical sense, but a complex structure based on coordination between public authorities, users, market players and informal sector providers. Modes of governance can thus be defined as a compromise, combining the three dimensions of public regulation, the market and citizen involvement [BIE 06], p. 44. Despite the inadequacies of public policies, the state retains responsibility, within these systems, for defining long-term objectives and ensuring that they are implemented, especially in terms of infrastructure. The state must also organize the mode of governance, and the public sector is ultimately responsible for the organization and adaptation of water services [BIE 06], p. 55.

NOTES

1. [VAI 06], p. 183.
2. Such policy instruments are intermittent supply, reduction of water losses (detection and repair of leaks), routine installation of meters, pricing reforms, installation of water-saving devices, wastewater recycling, public education and awareness programmes.
3. 'In today's environment, where publics are calling for less governmental oversight, regulation and control, and increasing participation in planning and management activities, top-down approaches are becoming less desirable or acceptable,' [LOU 05], p. 25.
4. More specifically, the report states that: 'Prices of water for irrigation and drinking water are in many countries well below the full cost of the infrastructure and personnel needed to provide that water, which comprises the capital charges involved, the operation and maintenance (O&M) costs, the opportunity cost, economic externalities and environmental externalities. . . . Charging for water at less than full cost means that the government, society and/or environment 'subsidizes' water use and leads to sub-optimal use of the resource.' [LOU 05], p. 27.
5. For a critical discussion of the pros and cons of water supply privatization, see [KAN 07].
6. [WHO 05].
7. Expression used by Mancur Olson in his famous article 'Big Bills Left on the Sidewalk: Why Some Nations are Rich and Others Poor' [OLS 96].
8. Litres per capita per day.
9. 'When we realise that the European countries subsidized initial infrastructure throughout its long construction period, and continued to provide subsidies here and there, how can we expect the countries of southern Europe to operate on a full cost recovery basis? Increases in prices would be completely unacceptable, even if today they are well below what they should be; it is impossible to rationalize water service management (by getting closer to a situation where prices reflect the cost of water supply) so long as these services remain rationed (with not all of the population having a water supply)' [Transl], [BAR 01].
10. See, for example, the recent article by Iago Otero et al., which is informed by political ecology theories and methods of environmental history [OTE 09].

Bibliography

[ADB 08] Asian Development Bank, 'The Hows and Whys of Water Connection Charges', *Water for All*, January 2008, p. 8.

[ADB 07] Asian Development Bank, *Benchmarking and Data Book of Water Utilities in India*, 2007, p. 73.

[AGE 06] Agence de l'eau Rhône – Méditerranée – Corse, Le prix de l'eau en 2005 dans les bassins Rhône - Méditerranée et Corse, Octobre 2005, .http://sierm.eaurmc.fr/eau-potable/prix/index.php,

[ALL 06] Allen, A., J.D. Dávila and P., Hofmann *Governance of Water and Sanitation Services for the Peri-urban Poor: A Framework for Understanding and Action in Metropolitan Regions*, Development Planning Unit, UCL, London, 2006, p. 126.

[ANA 01] Anand, P.B., 'Consumer Preferences for Water Supply? An Application of Choice Models to Urban India', Discussion Paper 2001-145, UNU-WIDER Discussion Papers Series, The United Nations University, World Institute for Development Economics Research, Helsinki, 2001.

[ANG 08] Angueletou-Marteau, A., 'Etalement urbain et périurbanisation des grandes métropoles indiennes, le cas de Mumbai', in J.M. Zaninetti and I. Mareti (eds), *Etalement urbain et ville fragmentée à travers le monde, actes du colloque international d'Orléans: Etalement urbain à travers le monde, des opinions aux faits*, 26, 27, 28 September 2007, Orléans, PUO, 2008, pp. 55-74.

[ARR 02] Arrus, R., MEDUSE (MEDiterranée, Usages Sectoriels de l'Eau): une vision prospective des usages de l'eau en Méditerranée, Roma – Plan Bleu, 2002.

[ARR 00] Arrus, R., 'Mutations dans les modes d'usage de l'eau dans le Bassin méditerranéen', in Les modes d'usage de l'eau Echelles et modèles de gestion de l'eau en Méditerranée, ed. ARRUS R., Economies et sociétés, Paris, 2000.

[ARR 93] Arrus, R., A. Landreau and J-P Marchal, Schéma d'aménagement et de gestion des eaux: Contribution méthodologique aux confrontations ressources-besoins – Application aux Pyrénées orientales. Rapport BRGM R 37835, Grenoble, 1993.

[AUS 02a] Ausaid, Australia-India Development Cupertino, Water Supply Master Plan, Bangalore Water Supply and Environmental Sanitation Master Plan, Bangalore Water Supply and Sewerage Board, Bangalore, 2002.

[AUS 02b] Ausaid, Australia-India Development Cupertino, Public Fountain Detailed Use Survey Report, Bangalore Water Supply and Environmental Sanitation Master Plan, Bangalore Water Supply and Sewerage Board, Bangalore, 2002.

[AUS 02c] Ausaid Australia-India Development Cupertino (), Baseline Survey, Bangalore Water Supply and Environmental Sanitation Master Plan, Bangalore Water Supply and Sewerage Board, Bangalore, 2002.

[AUS 01a] Ausaid, Australia-India Development Cupertino, Extension of Water Supply in the BMA and Satellite Towns, Bangalore Water Supply and Environmental Sanitation Master Plan Project, Bangalore Water Supply and Sewerage Board, Bangalore, 2001.

[AUS 01b] Ausaid, Australia-India Development Cooperation, Strategic Action Paper Water Supply Tariffs and Financing Bangalore Water Supply and Environmental Sanitation Master Plan, Bangalore Water Supply and Sewerage Board, Bangalore, 2001.

[BAR 08] Barraqué, B., Les grandes villes et l'eau: économie institutionnelle, Responsabilité & Environnement, no. 49, January 2008, pp. 51-5.

[BAR 01] Barraqué, B., Cinq paradoxes dans la politique de l'eau, Responsabilité & Environnement, no. 25, 2001.

[BAS 05] Basu, K., 'New Empirical Development Economics: Remarks on Its Philosophical Foundations', *Economic and Political Weekly*, vol. 40, no. 40, 2005, pp. 4336-9.

[BIE 06] Bied-Charreton, M., R. Makkaoui, O. Petit and M. Requier, *Mondes en Développement*, vol. 34, no. 135, 2006/3.

[BMR 95] BMRDA, Draft Regional Plan for Bombay Metropolitan Region 1996-2011, BMRDA, Bombay, 1995, p. 589.

[BOU 05] Boudis, M., R. Arrus, P-A Davoine, G-EAU: système d'aide à la décision pour la simulation spatio-temporelle de la demande en eau urbaine. Revue Internationale de Géomatique, *Europen Journal of GIS and Spatial Analysis*, Cassini'04, vol. 15 no. 2, ed. Martin H., Hermès, Paris, 2005, pp. 175-94.

[BRA 05] Braadbaart, O., 'Privatizing Water and Wastewater in Developing Countries: Assessing the 1990s' Experiments', *Water Policy*, vol. 7, no. 4, 2005 , pp. 329-44.

[BRI 02] Brianne, X., Contribution à la réalisation de G-EAU, outil de simulation de la demande en eau urbaine: cartographie des résultats de la simulation, MA dissertation supervised by Davoine P-A. and ARRUS R., Institut de Géographie Alpine, Grenoble, 2002.

[BRI 95] Briscoe J. and H.A. Garn, 'Financing Water Supply and Sanitation Under Agenda 21', *Natural Resources Forum*, vol. 19, no. 1, 1995, pp. 59-70.

[BUC 62] Buchanan, J.M. and T. Gordon, *The Calculus of Consent: Logical Foundations of Constitutional Democracy*, Ann Arbor, Paperback, 1962.

[BUD 03] Budds, J. and G. McGranahan 'Are the Debates on Water Privatization Missing the Point? Experiences from Africa, Asia and Latin America', *Environment and Urbanization*, vol. 15, no. 2, 2003, pp. 87-14.

[BUT 06] Butler, D. and F.A. Memon, *Water Demand Management*, IWA Publishing, London, 2006.

[BWS 09] BWSSB, Bangalore Water Supply and Sewerage Board, Annual Performance Reports, Bangalore, 2009.

[BWS 07] BWSSB, Bangalore Water Supply and Sewerage Board, *Handbook of Statistics*, Bangalore, 2007.

[BWS 06] BWSSB, Bangalore Water Supply and Sewerage Board, Annual Performance Reports, Bangalore, 2006.

[BWS 02] BWSSB, Bangalore Water Supply and Sewerage Board, *Handbook of Statistics*, Bangalore, 2002.

[BWS 01] BWSSB, Bangalore Water Supply and Sewerage Board, *Handbook of Statistics*, Bangalore, 2001.

[CEP 08] Communauté de l'Eau Potable, Sécurisation de l'alimentation en eau potable, sur le périmètre du futur Scot de la région urbaine grenobloise (Isère 38), Jérémy RUZAND, June 2008.

[CHA 03] Charankar, P.K. and V.G. Sahasrabudhe, *Benchmarking (Performance and Process) of Water and Sanitation Utilities for Performance Improvement*, 35th Annual Convention, Indian Water Works Association, 10-13 February, New Delhi, 2003.

[CHO 96] Choe, K., R.C.G. Varley and H.U. Bijlani, *Coping with Intermittent Water Supply: Problems and Prospects, Dehra Dun India*, Environmental Health Project, Activity Report no. 26, 1996, p. 59 and Appendix.

[COA 60] Coase, R., 'The Problem of Social Cost', *Journal of Law and Economics,* vol. 3, no. 1, 1960, pp. 1-44.

[COI 01] *Census of India*, Maharashtra Provisional Population Totals, Series 28, Paper 2, 2001.

[COI 91] *Census of India*, Maharashtra Provisional Population Totals, 1991.

[COL 00] Colby B.G., 'Cap-and-Trade Policy Challenges: A Tale of Three Markets', *Land Economics*, vol. 76, no. 4, 2000, pp. 638-58.

[CON 04] Conan, H., 'Small Piped Water Networks: Helping Local Entrepreneurs to Invest', Manila, ADB, 2004, p. 42.

[CRA 94] Crane, R., 'Water Markets, Market Reform and the Urban Poor: Results from Jakarta Indonesia', *World Development*, vol. 22, no. 1, 1994, pp. 71-83.

[DAM 01] Damme, H.V., 'Domestic Water Supply Hygiene and Sanitation', in S. Ruth Meinzen-Dick and Mark W. Rosegrant (eds.), *Overcoming Water Scarcity and Quality Constraints, a 2020 Vision for Food, Agriculture and Environment*, Focus 9, International Food Policy Research Institute, Washington D.C., 2001.

[DIN 00] Dinar, A. (ed.), *The Political Economy of Water Pricing Reforms*, Oxford University Press, Oxford, 2000.

[DUM 00] Dumol, M., *The Manila Water Concession: A Key Government Official's Diary of the World's Largest Water Privatization*, The World Bank, Washington, D.C., 2000.

[DUP 07] Dupont, V., 'Conflicting Stakes and Governance in the Peripheries of Large Indian Metropolises: An Introduction', *Cities*, vol. 24, no. 2, 2007, pp. 89-94.

[DUP 06] Dupont, V., Dynamiques périurbaines: Population, habitat et environnement dans les périphéries des grandes métropoles, Centre Polpulation et Développement, La Chronique, Groupement d'intérêt scientifique INED-IRD-Paris I-Paris V-Paris X, no. 50, février 2006.

[DUP 04] Dupont, V., 'Urban Development and Population Redistribution in Delhi: Implications for Categorizing Population', in T. Champion and G. Hugo (eds.), *New Forms of Urbanization: Beyond the Urban-Rural Dichotomy*, Aldershot, Ashgate, 2004, pp. 171-90.

[FER 91] Fernandez R., D. Rodrik 'Resistance to Reforms: Status Quo Bias in the Presence of Individual-Specific Uncertainty', *American Economic Review*, vol. 81, no. 5, 1991, pp. 1146-55.

[FRE 93] Freeman, M.A., *The Measurement of Environmental and Resource Values*, Resource for the Future, Washington, D.C., 1993.

[GAL 05] Galiani, S., P. Gertler and E. Schargrodsky, 'Water for Life: The

Impact of the Privatization of Water Services on Child Mortality', *Journal of Political Economy*, vol. 113, no. 1, 2005, pp. 83-120.

[GAM 07] Grenoble-Alpes-Métropole, Rapport annuel sur le prix et la qualité du service public d'assainissement intercommunal de l'agglomération grenobloise, 2007.

[GAM 03] Gambiez, M. and E. Lacour, 'Rural Impact of Farmers Selling Water to Chennai Metropolitan Water Board: A Case Study of Magaral Panchayat', available at www.cerna.ensmp.fr/Documents/cerna_globalisation/GambiezLacour.pdf, 2003.

[GAR 93] Garadi, A., 'Prospective des besoins en eau et anticipation de la demande. PhD thesis, Université Pierre Mendès France, Grenoble, 1993.

[GLE 02] Gleick, P.H., G. Wolff, E.E.L. Chalecki and R. Reyes, *The New Economy of Water: The Risks and Benefits of Globalization and Privatization of Fresh Water*, A Report of the Pacific Institute for Studies in Development, Environment, and Security, Oakland, California, 2002.

[GoM 03] GoM, Maharashtra State Water Policy, GoM, Irrigation Department, July, 2003.

[HAN 06] Hanemann, M.W., 'The Economic Conception of Water', in P.P. Rogers, M.R. Llamas, and L. Martinez-Cortina (eds.), *Water Crisis: Myth or Reality?*, Taylor & Francis, London, 2006.

[HIN 07] 'Groundwater in Chennai Declining', *The Hindu*, 7 May 2007.

[HODG 06] Hodgson, G.M., 'What are Institutions?', *Journal of Economic Issues*, vol. XL, no. 1, 2006, pp. 1-25.

[HOE 01] Hoek W. van Der, 'Emerging Water Quality Problems in Developing Countries', in Ruth S. Meinzen-Dick and Mark W Rosegrant (ed.), *Overcoming Water Scarcity and Quality Constraints, A 2020 Vision for Food, Agriculture and Environment, Focus 9*, International Food Policy Research Institute, Washington D.C., 2001.

[HUG 80] Hugon, P., Les petites activités marchandes dans les espaces urbains africains (essai de typologie), Revue Tiers Monde, vol. 21, no. 82, 1980, pp. 405-26.

[IND 02] India Government, National Water Policy, Ministry of Water Resources, Government of India, New Delhi, 2002.

[IND 97] India Government, National Water Policy, Ministry of Water Resources, Government of India, New Delhi, 1997.

[INS 05] INSEE Rhône-Alpes, Portrait de l'agglomération grenobloise, January 2005.

[JAG 01] Jaglin, S., Villes disloquées? Ségrégations et fragmentation urbaine en Afrique australe, Annales de géographie, no. 619, 2001, pp. 243-65.

[JAL 01] Jalan, J., and M. Ravallion, 'Does Piped Water Reduce Diarrhea for Children in Rural India?', Policy Research Working Paper 2664, World Bank, Washington D.C., 2001.

[JAN 06] Janakarajan, S., M.-H. Zérah and M. Llorente, 'Urban Water Conflicts in Indian Cities: Man-made Scarcity as a Critical Factor', MIDS Working Paper No. 196, Madras Institute of Development Studies, Chennai, 2006.

[KAN 07] Kanbur, R., 'Development Disagreements and Water Privatization', in www.arts.cornell.edu/poverty/kanbur/WaterPrivatization.pdf, 2007.

[KEM 06] Kemper, K.E., 'Markets for Tradable Water Rights', in *Overcoming Water Scarcity and Quality Constraints*, A 2020 Vision for Food, *Agriculture and Environment, Focus 9*.

[KJE 06] Kjellén, M., and G. McGranahan, 'Informal Water Vendors and the Urban Poor', IIED, Human Settlements Discussion Paper Series, Theme: Water 3, p. 26, 2006.

[KJE 00] Kjellén, M., 'Complementary Water Systems in Dar es Salaam, Tanzania: The Case of Water Vending, *Water Resources Development*, vol. 16, no. 1, 2000, pp. 143-54.

[KRI 01] Krishnakumar A., 'Chennai's Agony', *Frontline*, vol. 18, no. 13, 23 June-6 July, 2001.

[KUI 97] Kuik, O.J. and M.V. Nadkarni, F.H. Oosterhuis, G.S. Sastry and A.E. Akkerman, *Pollution Control in the South and North: A Comparative Assessment of Environmental Policy Approaches in India and the Netherlands*, Sage Publication, New Delhi, 1997.

[KUN 02] Kundu et al., *Changing Role of State in Urban Governance: Provision of Basic Amenities to Poor in the Context of Unplanned Growth in Metropolitan Peripheries of Delhi and Hanoi*, Institute of Human Development, Delhi, 2002.

[LAK 07] Lakshmi, G. and S. Janakarajan 'Intricacies of Chennai Metropolitan Water Laws', *The ICFAI Journal of Urban Policy*, vol. 2, no. 1, 2007, pp. 29-41.

[LEE 94] Lee Yok-shiu F., 'Urban Water Supply and Sanitation in Developing Countries', in James E. Nickum and K. William Easter (eds), *Metropolitan Water Use Conflicts in Asia and the Pacific*, Chapter 2, East-West Centre and United Nations for Regional Development, Boulder San Francisaco and Oxford: West View Press, 1994.

[LLO 03] Llorente, M. and M.H. Zérah, 'The Urban Water Sector: Formal Versus Informal Suppliers in India, *Urban India*, vol. XXII, no. 1, January-June, 2003.

[LLO 02] Llorente, M., Une approche néo-institutionnelle de la gestion urbaine de l'eau à Delhi: quelle régulation pour quel service?, Thèse de doctorat de sciences économiques, Université de Paris X Nanterre, 2002.

[LOB 06] Lobina, E., D21: Watertime Case Study – Grenoble, France, A Research Project Supported by the European Commission, 2006, http://www.watertime.org .

[LOU 05] Loucks, D.P. and E. Van Beek, *Water Resourcs Systems Planning and Management. An Introduction to Methods, Models and Applications*, Studies and Reports in Hydrology, UNESCO Publishing, 2005.

[LOV 93] Lovei, L. and D. Whittington, 1993, 'Rent-extracting Behavior by Multiple Agents in the Provision of Municipal Water Supply: A Study of Jakarta, Indonesia', *Water Resources Research*, vol. 29, no. 7, pp. 1965-74.

[MAR 06] Maria, A., 'Quels modèles techniques et institutionnels assureront l'accès du plus grand nombre aux services d'eau et d'assainissement dans les villes indiennes?', PhD thesis in economics, Paris Dauphine, 2006, p. 282.

[MAT 01] Mathian, H. and M. Piron, 'Echelles géographiques et méthodes statistiques multidimensionnelles', in *Modèles en analyse spatiale*, ed. Sanders L., Information Géographique et Aménagement du Territoire, Hermès, Paris, 2001, pp. 61-103.

[MCG 06] McGranahan, G., C. Njiru, M. Albu, M. Smith, D. Miltin, How Small Water Enterprises Can Contribute to the Millennium Development Goals.' Evidence from Dar es Sallam, Nairobi, Khartoum, Accra, Water, Engineering and Development Centre, Loughbrough University, 2006, p. 47.

[MCI 03] McIntosh, A.C., *Asian Water Suppliers: Reaching the Urban Poor*, ADB, International Water Association, 2003, p. 139.

[MCN 92] McNeill, D., *Water as an Economic Good, Development and Management Issues*, 1992.

[MED 06] Ministère de l'écologie et du développement durable, La gestion des services liés à l'utilisation de l'eau, Rapport final, Direction de l'eau, TNS Sofres, septembre 2006.

[MEI 01] Meinzen-Dick, R.S. and M.W. Rosegrant, 'Overview', in *Overcoming Water Scarcity and Quality Constraints: A 2020 Vision for Food, Agriculture and Environment*, Focus 9, ed. Ruth S. Meinzen-

Dick and Mark W. Rosegrant, International Food Policy Research Institute, Washington DC, 2001.

[MEN 99] Menard C. and M.M. Shirley, 'Reforming Contractual Arrangements: Lessons from Urban Water Systems in Six Developing Countries', Paper presented at the ISNPE Meetings in Washington, D.C., 1999.

[MIL 01] Milbert, I., 'Les villes indiennes au coeur de la libéralisation de l'économie', *Revue Tiers Monde*, t. XLII, no. 165, janvier-mars, 2001, pp. 175-87.

[MIR 80] Miras de, C., 'Le secteur de subsistance dans les branches de production à Abidjan', *Revue Tiers Monde*, vol. XXI, no. 82, 1980, pp. 353-72.

[MOE 02] Moench M., and S. Janakarajan, 'Water Markets, Commodity Chains and the Value of Water', MIDS Working Paper No. 172, Madras Institute of Development Studies, Chennai, 2002.

[MOR 05] Morris, L. and L.F.G. Cabrera, 'The Involvement of Private Sector in Water Servicing: Effects on the Urban Poor in the Case of Aguascalientes, Mexico', in J. Chenoweth and J. Bird (eds.), *Business of Water Supply and Sustainable Development*, Green Management International Publisher, Sheffield, UK, 2005.

[MMR 03] MMRDA, 'Regional Plan of Mumbai Metropolitan Region', [online version http://www.regionalplan-mmrda.org/, consulté le 03/11/2008] , 2003.

[MMR 05] MMRDA, 'Transportation Study for the Region of Mumbai', Intermediate Report, 2006.

[NAT 04] National Water Development Agency (NWDA), Interbasin Water Transfer Proposal, Ministry of Water Resources, New Delhi, 2004.

[NJU 04a] Njiru, C., and M. Albu, 'Improving Access to Water Through Support to Small Water-providing Enterprises', *Small Enterprise Development*, vol. 15, no. 2, 2004, pp. 30-6.

[NJU 04b] Njiru, C., 'Utility-small Water Enterprise Partnerships: Serving Informal Urban Settlements in Africa', *Water Policy*, vol. 6, no. 5, 2004, pp. 443-52.

[NOR 91] North D.C., 'Institutions', *Journal of Economic Perspectives*, vol. 5, no. 1, 1991, pp. 97-112.

[OEC 03] OECD, *Improving Water Management: Recent OECD Experiences*, IWA Publishing, Paris, 2003.

[OKU 88] Okun, D.A., 'The Value of Water Supply and Sanitation in

Development: An Assessment', *American Journal of Public Health* 78(11), 1988, pp. 1463-7.

[OLI 04] Oliveau, S., 'Modernisation villageoise et distance à la ville en Inde', Thèse Paris I, Géographie, Université Paris I Panthéon Sorbonne, 288 p., 16 novembre 2004.

[OLS 96] Olson, M., 'Big Bills Left on the Sidewalk: Why Some Nations are Rich and Others Poor', *Journal of Economic Perspectives*, vol. 10, 1996, pp. 3-24.

[OTE 09] Otero I., G. Kallis, R. Aguilar, V. Ruiz, 'Water Scarcity, Social Power and the Production of an Elite Suburb: The Political Ecology of Water in Catalonia, Matadepera', *Ecological Economics*, 2009, p. 12.

[PET 09] Petit, O., B. Romagny, 'La reconnaissance de l'eau comme patrimoine commun: quels enjeux pour l'analyse économique?', *Monde en développement 2009/01*, no. 145, 2009, pp. 29-54.

[PUM 97] Pumain D., and T. Saint-Julien, 'Analyse spatiale' (I), Colin Armand, collection Cursus, Paris, 1997.

[PUM 92] Pumain, D. and L. Sanders, 'La formalisation du changement dans trois modèles de dynamique urbaine: une étude comparative', *Revue d'Economie Urbaine et Régionale*, no. 5, 1992, pp. 773-94.

[RAG 02] Raghupathi, U.P., V. Viven Foster, Water Tariffs and Subsidies in South Asia: A Scorecard for India, Paper 2, PPIAF and Water and Sanitation Programme, World Bank, Washington, DC, 2002.

[RAG 03] Raghupathi U.P., 'Small-scale Private Water Providers – A Growing Reality', *Urban Finance Newletter*, vol. 6, no. 3, September, 2003.

[REG 07] Régie des eaux de Grenoble, Rapport d'activité, 2007.

[REG 06] Régie des eaux de Grenoble, Rapport d'activité, 2006.

[REN 02] Renzetti, S., 'The Economics of Water Demands' in *Natural Resource Management and Policy*, ed. A. Dinar and D. Zilberman, Series Editions. Kluwer Academic Publishers, London, 2002.

[ROD 91] Rodrik, D. and R. Fernandez, 'Resistance to Reform: Status Quo Bias in the Presence of Individual-Specific Uncertainty', *American Economic Review*, vol. 81, no. 5, 1991, pp. 1146-55.

[ROG 02] Rogers, P., R. de Silva and R. Bhatia, 'Water is an Economic Good: How to Use Prices to Promote Equity, Efficiency and Sustainability', *Water Policy*, vol. 4, no. 1, 2002, pp. 1-17.

[RUE 07] Ruet, J., M. Gambiez, and E. Lacour, 'Private Appropriation of Resource: Impact of Peri-urban Farmers Selling Water to Chennai Metropolitan Water Board', *Cities*, vol. 24, no. 2, 2007, pp. 110-21.

[RUE 01] Ruet, J., V.S. Sravana and M.H. Zerah, 'The Water and Sanitation Scenario in Indian Metropolitan Cities: Resources and Management in Delhi, Calcutta, Chennai, Mumbai', Occasional Paper, CHS, New Delhi, 2001.

[SAL 01] Saleth, R.M., *Water Pricing Potential and Problem in Overcoming Water Scarcity and Quality Constraints: A 2020 Vision for Food, Agriculture and Environment*, Focus 9, ed. Ruth S. Meinzen-Dick and Mark W. Rosegrant, International Food Policy Research Institute, Washington DC, 2001.

[SAL 04] Saleth, R.M. and A. Dinar, *The Institutional Economics of Water: A Cross-Country Analysis of Institutions and Performance*, Edward Elgar: Cheltenham, 2004.

[SAL 97] Saleth, R.M. and A. Dinar, *Satisfying Urban Thirst: Water Supply Augmentation and Pricing Policy in Hydrabad City*, India, World Bank Technical Paper No. 395, World Bank, 1997.

[SAL 96] Saleth, R.M., *Water Institutions in India: Economics Law and Policy*, Commonwealth Publishers, New Delhi, 1996.

[SAM 54] Samuelson, P.A., 'The Pure Theory of Public Expenditure', *The Review of Economics and Statistics*, vol. 36, no. 4, 1954, pp. 387-9.

[SAN 93] Sanders L., 'Modèles de la dynamique urbaine: une approche critique'. In Lepetit et D. Pumain, ed., *Temporalités Urbaines*, Paris, Economica, pp. 3-41, 1993.

[SAN 98] Sanders, L., 'La dynamique d'un système de villes: les apports d'une modélisation par la synergétique', *Cahiers de Géographie du Québec*, vol. 42, no. 117, 1998, pp. 367-77.

[SAS 07a] Sastry, G.S., 'Growth and Development Issues of Emerging Greater Bangalore: A Development Policy Perspective', *The ICFAI Journal of Urban Policy*, vol. 2(2), October, 2007: 40-55.

[SAS 07b] Sastry, G.S., 'Issues of Urban Water Management: A Study of Unaccounted for Water in Bangalore', *The ICFAI Journal of Urban Policy*, vol. 2(1), April, 2007: 7-28.

[SHO 08] Shogren, J.F., and L.O. Taylor, 'On Behavioral-Environmental Economics', *Review of Environmental Economics and Policy*, vol. 2, no. 1, February 2008, pp. 26-44.

[SIE 07] Syndicat intercommunal Des Eaux De La Region Grenobloise Rapport d'activité, 2007.

[SRI 08] Srinivasan V., 'An Integrated Framework for Analysis of Water Supply Strategies in a Developing City: Chennai, India, Dissertation, Doctor of Philosophy, Stanford University, July 2008, p. 342.

[THI 03] Thippeswamy, M.N., *Problems of High Proportion of Unaccounted for Water*, Bangalore Water supply and Sewerage Board, Bangalore, 2003.

[THO 98] Thobani, M., 'Meeting Water Needs in Developing Countries: Resolving Issues in Establishing Tradable Water Rights', in K. William Easter, Mark W. Rosegrant and Ariel Dinar (eds.), *Markets for Water: Potential and Performance*, Kluwer Academic Publishers, Boston, 1998, pp. 35-50.

[TIM 07] Times of India, The Karnataka Groundwater (Regulation and Control of Development and Management) Bill, 2007, *Times of India*, 22 May 2007.

[TIM 08] *Times of India*, 30 July 2008.

[TRI 06] Triche, T., S. Requena, and M. Kariuki, 'Engaging Local Private Operators in Water Supply and Sanitation Services. Initial Lessons from Emerging Experience in Cambodia, Colombia, Paraguay, the Philippines and Uganda', vol. 1, Overview of Experience, World Bank, Water Supply and Sanitation Working Notes no. 12, 2006, p. 51.

[UNE 09] UNESCO, Water in a Changing World: The United Nations World Water Development, Report 3, World Water Assessment Programme, UNESCO Publishing, 2009.

[UNE 03] UNESCO, World Water Assessment Report, and UNESCO: Paris, 2003.

[UNH 03] UNHSP, Water and Sanitation in Cities of the World, United Nations Habitat and Settlement Programme, UNHSP: Nairobi, 2003.

[USA 02] USAID, Watergy, Alliance to Save Energy, Washington DC, 2002.

[VAI 06] Vairavamoorthly, K. and M.A.M. Mansoor, 'Demand Management in Developing Countries', in *Water Demand Management*, ed. D. Butler and Memon F. Ali, IWA Publishing, London, 2006.

[VAR 08] Varone, F., S. Nahrath and J.-D. Gerber, Régimes institutionnels de ressources et théorie de la régulation, Revue de la régulation [online], no. 2, January 2008, http://regulation.revues.org/index2623.html

[VEN 05] Venkatachalam, L., 'Demand-Side versus Supply-Side Approach: The Case for Sustainable Management of Water Supply in Developing Countries – A Case Study', in J. Chenoweth and J. Bird (eds), *Business of Water Supply and Sustainable Development*, Green Management International Publisher, Sheffield, UK, 2005, pp. 238-50.

[VEN 03] L. Venkatachalam, 'Theories of Failure, Failure of Theories and

Non-Market Valuation: A Survey', ISEC Working Paper No. 122, Institute for Social and Economic Change, Bangalore, 2003.

[VER 06] Véron J., L'urbanisation du monde, La Découverte, coll. Repères no. 447, 122 p., 2006.

[VYA 04] Vyas, S., 'Addressing Urban Infrastructure Needs of the Poor: The Tamil Nadu Experience of Public Private Partnerships', 2004, www.worldbank.org/wbi/reducingpoverty/

[WEG 99] Wegelin-Schurina, M., The SSIP Model and Community-based Providers of Water and Sanitation Services, UNDP Conference on public-private partnerships for the urban environment, Bonn, 1999.

[WHI 93] Whittington, D., D.T. Lauria, A. Wright, K. Choe, J. Hughes, V. Swarna, 'Household Demand for Improved Sanitation Services in Kumasi, Ghana: A Contingent Valuation Study', *Water Resources Research*, vol. 29, no. 6, 1993 , pp. 1539-60.

[WHI 91] Whittington, D., D.T. Lauria, X. Mu, 'A Study of Water Vending and Willingness to Pay for Water in Onitsha, Nigeria', *World Development*, vol. 19, no. 2/3, 1991, pp. 179-98.

[WHO 05] WHO/UNICEF, *Water for Life: Making it Happen*, World Health Organization and United Nations Children Emergency Fund, Geneva, 2005.

[WHO 87] WHO, *The International Drinking Water Supply and Sanitation Decade, 1981-90*, Geneva, WHO, 1987.

[WIL 00] Williamson, O. 'The New Institutional Economics: Taking Stock, Looking Ahead', *Journal of Economic Literature*, vol. 38, no. 3, 2000, pp. 595-613.

[WOO 00] Woolcock, M. and D. Narayan, 'Social Capital: Implications for Development Theory, Research and Policy', *World Bank Research Observer*, vol. 15, no. 2, 2000, pp. 225-49.

[WOR 92] World Bank, World Development Report-1992, Development and the Environment, World Bank, Washington DC, 1992.

[WUN 08] Wunder, S., S. Engel and S. Pagiola, *Taking Stock: A Comparative Analysis of Payments for Environmental Services Programs in Developed and Developing Countries, Ecological Economics*, vol.65, no. 4, 2008, pp. 834-52.

[WUN 05] Wunder, S., 'Payment for Environmental Services: Some Nuts and Bolts', Occasional Paper No. 42, Centre for International Forestry Research, Bogor, Indonesia, 2005.

[ZER 00] Zérah, M.H., *Water: Unreliable Supply in Delhi*, Manohar, Centre de Sciences Humaines, New Delhi, 2000, p. 168.

Index